THE TIMELY PEARL
A 12th CENTURY TANGUT-CHINESE
GLOSSARY
VOLUME I., THE CHINESE GLOSSES

The research was supported by a grant from THE NATIONAL ENDOWMENT FOR THE HUMANITIES Grant RT-24850-76-1100

Indiana University Uralic and Altaic Series
Volume 142
Denis Sinor, Editor

Luc Kwanten

THE TIMELY PEARL
A 12th CENTURY TANGUT-CHINESE GLOSSARY
VOLUME I., THE CHINESE GLOSSES

Research Institute for Inner Asian Studies
Indiana University, Bloomington
1982

THE TIMELY PEARL

ISBN No. 0-933070-10-1
Library of Congress Catalogue Number 82-062332

Other Volumes in the Uralic and Altaic Seris:

131. STUDIES IN FINNO-UGRIC LINGUISTICS IN HONOR OF ALO RAUN. Edited by Denis Sinor. Bloomington and Louvain, Edition Peeters, 1977, 440 pp., 2100.-FB., $70.

132. CHEREMIS LITERARY READER, WITH GLOSSARY, by Thomas A. Sebeok, Bloomington and Louvain, Edition Peeters, 1978, 120 pp., 500-FB., $17.

133. THE POLITICAL ROLE OF MONGOL BUDDHISM, by Larry W. Moses. Bloomington, 1977. 299-x pp., 500.-FB., $14.95.

134. PROCEEDINGS OF THE EIGHTEENTH MEETING OF THE PERMANENT INTERNATIONAL ALTAISTIC CONFERENCE, BLOOMINGTON, JUNE 29-JULY 5, 1975. Edited by Larry V. Clark and Paul A. Draghi. Bloomington and Louvain, Edition Peeters, 1978, 212 pp., 1000-FB., $34.

135. PRELIMINARY STUDIES IN TURKIC HISTORICAL PHONOLOGY by Vilhelm Grønbech, translated by John R. Krueger. Bloomington, 1979, 162 pp. $8.

136. THE STRUCTURE OF THE TURKIC LANGUAGES By Kaare Grønbech, translated by John R. Krueger. Bloomington, 1979, 188 pp. $8.

137. TANGUT (HSI HSIA) STUDIES: A BIBLIOGRAPHY, by Luc Kwanten and Susan Hesse. Bloomington, 1980, 125 pp. $8.

138. BETWEEN THE HAMMER AND THE ANVIL? CHINESE AND RUSSIAN POLICIES IN OUTER MONGOLIA, 1911-1921, by Thomas E. Ewing. Bloomington, 1980, 300 pp. $20.

140. A REVERSE INDEX OF MANCHU, by William Rozycki with the Assistance of Rex Dwyer. Bloomington, 1981, 189 pp. $14.

141. FOLKLORICA: FESTSCHRIFT FOR FELIX J. OINAS, Edited by Egle Victoria Žygas and Peter Voorheis. Bloomington, 1982, 348 pp., $19.

These volumes can be ordered in Europe from Edition Peeters, P.B. 41; B-3000 Leuven (Belgium), and in the United States from Uralic and Altaic Series, Research Institute for Inner Asian Studies, Goodbody Hall, Bloomington, Indiana 47405.

TO
BOB AND CLAIRE

CONTENTS

PART I

INTRODUCTION

At the beginning of the twentieth century, the area through which the old Silk Road travelled was the subject of an intense curiosity on the part of European explorers. The scientific observations made by expeditions like those of Sven Hedin, Sir Aurel Stein and F. von Le Cocq, to mention but a few, are well-known and need not be elaborated upon. In 1908, the Russian geographer P.K.Kozlov undertook an exploration of the region from Mongolia to Amdo, the Tibetan territory around Lake Kokonor. Crossing the Kansu corridor, he learned from the local inhabitants that he was near the ruins of a city known to them as Qaraqoto, the Black City. Fortunately, P.K. Kozlov made a detour to explore this, as yet, unvisited site.

Whereas Kozlov's expedition contributed substantially to our knowledge of the geography, flora and fauna of the region, its fame rests not only on the discovery of Qaraqoto, the Etsina of Marco Polo,[1] but upon the discovery within a partially ruined stupa in that dead city of a major hoard of materials in the Hsi Hsia script.[2] Until that discovery, which took place in 1908, only a printed and an epigraphical text, as well as a few numismatic items, were known to exist in that script. In fact, the Hsi Hsia script had been identified a mere seven years before Kozlov's discovery by the French scholar G. Deveria.[3] Until that time, it was customary to refer to it as a variant of the Jurchen script created during the Chin dynasty, a dynasty of foreign origins which ruled northern China between 1115 and 1234.

The existence of a Hsi Hsia state between the 10th and 13th history was known, albeit very inadequately, and the little that was known did no indicate a high cultural level. The discovery made by Kozlov forced a change, for it became apparent that Hsi Hsia had a flourishing culture with an extensive written literature. This came as quite a surprise to the scholarly world.

It had been suspected that the Hsi Hsia state had a Buddhist orientation. This was amply confirmed by the discovery. The bulk of the material brought back to St. Petersburg by P.K. Kozlov was later identified as translations of Chinese and Tibetan Buddhist materials.

Not all the material thus discovered were Buddhist texts. A small number of materials had the appearance of Chinese rhyme dictionnaries and quite obviously dealt with certain, as yet not properly identified, aspects of the language. In addition to a few Tibetan pages and a Persian prayer book, the Qaraqoto treasure yielded one bilingual Hsi Hsia-Chinese text, the **Fan-Han Ho-shih Chang-chung-chu**. In fact this was the only bilingual text recovered, hence the only non-mute text in the collection. It is this text which is the object of the present study.

I wish to take this opportunity to thank Prof. E.I. Kychanov of the Institut Vostokovedeniya in Leningrad for having provided me with an excellent microfilm of this document and for all the assistance he gave me during my stay at the Institute in the summer of 1977.

THE DOCUMENT

The bilingual document recovered is a woodblock print on coarse paper in a satisfactory state of preservation. The paper measures 23 x 15.5 cm and the printed surface measures 18.7 x 12 cm. The book was printed for butterfly stitching. Each page is divided into three printed columns. In turn these are divided into four parts, two of which are in Hsi Hsia script, the other two in Chinese. Starting from left to right, the first column is a Hsi Hsia phonetic gloss, the second column is the Chinese character thus glossed, the third column is the Hsi Hsia translation of the Chinese character and the fourth column is a Chinese phonetic gloss for that Hsi Hsia character.

The work has a preface in Chinese and in Hsi Hsia. The original inventory listed a manuscript of 125 pages. A detailed examination of the document reveals that there are in fact two slightly different editions, both incomplete, and with a total of 85 pages. The 40 remaining pages are duplicate fragments of other copies of the same editions.

The work is a Hsi Hsia-Chinese glossary of basic terms and phrases, divided into three major chapters : Heaven, Earth and Man. These are further subdivided into three subchapters: Heaven Itself, Heavenly Bodies, Phenomena of Heaven; Earth Itself, Earthly Bodies, Phenomena and Products of Earth; Man Himself, Physical Aspects of Man and, finally, the Affairs of Man. It provides a basic vocabulary as well as a very basic grammar through the use of sentences each having about four Hsi Hsia characters on the average.

Not much is known about the author, a Tangut named Ku-le-mao-ts'ai, in Chinese transcription, other than that he was fluent in both languages and that he compiled this study guide for use by both Chinese and Tanguts, for "the two languages are not mutually understood." The preface is dated with a Hsi Hsia **nien-hao** and it corresponds to the year 1190 A.D. There are no indications on the document as to the year in which the work was printed, or reprinted. In its presentation, the work is quite anticipatory of the much better known **Hua-i i-yü** 華夷譯語, which, in fact does not provide a foreigner with a guide to the pronunciation of Chinese.

The first scholar to examine and study the document was the Russian Orientalist A.I. Ivanov. He presented his findings to the Academy of Sciences in St. Petersburg in 1909 and subsequently published his address. In it he gave a brief description of the document, a list of some 300 words, their translation as well as their pronunciation. A photograph of a single page was published together with the text.[1]

A.I. Ivanov had realized the importance of the document for the reconstruction of the phonology of the Hsi Hsia language, but his brief study suffered serious defects, the least of which was not the fact that he had used contemporary Chinese to render Chinese of the 12th century. His major mistake was that he had read the phonetic glosses from left to right rather than the opposite. This error remained undetected for more than twenty years when a handwritten fragmentary copy of the document began to circulate in China.[2] It is on the basis of Ivanov's article that the famous scholar Berthold Laufer made his study of the phonology of the Hsi Hsia language and attributed it a space in the Sino-Tibetan linguistic group.

In spite of its obvious importance, the document has not been the subject of a great deal of scholarly interest. The only other scholarly works dealing with the document as such are brief descriptions by Hashimoto Mantaro and Nishida Tatsuo.[3]

One of the most outstanding early scholars in Hsi Hsia philology was the Russian Nikolai Alexandrovich Nevskii (1892-1945)3. Under his influence a number of studies were published in both China and Japan. Among the Chinese scholars active in this field was Lo Fu-ch'eng who, in 1924, published a facsimile of a handwritten copy of the Leningrad document. The content of this copy does not correspond to the document itself. Published privately this "facsimile" is extremely rare.[4]

Another copy of the document has been made available by Nishida Tatsuo in volume I of his **Sei-kago no kenkyu**.[5] Although based on the Leningrad document, it differs substantially from that document as well as from the Lo Fu-ch'eng copy. It appears to have been heavily edited. Furthermore, it is not a facsimile but an edited version printed in the Western tradition and omitting all Hsi Hsia phonetic glosses.

The major advantage of Nishida's edition is that it is the only one that provides us with a translation of the document. By and large, the translations can be accepted although an important number of emendations have to be made.

Thus in spite of its obvious importance to a scientific approach to the study of the Hsi Hsia language, the document has not received the attention it deserves.

THE PHONOLOGICAL HYPOTHESIS

Among the numerous languages of the Sinitic area, the dead language of the state of Hsi Hsia 西夏 (984-1227), located on the northwestern fringes of Sung China, presents some of the most baffling problems to the student of the area. Known to the Turkic world as Tangut and to the Chinese as Tang-hsiang 党項 ,[1] the inhabitants of this state, early in the 11th century, developed an extremely complex script, the organizing principles of which are not yet understood.[2] The script remained in active use until well into the Yüan dynasty (1260-1368), after which it fell into oblivion. Its rediscovery, at the end of the 19th century, and the beginning of Hsi Hsia studies cannot be entered into here and has been discussed elsewhere.[3]

The first scholar to attempt a phonetic reconstruction of the language was G. Morisse. His comparison, in 1904, of the Chinese version of the **Saddharmapuṇḍarīka** with its Hsi Hsia translation permitted him to reconstruct a small number of phonemes. The majority of the Hsi Hsia characters, however, remained mute and Morisse's phonetic reconstruction was done on the basis of the contemporary pronunciation of Chinese rather than on the Chinese dialect of the Northwest in the 10th to 13th century. Chinese historical linguistics were still in their infancy and Morisse could not have done any better.[4]

When Morisse undertook his study, only two epigraphical texts were known to exist in the Hsi Hsia language and they had no direct equivalent in Chinese. The paucity of the available material made it evident that any attempts at phonetic reconstruction of the language were bound to fail. Four years later, P.K. Kozlov made his discovery in Qaraqoto and the availability of the **Fan-Han ho-shih chang-chung-chu** 番漢合時掌中珠 (henceforth **CCC**) was a crucial key to an accurate and scholarly reconstruction.

In 1909, A.I. Ivanov published a brief description of the **CCC** as well as a list of some 300 words, their translation and their pronunciation in the Peking dialect.[5] Other than a photograph of a single page, no facsimile was made available. Ivanov's translations are guess work, often erroneous, and his phonetic reconstruction was all but useless. This did not become evident, however, until some twenty years later when handwritten, fragmentary copies of the CCC began to circulate in China and Japan.[6]

A.I. Ivanov's communication attracted the attention of the well-known scholar Berthold Laufer who undertook an etymological study of the language on the basis of Ivanov's wordlist. His results, published in 1916, established the Sino-Tibetan hypothesis on which all current studies are based.[7] Laufer's work, however, compounded the errors made by Ivanov. He accepted the Russian scholar's translation at face value and failed to realize that in many instances Ivanov read the material wrongly. Although Laufer corrected the Chinese readings, his own readings still reflected a near contemporary reading far removed in time and space from the dialect known to the Tangut author of the **CCC**.

The major difficulty with Laufer's study is not its weak phonetic reconstruction, but the fact that he assumed that the words in Ivanov's list were basic semantic units. As he was unable to examine the **CCC** directly, he could not do anything else.

Laufer, like Ivanov, assumed that the Hsi Hsia characters were similar to Chinese characters; hence, they assumed that the character for **man**, to give but one example, was always the same, regardless of its functions. A detailed examination of the **CCC**, however, reveals this to be an erroneous assumption. The word **man** is rendered by a number of Hsi Hsia characters all of which are translated by the Chinese **jen** 人 . This observation, combined with Laufer's erroneous phonetic reconstruction, seriously calls into question his entire hypothesis, at least for the time being.

The example of **man** is not the exception and the majority of Laufer's words fall into this category. In the examples hereafter, the Hsi Hsia character is followed by its Chinese phonetic gloss. At this point of our research, it is not possible to give precise definitions of each word and its grammatical functions.

1. <u>man - Chinese **jen** 人</u>

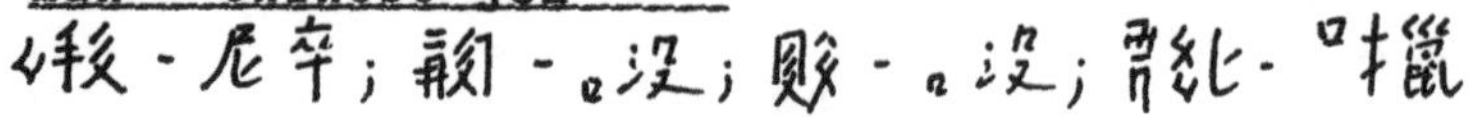

2. <u>heaven - Chinese **t'ien** 天</u>

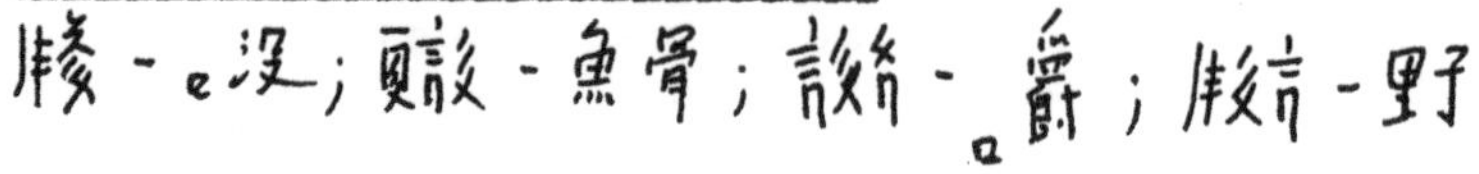

3. <u>fire - Chinese **huo** 火</u>

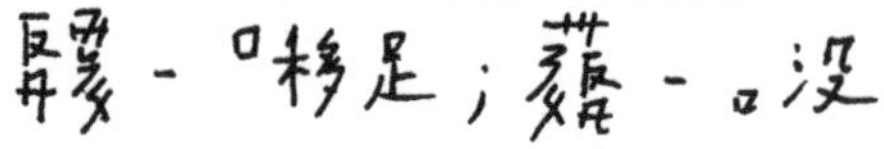

4. <u>white - Chinese **pai** 白</u>

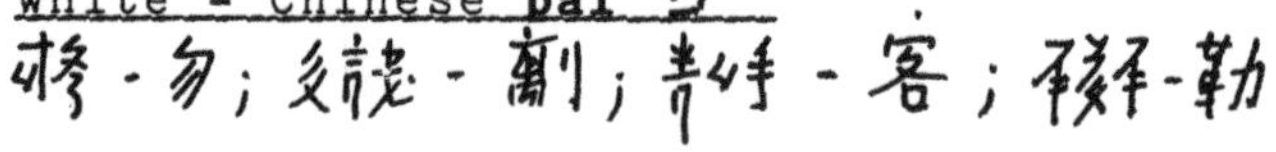

The character 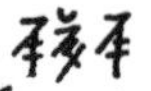, always glossed as 勒, means not only **pai** 白 but also **yin** 寅 and **hu** 虎.

5. <u>day - Chinese **jih** 日</u>

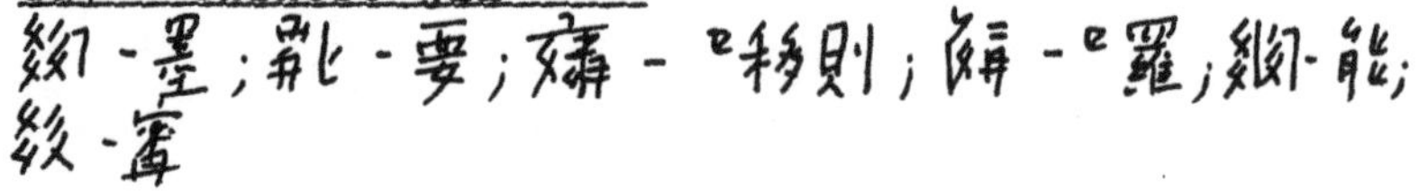

From these examples, and many others could be cited, it is obvious that the CCC does not support Laufer's hypothesis, at least not in its present form. It is equally obvious that the **CCC** as a native, bilingual document is of the utmost importance for both the phonology and the lexicography of the language. Until recently, however, it has been treated as merely an interesting but external source of data on the language.[8] A thorough understanding of the **CCC**, however, is essential to any successful reconstruction of the language and its omission from research has hampered the extant attempts at reconstruction.

The **CCC** was not the only linguistic document recovered in Qaraqoto. A number of the works obviously deal with some, as yet unknown aspect of the Hsi Hsia language. Unlike the **CCC**, however, they are completely mute and contain not a single Chinese character. At present, these works are best known under their reconstructed Chinese titles. These titles, the correctness of which is by no means certain, are **T'ung-yin** 同音, **Wen-hai** 文海, **Wen-hai pao-yün** 文海寶韻, **Wen-hai tsa-lei** 文海雜類, and the **Wu-ying ch'ieh-yün** 五聲切韻. This last work, apparently, has been lost again. It is commonly assumed that these works are phonological rhyme dictionaries based upon a Chinese model.

Fascinating as this may be, one important factor cannot be forgotten, namely that these texts are mute. There is no indication in them as to the pronunciation of the Hsi Hsia characters. They have to be studied through translation and, as I have pointed out elsewhere, the existing "dictionaries" of the Hsi Hsia language are far from satisfactory.[9]

The lexicographical problem is a serious one for most of the "dictionaries" are merely educated guess work, and their definitions are frequently unattested by the material. Under these circumstances, serious doubts arise as to our ability to read a technical, linguistic work when the meaning of its words have been merely guessed at. The correct lexicographical study of the language has to proceed from a comparative study of Hsi Hsia translations from Chinese, or other languages if they can be found. Until now, only one such study has been published and its glossary is a substantial improvement over the "dictionaries".[10] Still, our knowledge is far from sufficient to read anything but known translations, technical works are still inaccessible.

Of the so-called phonological works recovered from Qaraqoto two have been published, namely the **Wen-hai** and the **T'ung-yin**, the former in facsimile.[11] The **T'ung-yin** is the primary source for the phonetic reconstruction proposed by Nishida Tatsuo and M.V.Sofronov. As it is available only in

Sofronov's study notes,[12] the **Wen- hai** will serve to examine the rhyme dictionary hypothesis. The **CCC** will provide the phonological data in accordance with Lo Ch'ang-pei'a study of the dialects of the Northwest in the Ü0th century[13]. Until and if later-date material from northwestern China becomes available, we have to postulate a 10th-century reading for 12th-century glosses.

The interpretation given by Nishida Tatsuo, M.V. Sofronov and E.I. Kychanov to the **Wenhai**, the **Wen-hai pao-yun** and the **Wen-hai tsa-lei** is that they are rhyme dictionaries based on a Chinese model although they are uncertain as to whether they follow the **Ch'ieh-yün** or the **Kuang-yün**.[14]

If the assertion is correct that the **Wen-hai** is a rhyme dictionary and that the information it contains is primarily of a phonological nature, the lessons that can be drawn from the **CCC** should either support it or, at least, not contradict it completely. Hence, if in the **CCC**, a Hsi Hsia character **A** has the Chinese phonetic gloss **Y**, other Hsi Hsia characters with identical Chinese phonetic glosses, they should be found under the same rhyme heading, or a very similar one, in the **Wen-hai**.

The **CCC** contains a number of Hsi Hsia phonetic glosses that are identical with the Chinese phonetic gloss of the Hsi Hsia character that translates the Chinese word. One such character is 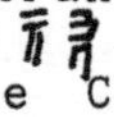 . It is the Hsi Hsia phonetic gloss for the Chinese word **ming** 名 ; it is also the Hsi Hsia character that translates this word and is itself glossed as **ming** 名 . Although this one character would be the most appropriate for our purposes, it is not attested in the **Wen-hai**. A number of other Hsi Hsia characters are glossed as **ming**. Their examination reveals :[15]

1) 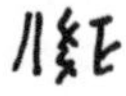 Wen-hai no. 354 rhyme heading 

2) 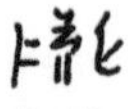 Wen-hai no. 458 rhyme heading 

3) 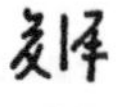 Wen-hai no. 1343 rhyme heading 

4)  Wen-hai no. 1880 rhyme heading 

Phonetic Reconstruction

Sofronov				Nishida			
Character		Rhyme		Character		Rhyme	
mi	1491	źwei	3949	miɦ	041-081	tshiɦ	204-053
mI̭e	1257	tsi̭e	2301	mIɦ	068-091	tši	269-053
mi̭e	2375	*		mɤeɦ	208-062	*	
mbI̭ẹ	4336	tśi̭e	4609	mɛ̣	010-113	tšɛ̣	182-072

The examples above already are a contradiction of the hypothesis of the **Wen-hai**. None of the rhyme headings, however, are attested in the **CCC**, but, if the hypothesis about the **Wen-hai** is correct, the characters under the rhyme have the same phonological structure. If we take the rhyme [illegible] , we find that among the characters listed are [illegible] , glossed as 皮 in the **CCC**, and [illegible] glossed as 沒 .

Character	Sofronov		Nishida	
[illegible]	phi	4886	039-081	phi
[illegible]	mI	1649	259-051	mʉɦ

When we reconstruct the glosses, we obtain in Middle Chinese **b'jiḙ** and **muɔt**, in 10th-century Northwestern Chinese this results in **b'wi** and **'bur**. It does appear that we are far from an accurate phonetic reconstruction and from the system postulated for the **Wen-hai**.

In the above example, we examined Hsi Hsia characters with identical Chinese glosses in the **CCC**. Another approach is to examine the entries under a specific rhyme heading in the **Wenhai** and compare it with the data from the **CCC**. The rhyme thus examined carries the no. **772** and its gloss 腰 can be reconstructed in 10th NW Chinese as **yau**. Under the heading are listed 17 characters divided into four groups by means of a small circle.

Character		Wen-hai	Sofronov		Nishida	
Group 1						
1		0759	2955	ki̭a	kǐaɦ	246-062
2		0760	1995	khi̭ah	khǐaɦ	007-10f
3		0761	0055	tśi̭a	-kʷiɦ	193-051
4		0762	2738	tśi̭a	ndžǐě	236-142
Group 2						
5		0763	0076	tśhi̭a	tšhǐa	001-081
6		0764	0074	tśhi̭a	tšhaǐ	001-091
7		0765	0073	tśhi̭a	*	
8		0766	0072	tśhi̭a	*	
Group 3						
9	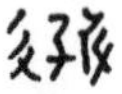	0767	3921	śi̭a	mbiɦ	204-12g
10	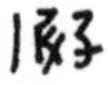	0768	1526	tśhi̭a	*	
11	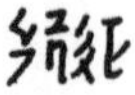	0769	4269	nI̭a	nhǐaɦ	181-115
12	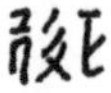	0770	4479	nI̭a	khʷiɦ	107-063
13		0771	0936	nI̭a	ňžǐew	017-123
Group 4						
14	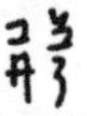	0772	4497	.I̭a	*	116-061
15		0773	3656	śi̭wa	ŋgiɦ	204-11k
16		0774	2298	śi̭wa	BǏẓ	269-066
17		0775	1527	tśhi̭a	*	

Examining this example this example we note that in spite of the fair degree of consistency offered by Sofronov's reconstruction, in contrast to Nishida's, a number of serious problems do arise.

First, the basis for the alternation between **i̭a** **I̭a** and **i̭a** ~ **I̭a** ~ **iwa** is not provided and Sofronov's study of medials does not provide a satisfactory explanation.[16] Second, in accordance with this reconstruction the name of the rhyme is **.I̭a** whereas the phonetic reconstruction yields **yau**. Third, if we accept the hypothesis about the nature of the **Wen-hai**, we can expect that the principal vowel combination within the rhyme is **.I̭a**. Out of the seventeen characters listed under this rhyme, only four have this vowel combination. Finally, no explanation is given for the variations of the initial consonant within the same group.

Neither Sofronov nor Nishida provide us with the external data on which they based themselves in assigning phonemes to the Hsi Hsia characters of the **T'ung-yin** and hence applied to the **Wen-hai**. Both these texts are mute. When we examine our only non-mute text, the **CCC**, only five out of the seventeen characters are attested and their glosses can be reconstructed as follows:

	Char	Gloss	Reconstructed[17]	
3	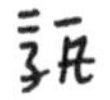	朝	t̂i̭äu/tau	tśi̭a/-kʷiɦ
12	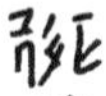	嘿	xək/heg	nI̭a/khʷIɦ
13		旋	zi̭wan/swan	nI̭a/ňžǐew
		乙	.i̭ɛt/yir	
14		腰	.i̭äu/yau	.I̭a/*
16		說	śi̭wat/swar	śi̭wa/BǏẹ

Two conclusions can be drawn from this examination. First, both consonant and vowel in the extant reconstructions cannot be accepted without any additional evidence to support it. Second, the **CCC** data indicate the existence of consonantal finals, a fact not reflected in the proposed reconstructions.

If serious doubt can be raised about the phonological structures derived from the **Wen-hai**, the same will apply to another hypothesis based on this work, namely the tones of the Hsi Hsia language. Although it is commonly accepted that the Hsi Hsia is a tonal language, the basis for this information is open to question. According to Sofronov's reading of the introduction to the **T'ung-yin**, which is not included in the reproductions in his study, the Tangut scholars refer to five tones that are identical with Chinese tones. In his notes to the **Wu-ying ch'ieh-yün**, which can no longer be located in the Leningrad collection, N.A. Nevskii stated that the language had three tones. The current interpretation of the **Wen-hai** is that it represents two tones, an even and a rising tone.

The only text that provides us with direct phonological information is the **CCC**. Although it does not permit us to make statements about the tonal nature of the language, a unique feature does permit us to assess whether or not Hsi Hsia tones, if they existed at all, were identical to Chinese tones. In contrast to later date Chinese-foreign language glossaries, the **CCC** uses Hsi Hsia characters as phonetic glosses for Chinese. It is these characters that provide us with tonal information, albeit incomplete. The examples below illustrate this unqiue material.

1. <u>Tangut Phonetic Gloss</u> 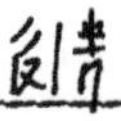

Sofronov 3167 śi̭on

Nishida 243-083 šɨ̌wõ̌

Renders	Tone	Middle Chinese	ÜO NW Chinese
上	4	źiang	śoṅ
常	2	źiang	śoṁ

2. Tangut Phonetic Gloss 

Sofronov 4024 thi

Nishida 319-Ü04 thiɦ

Renders	Tone	Middle Chinese	10 NW Chinese
體	3	t'iei	dye
涕	4	t'iei	dye
地	4	d'i	di
弟	4	d'iei	dye
堤	2	t'iei	dye

3. Tangut Phonetic Gloss 

Sofronov 0090 mIn

Nishida 102-052 meɦ

Renders	Tone	Middle Chinese	10 NW Chinese
名	2	mi̯äng	'beṅ
明	2	mi̯wɒng	'boṅ
面	4	mi̯än-	'beṅ
冕	3	mi̯än-	'beṅ

4. Tangut Phonetic Gloss 

Sofronov 4775 thIe

Nishida 230-031 thẽ

Renders	Tone	Middle Chinese	10 NW Chinese
天	1	t'ien	din
電	4	d'ien-	din

田	2	d'ien	din
甜	2	d'ien	din
殿	4	tien	tin

5. Tangut Phonetic Gloss 

Sofronov 3171 tśi̭on

Nishida 204-96p šʉ

Renders	Tone	Middle Chinese	10 NW Chinese
中	1	t̑i̭ung	cuṅ
鍾	1	ts'i̭wong	č'uṅ
忠	1	t̑i̭ung	cuṅ

When, in addition to the tone, the rhyme of the Chinese character is considered, it becomes immediately evident that to the Hsi Hsia phoneme, neither is of any significance. It thus appears that M.V. Sofronov may have misread the introduction to the **T'ung-yin**. The text seems to speak about the five Chinese tones and not about five Hsi Hsia tones.

As the **CCC** does not pay any attention to the Chinese tones, it is important to examine how the **Wen-hai** does it, at least on the basis of characters attested in the **CCC**. The Hsi Hsia character in example 1 is **wen-hai no. 1731** and the Hsi Hsia character in example 5 is **wen-hai no. 1718**; they are both under the rhyme heading which Sofronov reconstructs as **.ion**. The rhyme is divided into eight groups for a total of 33 characters. Examination of those attested by the **CCC** yields the following[18] :

Rhyme 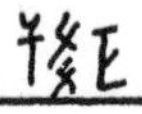

Sofronov : 2144 .i̭on

Nishida : 096-081 ʔyĭwõ

Wen-hai : 1734

<u>Group 1</u>

3) Wen-hai 1711

Sofronov 0650 ki̭on kĭʷõ Nishida 098-042

CCC 宮 Tone 1 ; ki̭ung/kuṅ

<u>Group 3</u>

6) Wen-hai 1715

Sofronov 3831 tśi̭on tšĭʷõ Nishida 204-108

CCC 張 , tone 01 tiang/con

9) Wen-hai 1718

Sofronov 3117 tśi̭on šʉ Nishida 204-06p

CCC 中 , tone 1, t̂i̭ung/cuṅ

鍾 tone 1, ts'i̭wong/č'oṅ

忠 tone 1, t̂i̭ung/cuṅ

10) Wen-hai 1719

Sofronov 4521 tśi̭on tšĭan̂ Nishida 263-031

CCC 張 , tone 1, t̂i̭ang/coṅ

悵 , tone 1, t̂'i̭ang/ coṅ

<u>Group 5</u>

21) Wen-hai 1731

Sofronov 3167 śi̭on šĭʷõ Nishida 243-083

CCC 上 , tone 4, źiang/soṅ

常 , tone 2, źiang/soń

Group 6

23)  Wen-hai 1733

Sofronov 5559 xi̭on xĭã̃ Nishida 032-071

CCC 香 , tone 1, xi̭ang/hoṅ

27)  Wen-hai 1737

Sofronov 2559 li̭on lu Nishida 028-092

CCC 龍 , tone 1, li̭wang/luṅ

Group 7

30)  Wen-hai 1740

Sofronov 1060 ngi̭on ŋgĭwõ Nishida 001-074

CCC 鵝 , tone 1, nga/ga

Examining these examples, it is evident that no information about tones in Hsi Hsia can be derived from the documents available to us. It furthermore raises serious questions about the hypothesis on which the extant reconstructions have been made. The **CCC** is very suggestive of a vowel harmony through vowel alternation between groups within identical rhymes.

Even though we are not in a position to examine the **T'ung-yin** directlyÜ9 it is fait to assume that reconstructions based upon it will yield similar results. As the examples below will indicate, this has not been the case. Furthermore, in many cases the proposed reconstructions contradict completely the **CCC** data.

1. Chinese Phonetic Gloss 勿

Middle Chinese : miuət; 10 NW Chinese : 'bur

Character	Wen-hai	Nishida			Sofronov
	2115	208-053	ŋvɨ	vi̭e	2371
	1134	061-051	ŋvɨɦ	wə	4095
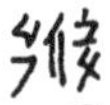	3801	181-09a	ŋvɨɦ	vi̭ə	4242
	0072	206-111	ŋvɣuɦ	vi̭u	3960
	4955	085-071	ŋvʉr	wə̣	0613

2. <u>Chinese Phonetic Gloss 沒</u>

Middle Chinese : muət; 10 NW Chinese : 'bor

Character	Wen-hai	Nishida			Sofronov
	1128	017-111	mʉ	mə	0991
	0884	075-082	mʉɦ	mə	1273
	2455	124-051	mɨr	mi̭ə	0029

3. <u>Chinese Phonetic Gloss 各</u>

Middle Chinese : kâk; 10 NW Chinese : kag

Character	Wen-hai	Nishida			Sofronov
	2434	261-101	kʉr	kwə̣	0455

4. <u>Chinese Phonetic Gloss 悟</u>

Middle Chinese : nguo- ; 10 NW Chinese : 'go

Character	Wen-hai	Nishida			Sofronov
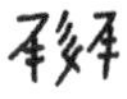	3078	080-083	ŋgu	ngu	5232
	3075	017-12d	ŋgu	ngu	0867

5. Chinese Phonetic Gloss 勒

Middle Chinese : lək; 10 NW Chinese : leg

Character	Wen-hai	Nishida		Sofronov	
	5140	210-055	ƚI	ldI̯ə̣	4023
	3295	050-010	lI	lde	4802
	*	041-112	ƚɨ	lə	1445
	3864	210-061	lɨ	lhI̯ə̣	4029
	*	204-066	lhɨ	lhə	3881
	4179	204-08c	ƚəw	ldeɰ	3346
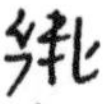	1182	181-062	lʉɦ	ldI̯ə̣	4305
	2156	164-041	ƚɨ̣	ldI̯ə̣	5126

A final point that needs to be examined is the consistency of the phonetic glosses. Chinese rhyme dictionaries are generally consistent in their use of phonetic symbols. As the **CCC** is our only document with glosses, the examination has to be restricted to it. It reveals that the Hsi Hsia author did not use a very consistent system, for he would use different Chinese characters for similar sounds.

1. Characters with Identical Middle Chinese

Character	Middle Chinese	10 NW Chinese
征	tśiäng	ceṅ
正	tśiäng	ceṅ
菊	ki̯uk	kug

鞠	ki̯uk	kug
西	siei	sye
恖	siei	sye
薛	si̯ät	sar
斜	si̯ät	sar
割	kât	kar
葛	kât	kar

2. <u>Characters with identical 10 NW Chinese</u>

Character	Middle Chinese	10 NW Chinese
征	tśiäng	ceṅ
成	źiang	ceṅ
之	tśi:	ci
知	ȶie̯	ci
西	siei	sye
星	sieng	sye
宜	ngjie̯	'ji
義	ngjie̯-	'ji

All of the above examples raise serious questions about the validity of the **Wen-hai**, and hence **T'ung-yin**, hypothesis. This all the more so as we are unable to verify the original. It is clear, however, that in spite of their internal consistency, the extant reconstructions are too often at odds with the CCC data and it becomes difficult to accept them.

Although the original of the **T'ung- yin** cannot be examined, we are in a position to express some opinion about it as Lo Fu-ch'eng published a poorly copied manuscript excerpt.[20] This fragment tends to indicate that it is a dictionary of **synonyms** and not of **homonyms** as is usually assumed. The Hsi Hsia synonymic usage of different Chinese phonetic glosses for the same Chinese lexemes mentioned above is clearly reflected in this document.

From the evidence that has been presented above, it is clear that, at least for the time being, we have to disregard the **Wen-hai** and the **T'ung-yin** as sources of internal evidence for the phonological structure of the language

It is a well-known fact that Chinese is not a very appropriate script to render sounds of other languages although Chinese scholars did develop a reliable and fairly consistent system for those purposes. The **CCC** was not compiled by a Chinese scholar and its transcription system is highly inconsistent. Hence, any attempt at reconstruction based on the **CCC** must be supplemented by data from other reliable, i.e. readable sources. Two such sources are available to us, namely Hsi Hsia transcriptions of identifiable Sanskrit names and Hsi Hsia transcriptions of identifiable Chinese names. In addition to these, we have a few Tibetan transcriptions of Hsi Hsia sounds.

The bulk of the material in Hsi Hsia script that has been identified is Buddhist in nature.[21] Although nearly all texts seem to have been translated from the Chinese, the Sanskrit transcriptions differ from the usual Chinese manner for transliterating Sanskrit. Thus the Sanskrit data provides a means to modify the **CCC** data and, hence, to approach more closely the original Hsi Hsia sound. Neither Sofronov nor Nishida, at least not in an identifiable manner, take Sanskrit data into consideration when they reconstruct the sound of this dead language.

In the examples below, a number of Sanskrit names have been extracted from the Hsi Hsia translation of the **Suvarnaprabhasa**. The Hsi Hsia translation differs sufficiently from the Chinese model to be considered an original text, not a slavish translation. The Sanskrit examples were chosen so that the Hsi Hsia character functions not only as a phonetic gloss for the Sanskrit but is also an attested morpheme in the language itself. The reconstruction is done in accordance with Lo Ch'ang-pei and the proposed reconstruction combines both **CCC** and Sanskrit data.

Character	Nishida		Sofronov		Proposed
arhat					
	255-067	ʔa	a	0489	a
	008-111	lɔɦ	lo	1873	r(a)/la
	157-065	ɮzar	ʐạ	1760	xan
bhikṣu					
	039-081	phi	phi	4886	bhiɣ/vi
	074-071	tsɪ̆u	tśhê	5425	cu
bhagavān					
	204-05j	phɔɦ	pho	3729	bhaɣ / va
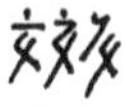	220-121	kɔr	kha	3059	ka
	044-092	xʷɔ̃	xwân	3126	van
Rāhula					
	008-111	lɔɦ	lo	1873	r(a)/la
	145-065	xəw	xeɰ	3269	ɣo
Indra					
	108-002	ʔɪ̆	.I̭en	4354	in
	039-098	thɔɦ	thon	1584	da/dai
	008-111	lɔɦ	lo	1873	r(a)/la

brāhman

	204-05j	phɔɦ	pho	3729	bhaɣ /va
	008-111	lɔɦ	lo	1873	r(a)/la
	007-08d	mẽ	men	1932	man/men

Śakyamuni

	*		śi̭ə	1042	sä
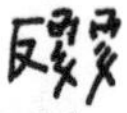	255-145	kɣa	ka	0549	ka
	259-053	mɔɦ	mo	1642	ma
	007-065	niɦ	ni	2104	ni

Licchavi

	108-081	li	lI̭e	4361	li
	220-041	šwã	śi̭a	0138	ča
	039-081	phi	phi	1614	bhiɣ /vi

Vipasyana

	039-081	phi	phi	1614	bhi ɣ /vi
	108-141	pa	pa	4362	pa
	*		śi̭a	2355	sia
	041-102	now	no	1403	na

dharani

	039-098	thɔɦ	thon	1584	da/dai
	008-111	lɔɦ	lo	1873	r(a)/la
	007-065	niɦ	ni	2104	ni

From the examples quoted above, it is obvious that the proposed reconstruction yields a phonetic scheme that can accomodate both Chinese and Sanskrit data. This methodology can be applied successfully to the Hsi Hsia transcription of Chinese names provided that they are first reconstructed according to the Lo Ch'ang-pei's study. The examples below are taken from the Hsi Hsia translation of the **Lun-yü**.

<u>Chinese Names</u> :

1. Chi Lu	=	Kji Lo
2. Jan Yu	=	Zam 'Weu
3. Tzu Yu	=	Tsi Eu
4. Yen Yuan	=	'Gan Wen
5. Jan Pai-niu	=	Zam Pag-'geu

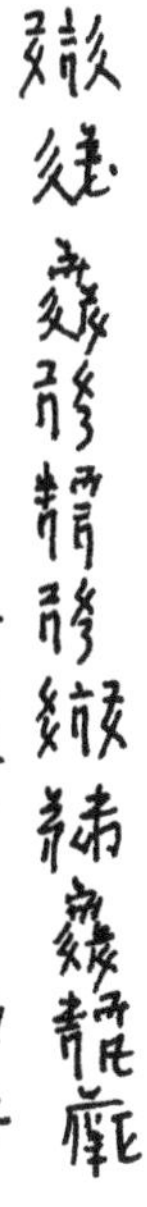

Character	Nishida		Sofronov		Proposed
1. 季	230-091	kʷiɦ	kwi	4752	ɣi
路	204-07f	lu	lu	3593	lo
2. 冉	*		ẓi̯a	2539	źam
有	107-051	ʔyɣəw	.êɥ	4491	yö
3. 子	186-081	tsɨɦ	tsə	1724	ći
游	107-051	ʔyɣəw	.êɥ	4491	yö
4. 顏	211-092	-ŋa	ngâɥ	5722	ɣan
淵	*		.i̯wan	2427	wen
5. 冉	*		ẓi̯a	2539	źam
伯	139-101	pi̯ẽ	pê	1693	paɣ
牛	007-09j	niw	ngi̯əɥ	1854	ɣö

As was suggested earlier, the evidence from both the **CCC** and the **Wen-hai** was suggestive of a vowel alternation within each so-called rhyme.

This is further confirmed, and expanded, by the data obtained from Chinese and Sanskrit transliterations. The evidence strongly suggest that each Hsi Hsia character can have more than one phonetic reading, but that each reading will present a common characteristic, usually in the consonants whether they be initials or finals.

Before proceeding with the elaboration of a new research hypothesis, to replace or emendate the one suggested by Laufer more than half a century ago, a few words have to be said about the Tibetan transliterations of Hsi Hsia characters. These were published by N.A. Nevskii more than sixty years ago and all the material on which he based his study have, apparently, been lost again.[22] The only available evidence for Tibetan transcriptions are a few photographs in Sir Aurel Stein's **Innermost Asia**, but the script in these photographs is nearly illegible and cannot be used for scholarly purposes.[23]

Nevskii's reconstruction of the **CCC** glosses is the same as that of Laufer. He also accepts the latter's hypothesis, and consequently, all of the above remarks apply to Nevskii's study as well. Although the Nevskii material cannot be verified and even though his Tibetan orthography is sometimes dubious, the Tibetan transliterations basically do not contradict the reconstruction methodology that has been suggested.

Character	Gloss	10NW Chinese	Tibetan
[illegible]	没	'bor	bor
[illegible]	名	myeṅ	dbe/bi
[illegible]	名	myeṅ	bi
[illegible]	盈	iän	gyi
[illegible]	悟	'go	'gu

From all that precedes, it is evident that we have

to rely on material the reading of which is far from certain. Works such as the **Wen-hai** and the **T'ung-yin** will remain inaccessible until the proper lexicographical and grammatical studies have been completed. The extant hypothesis about the nature of these two works has not led to a scholarly acceptable solution to the problem of the Hsi Hsia language, merely to an interesting but sterile scholarly exercise.

The elaboration of a working hypothesis about the nature of the Hsi Hsia language, at least sufficient to elaborate a theoretical framework within which to place the phonological data, is possible without flights of fancy. There are three sources of information to assist us in this endeavor. First, there is the phonological data of the type mentioned above. Second, we have at our disposal the history of the state of Hsi Hsia, a history that cannot be ignored. Third, there are a substantial number of texts known to be translated from the Chinese whose lexicography and grammar can be studied without great difficulties. It is the combination of these three points that allows us to elaborate a sound working hypothesis.[24]

Ever since the publication of Laufer's study, the assumption is made that the Tangut are a Tibetan people, and hence, that the language belongs to the Sino-Tibetan group, and that it is related in particular to Lolo.[25] In spite of the fact that Laufer compared 10-12th century data from Central Asia with often inaccurately recorded data from 19th century Southwest China, no questions have been raised about his study.

The history of the Hsi Hsia state cannot be entered into here and is readily available elsewhere.[26] The Tangut-Tibetan equation is based on ethnograpical statements made in the Chinese official histories, data which more often than not teach us something about Chinese perceptions of foreign people than about these people themselves. If traditional Chinese ideas are to be believed, the Tibetans themselves are descendants from the Hsien-pi, probably a Turkic people, through the Southern Liang dynasty (397-414).[26] The Chinese considered the Tangut to be a Western Ch'iang people who moved from the Hsi-chih region, to the southeast of Lake Kokonor, to the Hsia prefecture, modern Heng-shan in Shansi province, during the latter part of the T'ang dynasty (618 - 906). Be that as it may, by the time of the Northern Sung (960-1125), it is no longer certain that the name designated the same people as during the T'ang. As to a Tang-hsiang connection with the Lolo, Chinese contemporary sources are completely silent about it.

By the time of the creation of the Hsi Hsia script, in the early 11th century, the area in which the Tang-hsiang has settled, had become the center of a powerful empire whose territory extended from inside the Great Bend of the Yellow River into Central Asia and which included the Uighur principalities of Kan-chou and Sha-chou.[27] Its population was far from homogeneous. It included Chinese, Uighur and other Turkic peoples, as well as some Persians and a small group of Tibetans, the latter mostly and around modern Tun-huang. Politically, the Tangut state had no known contacts with Central Tibet and conquered the Eastern Tibetan principalities late in the 12th century. In fact, Tanguts and Tibetans were enemies throughout the history of the Hsi Hsia state.

Who were the Tanguts of the 11th century and thereafter? Its rulers claimed to be descendants of the Toba of the Northern Wei (386-534) and they did carry the name T'o-pa 拓拔. In fact, the Hsi Hsia rulers claimed legitimacy over the Sung.[28] Whereas this claim is generally dismissed, the evidence from Turkic materials cannot be ignored. The history of the Northern Wei itself indicates that a great many Toba returned to the steppe, in fact to the region where the Hsi Hsia state arose.[29] The Tang-hsiang who settled in that region were a small group and were, most likely absorbed by the native population. The history of the region between the middle of the 9th and the end of the 10th century can be reconstruted with only great difficulties as the sources are virtually silent about it. What seems certain is that the name Tang-hsiang persisted in the Chinese annals but that the people covered by that name were no longer a homogeneous group and that the name had become a general designation for the different people residing in the Kansu corridor.

The lesson that can be drawn from the history of the state of Hsi Hsia, and which has to be considered in the elaboration of a working hypothesis about the language, is that rather than looking for a Tibetan connection, a Central Asian approach may be much more fruitful. It was the Turkic and the Chinese world that exerted a great influence on the Hsi Hsia state, not the Tibetan world.

The examination of the third source for the hypothesis, the Hsi Hsia translations of such Chinese classics as the **Lun-yü**, makes it even more clear that the Sino-Tibetan hypothesis, at least in its present form, cannot be accepted outright. The grammatical data derived from this material are often in contradiction with our knowledge of Sino- Tibetan linguistics and suggestive of Altaic linguistics. The language does present a number of syntactic features, such as verbal declensions, pronominal comjugations, that are more closely related to Altaic languages than to Sino-Tibetan languages. As was stated above, there are even suggestions, albeit it only mute and graphic ones, of vowel harmony. Details of the grammatical features cannot be discussed at length and a few examples will have to suffice.[30]

In the case of the personal pronouns, we find a number of nominal and oblique forms, as well as a usage which strongly resembles that of these pronouns in Altaic languages.[31]

First Person		Nishida		Sofronov	
nominal		204-08n	ŋhaɦ	nga	3818
oblique		238-062	mʉɦ	mI	2524
Second Person					
nominal	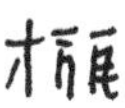	100-121	niɦ	ni	0591
oblique		- not attested -			

<u>Third Person</u>

nominal  074-041 thaɦ tha 5423

oblique  041-081 miɦ mi 1491

Verbal negation is produced by three attested characters, each of which is always appended to the verb and all of which have identical meanings and functions. The use of each character appears to be conditioned by the vowel of the verb as well as by its tense. The tenses are indicated by other characters that follow the negation. Although I suspect the existence of a 4th character, it has not yet been found. The attested characters are :

Character	Nishida		Sofronov	
	238-072	mɯɦ	mI	2530
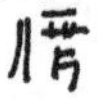	041-08c	Tĭaɦ	nI̭au	1348
	204-058	meɦ	mIn	3510

A few examples of the syntactic structure will have to suffice. The examples below have been taken from the Hsi Hsia **Lun-yü**.[32]

1) a.

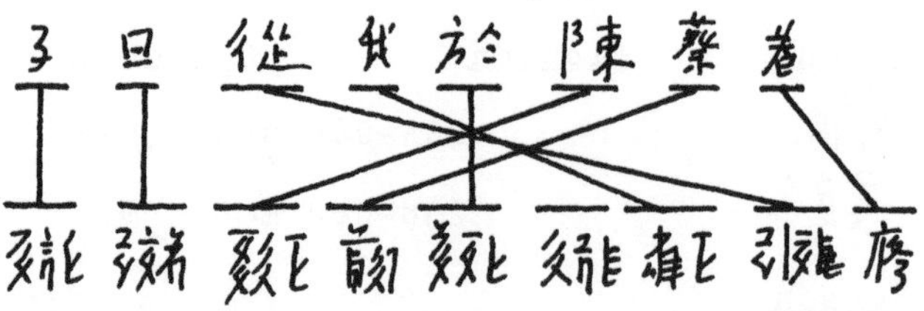

b.

a. The master said : Of those who went with me to Ch'en and Ts'ai...
b. The master said : When I went to Ch'en and Ts'ai...

2) a. b.

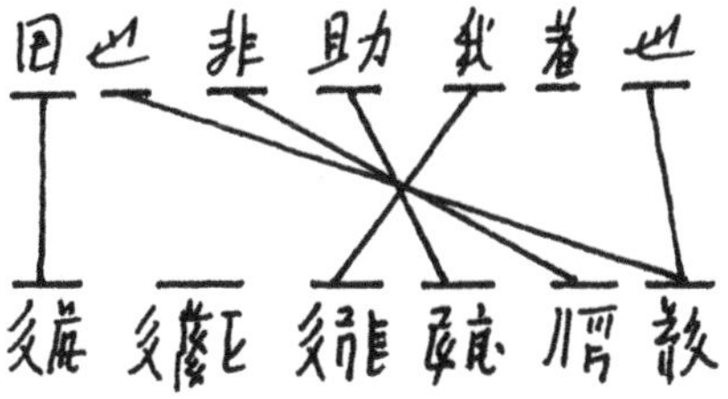

a. As to Hui, he was no help to me ...
b. From Hui, I received no assistance.

3) a. b.

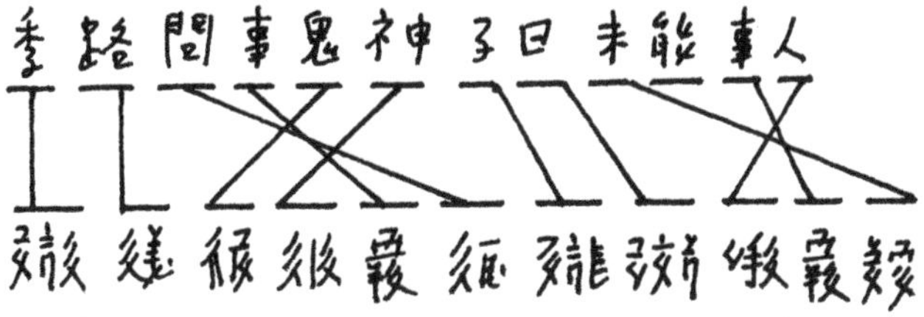

a. Ch'i Lu asked about the affairs of ghosts and spirits. The master said : not being able to handle the affairs of man...
b. Ch'i Lu asked about handling ghosts and spirits. The master said : not being able to handle man...

As a conclusion to all the preceding arguments it can be stated that it is premature to advance and to accept a Sino-Tibetan hypothesis for the language and to attempt a phonetic reconstruction using that hypothesis as the theoretical framework. The evidence that is available to us strongly suggests a **Mischsprache**, a hybrid language combining Sinitic elements, primarily Chinese, and Altaic elements, primarily Turkic. The linguistic as well as the historical evidence supports the possibility of a hybrid language. Our present inability to determine what constitutes the basic elements of the language requires us to use a very open-ended hypothesis. It is obvious that the model must be capable of accommodating both Altaic and Sinitic features.

The intent of this study has not been to reject the Sino-Tibetan hypothesis and to replace it with an Altaic one but merely to question the extant reconstructions and provide basic data for the elaboration of a reconstruction based on the all known facts of the language. It is also intended to point out that proper lexicographical and grammatical studies are needed before such apparent technical works as the **Wen-hai** and the **T'ung-yin** can be used successfully. It is only when these tasks have been completed that we will be able to determine whether Hsi Hsia has a legitimate place within the Sino-Tibetan languages. Until then it has to be treated as the mute script of a language, alleged to be Sino-Tibetan, but once spoken in an area where the dominant languages were Turkic and Chinese dialects.

NOTES

I. INTRODUCTION

[1]A.C.Moule & P. Pelliot, *Marco Polo. The description of the World*, London, 1938,pp. 160-161.

[2]P.K. Kozlov, *Russkii Putesestvennik v Tsentral'noi Azii i Mertvyi Gorod Kharakhoto*, St. Petersburg, 1911; P.K. Kozlov, *Mongoliya I Amdo I Mertvyi Gorod Kharakhoto*, Petrograd, 1923, especially pp. 68-87; Sir Aurel Stein, *Innermost Asia*, Oxford, 1928, vol. I, pp. 429-506.

[3]G. Devéria, "L'écriture du royaume Si-hia ou Tangout," *Mémoires. Académie des Inscriptions et Belles Lettres de l"institut de France*, Paris, 1901, vol. XI, pt. 1, pp. 147-175.

II. THE DOCUMENT

[1]A.I. Ivanov, " Zur Kenntnis der Si Hia Sprache," *Izvestiya Imperatorskoi Akademii Nauk*, Series VI, vol. III, nos, 12-13, 1909, pp. 1221-1233.

[2]Lo Fu-ch'eng, *Fan-Han Ho-shih Chang-chung-chu*, Tientsin, 1924.
羅福成，番漢合時掌中珠

[3]Nishida Tatsuo, *Seikago no kenkyū*, 2 vols., Tokyo, 1964-67, vol I, pp. 179-185; Hashimoto Mantaro, "Shōchūjū no Tanguto-Kan taion kenkyū," *Chugokugo Gaku*,vol. 4, 1961,pp. 13-16.

[4]L.L. Gromkovskaya and E.I. Kychanov, *Nikolai Alexandrovich Nevskii*, Moscow, 1978.

[5]See note 2. There were at least two editions

published both in Tientsin, one in 1924 and one in 1928.

[6]Nishida Tatsuo, op.cit., vol I, pp. 186-223.

III. THE PHONOLOGICAL HYPOTHESIS

[1]L. Kwanten," The History of the State Hsi Hsia" in Handbuch der Orientalistik. China Abteilung, H. Franke, ed., (Leiden, forthcoming); R. Dankoff," Three Turkic Verse Cycles on Inner Asian Warfare," Eucharistion, Festschrift fur O. Pritsak. Harvard Ukrainian Studies, vol. III/IV, 1979-1980, pp.161-165.

[2]Nishida Tatsuo, Seikago no kenkyu, Vol. 2, pp. 225-253; Nishida Tatsuo, The Structure of the Hsi Hsia (Tangut) Characters, J.A. Matisoff, transl., Kyoto,1979.

[3]L.Kwanten & S. Hesse, Tangut (Hsi Hsia) Studies: A Bibliography, Uralic and Altaic Series, vol. 137, Bloomington, IN, 1980, pp.4-14.

[4]G. Morisse, " Contributions préliminaire à l'étude de l'écriture et de la langue Si-hia," Mémoires. Académie des Inscriptions et Belles-Lettres de l'Institut de France, 1st ser., pt. 2, vol. 11, 1904, pp. 313-362.

[5]See above, II. The Document, note 1.

[6]See above, II. The Document, note 2 & 4.

[7]B. Laufer, " The Si-hia Language. A Study in Indo-Chinese Philology, T'oung Pao, vol. 17, 1916, pp. 1-126. A detailed examination of the hypothesis as well as an complete analysis is provided in L. Kwanten, "The Phonological Hypothesis of the Hsi Hsia Language," T'oung Pao, (forthcoming).

[8]M.V. Sofronov and E.I. Kychanov, " Researches concerning the Phonetics of the Tangut Language," Acta Orientalia Hungaricae, vol. XVIII, 1965, pp.

339-340; Nishida Tatsuo, op.cit., pp, 525-527.

9L. Kwanten and S. Hesse, op.cit, pp. 37-39. These dictionaries are: N.A. Nevskii, Tangutskaya Filologiya. Issledovaniya i Slovar', 2 vols., Moscow 1960, vol. I, pp.173-601; vol. II, pp.7-666. This is a facsimile of the author's working notes. A substantial number of the entries have no definitions. Nishida Tatsuo, op. cit., vol. II, pp. 304-505. It is based on the author's study of the **T'ung-yin**. K.B. Keping, V.S. Kolokolov, E.I. Kychanov and A.P. Terents'ev-Katanskogo, More Pis' men, 2 vols.,Moscow, 1969. This is an alleged translation of the **Wen-hai**. The work of Nevskii is based on a comparison of Chinese and Hsi Hsia texts. The other works are nothing but guesswork an contain an exceedingly large number of unattested meanings. On these problems, L. Kwanten, "The Lexicography of the Hsi Hsia Language," Cahiers de Linguistique de l'Asie Orientale, (Paris), 1982, no. 2.

10 K.B. Keping, Sun' Tsi v Tangutskom Perevode, Moscow, 1979. This study contains a facsimile of the Tangut text on pp.381-454.

11K.B. Keping et al., op.cit.,vol. I, pp. 499 - 607.

12 M.V. Sofronov, Grammatika Tangutskogo Yazyka, 2 vols. Moscow, 1968, vol. 2, pp. 102-273.

13 M.V. Sofronov and E.I. Kychanov, Issledovaniya po Fonetike Tangutskogo Yazika, Moscow, 1963; M.V. Sofronov and E.I. Kychanov, " Researches Concerning the Phonetics of the Tangut Language," Acta Orientalia Hungaricae,Vol. XVIII, 1965, pp. 339-354; M.V. Sofronov, " The Decipherment and Analysis of Tangut Phonetics," in A. MacDonald, Ed., Etudes Tibétaines, Paris, 1976. pp. 65-74.

14 The **Wen-hai** numbers refer to the Russian entries in More Pis'men, not to the facsimile. The Sofronov numbers refer to the index in his Grammatika, vol. 2, pp.279-403. The Nishida numbers refer to his dictionary in Seikago no kenkyū, vol.

2, pp.305-505.

15 The reconstruction of Chinese is based on B. Karlgren, *Grammata Serica Recensa*, Stockholm, 1957 repr. for Middle Chinese. 10th Century Northwest China is based on Lo Ch'ang-pei, *T'ang Wu-tai hsi-p'ei fang-yün*, Shanghai, 1932.
羅常培, 唐五代西北方音

16 M.V. Sofronov, *Etudes Tibetaines*, see note 13.

17 The first section in the Chinese gloss is Middle Chinese, the second 10th NW Chinese. The reconstruction gives first that by Sofronov and then the one by Nishida.

18 Group 1 contains 3 characters; group 2 has 2 characters; group 3 has 5 ; group 4 has 3; group 5 has 9; group 6 has 6; group 7 has 4 and group 8 has 1 character.

19 A fragmentary manuscript copy of the **T'ung-yin** was published by Lo Fu-ch'eng, "Yun t'ung chu li, "*Kuo-li Pei-p'ing T'u-shu-kuan kuan-k'an*, vol. 4, no. 2, 1930, pp. 81-87. 羅福成, 韻統舉例, 國立北平圖書館館刊

20 Lo Fu-ch'eng, *op.cit.*, p. 82 for the word Heaven and p. 84 for the word Fire. Nishida Tatsuo, *op. cit.*, vol. 2., p. 526 refers to another edition by Lo. We presume that is the work authored by Liu Ch'u-jen, *Hsi Hsia kuo-shu tzu-tien yin-t'ung*, n.p., 1935. L. Kwanten and S. Hesse, *op.cit.*, entry no. 180. The name reads like a pseudonym and the authenticty of this work presents serious problems. Nevertheless, it also appears to be a dictionary of synonyms rather than homonyms.
劉楚人, 西夏國書字典同

21 L. Kwanten, " Het Boeddhisme en de Staat Hsi Hsia," Public Lecture, State University of Ghent, Belgium, December 15.1981. Nishida Tatsuo, *Seika-*

ban Kegon-kyo, 3 vols, Kyoto,1975-77, lists some 300 Buddhist titles in vol. 3, pp. 13-59.

[22]N. Nevskii, *A Brief Manual of the Si Hia characters with Tibetan Transcritions*, Research Review of the Osaka Asiatic Society, no. 4, §1926. I wish to thank Professor Nathan Sivin, University of Pennsylvania, for having provided me with this very rare work. During the summer of 1977, when I was in Leningrad, it proved impossible to examine this material.

[23]See Introduction, note 1.

[24]Because of the poor transliteration qualities of Chinese, this is absolutely necessary. Thus, for example, the Chinese **lo** renders both the Tibetan **blo** and the Turkic **ra**.

[25]B. Laufer, *op.cit.*, pp. 2-3.

[26] L. Kwanten, "A History of the State of Hsi Hsia, *loc. cit.*, see note 1. E. I Kychanov, *Ocherk Istorii Tangutskogo Gosudarstva*, Moscow, 1968; Okazaki Seiro, *Tanguto Kodaishi Kenkyu*, Kyoto, 1972.

[26]*Ch'ien T'ang Shu*, (Po-na ed.), 196A:1a.

[27] E. Pinks, *Die Uiguren von Kan-chou im fruhen Sung-Zeit*, Wiesbaden, 1968; L. Kwanten, *Imperial Nomads. A History of Central Asia*, Philadelphia, 1979, pp.50-56; L. Kwanten, " Chio-ssu-lo (997 - §065). A Tibetan Ally of the Northern Sung," *Rocznik Orientalistyczny*, vol. XXXIX, no. 2, 1977, pp. 97-106.

[28]*Sung shih*, (Po-na ed.), 485:13ff.

[29]The Tangut claim is rejected by O.Franke, *Geschichte des chinesischen Reiches*, Berlin 1948, vol. IV, p. 132. I feel that the subject needs sub-

stantially more research before the claim can be either accepted or rejected.

30We indicated this in a public lecture at Columbia University in 1977. L. Kwanten, The Analysis of the Tangut (Hsi Hsia) language: Sino-Tibetan or Altaic ?.

31W. Kotwicz, Les pronoms dans les langues altaiques, Mémoires de la Commission Orientaliste, no. 24, Krakow, 1936.

32A facsimile of the **Lun-yü** is available in V.S. Kolokolov and E.I. Kychanov, Kitaiskaya Klassika v Tangutskom Perevode, Moscow, §966, pp. 3-49. I am presently preparing a translation and a study of this Hsi Hsia text.

PART II

PHONOLOGICAL TABLES

ABBREVIATIONS

Nishida : Nishida Tatsuo 西田龍雄, **Seikago no kenkyu** 西夏語の研究, 2 vols., Tokyo, 1964-66.

Sofronov : M.V. Sofronov, **Grammatika Tangutskogo Yazyka**, 2 vols., Moscow, 1968.

More Pis'men : K.B.Keping, V.S. Kolokolov, E.I. Kychanov and A.P. Terent'sev-Katanskogo, **More Pis'men**, 2 vols., Moscow, 1969.

Middle Chinese : B. Karlgren, **Grammata Serica Recensa**, Stockholm, 1957 repr.

10 NW Chinese : Lo Ch'ang-pei 羅常培, **T'ang Wu-tai hsi-p'ei fang-yun** 唐五代西北方音, Shanghai, 1932.

N.L. : This character, as written in our document, can either not be found in this form in the the extant lists or has not been included in these lists.

MONOSYLLABIC GLOSSES

Gloss : **A** 阿

Middle Chinese : .â
10 NW Chinese : ʔa

No.	**Char.**	**Nishida**	**Sofronov**	**More Pis'men**
1	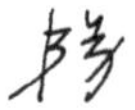	087-061 ʔa	5479 a	2770
2		204-09f a	3917 a	2770

GLOSS : **CHANG** 丈

Middle Chinese : d̑'i̭ang
10 NW Chinese : jaṅ

No.	**Char.**	**Nishida**	**Sofronov**	**More Pis'men**
1		026-131 tšoɦ	4980 tśhwôn	1708

GLOSS : **CHANG** 張

Middle Chinese : t̑i̭ang
10 NW Chinese : cȃṅ

No.	**Char.**	**Nishida**	**Sofronov**	**More Pis'men**
1		204-108 tšǐʷõ	3831 tśi̭on	1715
2		275-071 tšhʷIɦ	5579 tśi̭on	2196
3		159-071 tšã	3073 tśi̭on	4487

Gloss : CH'ANG 常

Middle Chinese : źi̯ang
10 NW Chinese : çôń

No.	Char.	Nishida	Sofronov	More Pis'men
1		N.L.	N.L.	N.L.

GLOSS : CHAO 召

Middle Chinese : d̂'i̯äu
10 NW Chinese : jau

No.	Char.	Nishida	Sofronov	More Pis'men
1		039-088 tšhĭaɦ	1599 tśiaɰ	3945

GLOSS : CHE 折

Middle Chinese : tśi̯ät
10 NW Chinese : jar̂

No.	Char.	Nishida	Sofronov	More Pis'men
1		017-128 šĭa	0793 śi̯a	0685
2	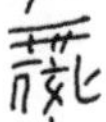	018-107 šĭa	0173 tśi̯a	0678
3		041-062 lu̯	1397 ldu̯	4521
4		265-001 lhi	2501 lhəɰ	3036
5		017-117 šĭa	0948 *	N.L.
6		N.L.	3067 śi̯a	0690

GLOSS : CH'E 徹

Middle Chinese : ngi̯ät
10 NW Chinese : 'gâr

No.	Char.	Nishida	Sofronov	More Pis'men
1	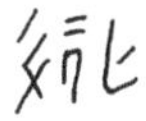	204-064 tšhĭa	3355 tśhi̭a	3604

GLOSS : **CHEN** 軫

Middle Chinese : tśi̭ĕn
10 NW Chinese : tsy̌an

No.	Char.	Nishida	Sofronov	More Pis'men
1		239-091 tšẽ	5146 tśi̭ə	1149

GLOSS : **CHEN** 貞

Middle Chinese : t̑i̭äng
10 NW Chinese : ceń

No.	Char.	Nishida	Sofronov	More Pis'men
1	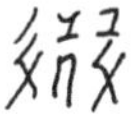	204-106 tšε̣	3622 tśi̭ẹ	1859

GLOSS : **CHENG** 正

Middle Chinese : tśi̭äng-
10 NW Chinese : çeń

No.	Char.	Nishida	Sofronov	More Pis'men
1	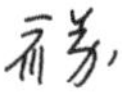	051-053 tšĭẽ	1146 tśi̭e	1393
2	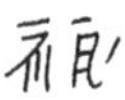	N.L.	1142 tśi̭e	1394

GLOSS : **CHENG** 征

Middle Chinese : tśiäng
10 NW Chinese : ceń

No.	Char.	Nishida	Sofronov	More Pis'men
1		218-041 tšεń	5366 tsi̭ei	3957

GLOSS : **CH'ENG** 悜

Middle Chinese : d̂'iäng
10 NW Chinese : jeń̂

No.	**Char.**	**Nishida**	**Sofronov**	**More Pis'men**
1	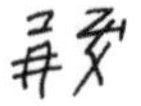	128-061 ʔwu-	4510 .u	N.L.
2		107-071 ʔu	4472 .u	3085

GLOSS : **CH'ENG** 成

Middle Chinese : źi̭äng
10 NW Chinese : ceń̂

No.	**Char.**	**Nishida**	**Sofronov**	**More Pis'men**
1		018-09b šĭẽ	0177 śi̭e	1399
2	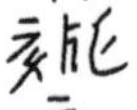	N.L.	N.L.	N.L.
3		035-061 še	1124 śi̭ei	3959

GLOSS : **CHI** 齊

Middle Chinese : dz'iei
10 NW Chinese : dzei

No.	**Char.**	**Nishida**	**Sofronov**	**More Pis'men**
1		204-10a' *	3358 z̀i̭e	4893

GLOSS : **CHI** 劑

Middle Chinese : dz'iei-
10 NW Chinese : dzei

No.	**Char.**	**Nishida**	**Sofronov**	**More Pis'men**
1	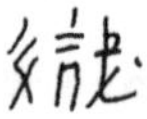	204-10a' *	3358 z̀i̭e	4893

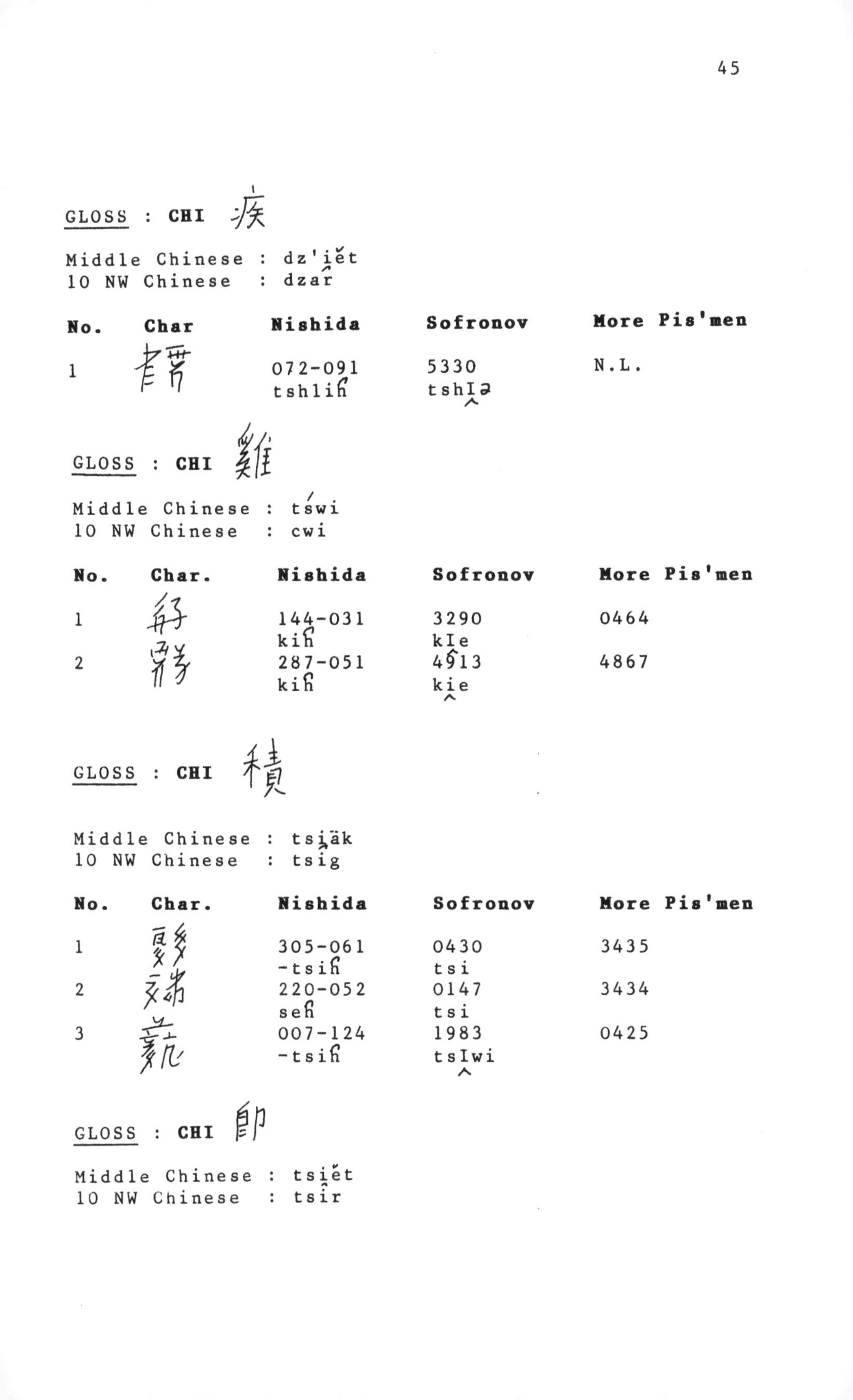

GLOSS : CHI 疾

Middle Chinese : dz'i̯ĕt
10 NW Chinese : dzar̂

No.	Char	Nishida	Sofronov	More Pis'men
1		072-091 tshliɦ	5330 tshI̭ə	N.L.

GLOSS : CHI 雞

Middle Chinese : tświ
10 NW Chinese : cwi

No.	Char.	Nishida	Sofronov	More Pis'men
1		144-031 kiɦ	3290 kIe	0464
2		287-051 kiɦ	4913 ki̭e	4867

GLOSS : CHI 積

Middle Chinese : tsi̯äk
10 NW Chinese : tsig

No.	Char.	Nishida	Sofronov	More Pis'men
1		305-061 -tsiɦ	0430 tsi	3435
2		220-052 seɦ	0147 tsi	3434
3		007-124 -tsiɦ	1983 tsI̭wi	0425

GLOSS : CHI 即

Middle Chinese : tsi̯ĕt
10 NW Chinese : tsir̂

No.	Char.	Nishida	Sofronov	More Pis'men
1	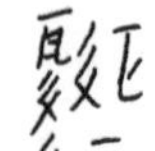	305-073 lạ	0419 lạ	1956
2	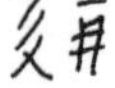	204-056 -lŏ̃	3400 lwon	4413
3		N.L.	0168 la	3565
4		017-084 kụ	0924 khụ	4498
5		016-071 lɔɦ	0160 lo	N.L.
6		026-091 lɔɦ	4944 lo	4310
7		017-11k lɔɦ	0804 lo	1573

GLOSS : **CH'I** 吃

Middle Chinese : ngi̯et
10 NW Chinese : 'gâr

No.	Char.	Nishida	Sofronov	More Pis'men
1	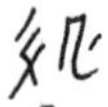	204-031 ŋgɨ̌	3568 ngÎ̯ə	1175
2		003-051 ŋgɨ̌	0037 ngI	3850
3		003-121 ŋgIr	N.L.	N.L.

GLOSS : **CH'I** 七

Middle Chinese : ts'i̯ĕt
10 NW Chinese : tsyar

No.	Char.	Nishida	Sofronov	More Pis'men
1		194-091 tshɨ	2814 tshI	0111

GLOSS : **CH'I** 其

Middle Chinese : kji
10 NW Chinese : gi

No.	Char.	Nishida	Sofronov	More Pis'men
1		N.L.	N.L.	N.L.
2		216-081 khiɦ	5787 ki	3419

GLOSS : **CH'I** 奇

Middle Chinese : g'jie
10 NW Chinese : gi ^

No.	Char.	Nishida	Sofronov	More Pis'men
1		039-071 kɔɦ	1590 ko	1556

GLOSS : **CHIA** 假

Middle Chinese : ka:
10 NW Chinese : ga

No.	Char.	Nishida	Sofronov	More Pis'men
1		181-097 kǐa̤	4152 kâ	3591

GLOSS : **CHIANG** 姜

Middle Chinese : ki̯ang
10 NW Chinese : kyań

No.	Char.	Nishida	Sofronov	More Pis'men
1		204-10c mIě	3469 mbệi	2019
2		017-122 -mbi	0885 mbê	3334

GLOSS : **CHIAO** 2 爵

Middle Chinese : tsi̯ak
10 NW Chinese : tsyag

No.	Char.	Nishida	Sofronov	More Pis'men
1		110-091 tshǐuɦ	2884 tshwu	N.L.
2	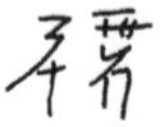	073-091 -tshǐu	5404 tshwu	N.L.
3		113-061 tsǐụ	0024 tsI̭wụ	1829
4		N.L.	N.L.	N.L.

GLOSS : **CHIH** 質

Middle Chinese : tśiĕt
10 NW Chinese : ciȓ

No.	Char.	Nishida	Sofronov	More Pis'men
1		236-052 nɨ̣	2693 ndI̭oɰ	1646

GLOSS : **CHIEH** 皆

Middle Chinese : kǎi
10 NW Chinese : ke

No.	Char.	Nishida	Sofronov	More Pis'men
1		018-111 kɛ	0226 kẹi	2020
2	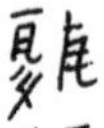	305-051 -kǐɛ	0411 kêi	1244
3		204-08f kǐɛ	3555 keɰ	1784

GLOSS : **CHIEH** 介

Middle Chinese : kǎi-
10 NW Chinese : kye

No.	Char.	Nishida	Sofronov	More Pis'men
1		041-103 kǐɛ	1472 kêi	1241

GLOSS : CHIEH 截

Middle Chinese : dz'iet
10 NW Chinese : dzyar

No.	Char.	Nishida	Sofronov	More Pis'men
1		144-063 rǐur	3201 ri̭u	2278
2		010-106 tshạ	4337 tshI̭e	1992
3		026-087 tshaɦ	4904 tsha	3638

GLOSS : CHIEN 堅

Middle Chinese : kien
10 NW Chinese : kyan

No.	Char.	Nishida	Sofronov	More Pis'men
1		205-083 ŧəw	N.L.	N.L.

GLOSS : CHIH 直

Middle Chinese : d̑'iək
10 NW Chinese : jig

No.	Char.	Nishida	Sofronov	More Pis'men
1		039-093 tšhi	1592 tśhi̭e	4971

GLOSS : CHIH 姪

Middle Chinese : d'iet
10 NW Chinese : dyar

No.	Char.	Nishida	Sofronov	More Pis'men
1		268-041 tšhɨɦ	1620 tśhi̭ə	0983

GLOSS : **CHIH** 只

Middle Chinese : tśi̯e:
10 NW Chinese : cin̂

No.	**Char.**	**Nishida**	**Sofronov**	**More Pis'men**
1		006-071 tšɨɦ	2928 tśi̭ə	0972

GLOSS : **CHIH** 之

Middle Chinese : tśi:
10 NW Chinese : ci

No.	**Char.**	**Nishida**	**Sofronov**	**More Pis'men**
1		007-144 tšʉ	1976 tśə̂	3797

GLOSS : **CHIH** 知

Middle Chinese : t̑ie̯
10 NW Chinese : ci

No.	**Char.**	**Nishida**	**Sofronov**	**More Pis'men**
1		007-12a tšIɦ	1938 tśi̭e	3359

GLOSS : **CH'IH** 吃

Middle Chinese : ki̯ət
10 NW Chinese : kîr

No.	**Char.**	**Nishida**	**Sofronov**	**More Pis'men**
1	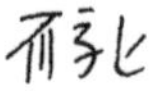	050-06i khiɦ	5284 *	N.L.
2		N.L.	0036 kI	N.L.
3		204-069 khIɦ	3666 vi̭o	1595

4	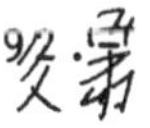	204-07d' khõ	3867 kI	N.L.
5	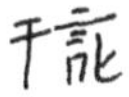	098-083 khɨr	0619 ki̭e	2538
6		026-021 tšiɦ	4885 śâ	N.L.
7		297-073 khɨ	5047 kI	1052
8		204-09f ŋgi	3611 *	N.L.
9		297-084 khɨ	5013 kI	3842

GLOSS : **CH'IH** 赤

Middle Chinese : ts'ĭăk
10 NW Chinese : c"ig

No.	**Char.**	**Nishida**	**Sofronov**	**More Pis'men**
1	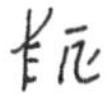	070-041 tšhi	3109 tśhi̭e	3361
2		070-101 tšhi	3112 tśhi̭ə	1151
3		N.L.	N.L.	N.L.
4		269-062 tšhɨɦ-	2303 tśhi̭ə	3805

GLOSS : **CHING** 井

Middle Chinese : tsi̭ăng:
10 NW Chinese : tseń

No.	**Char.**	**Nishida**	**Sofronov**	**More Pis'men**
1		026-116 tseɦ	4932 tsIn	4039

GLOSS : **CH'ING** 青

Middle Chinese : ts'ieng
10 NW Chinese : ts'eń

No.	Char.	Nishida	Sofronov	More Pis'men
1		039-11e tshlə w	1229 tshÎe	4131
2		235-053 -tsheɦ	262̂7 tshIn	1280
3		181-041 tsheɦ	4276 tshIn	1279
4		236-041 tshǐeɦ	2777 tshI̭e	1360

GLOSS : **CH'ING** 精

Middle Chinese : tsi̯äng
10 NW Chinese : tsîñ

No.	Char.	Nishida	Sofronov	More Pis'men
1		136-051 tsǐə̣r	1311 tsIə̣	2557
2		051-091 tsǐə̣r	11̂43 tsIə̣	2556
3		204-07g tseɦ	36̂0̣6 tsIn	4037
4	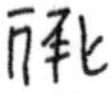	103-061 ⁿdzǐě	0303 ndzIe	2880
5	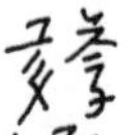	N.L.	456̂8 tsIn	1278
6	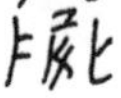	068-082 tsǐər	1262 *	4635
7	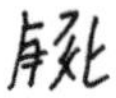	135-061 tšhɔ̆	1312 ndzI̭e	2688

GLOSS : **CH'ING** 請

Middle Chinese : ˛ts'i̯äng:
10 NW Chinese : ts'eñ

No.	Char.	Nishida	Sofronov	More Pis'men
1		236-041 tshǏeɦ	2777 tshI̭e	1360

GLOSS : **CH'ING** 慶

Middle Chinese : k'i̯ăng-
10 NW Chinese : k'ên̂

No.	Char.	Nishida	Sofronov	More Pis'men
1		N.L.	4987 khIn	5113
2		080-043 khen̆	5210 khIn	1271

GLOSS : **CH'ING** 京

Middle Chinese : ki̯ɒng
10 NW Chinese : ke

No.	Char.	Nishida	Sofronov	More Pis'men
1		217-051 ken̆	5794 kIn	5107

GLOSS : **CHIU** 久

Middle Chinese : ki̯ə̯u:
10 NW Chinese : kŷu

No.	Char.	Nishida	Sofronov	More Pis'men
1	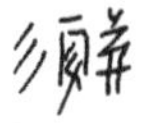	201-131 ŋɣu	3309 ndi	3413
2		135-031 ndɨ	1291 ndI	1043
3	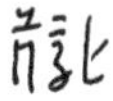	106-071 ɣʉh	1894 ,we	3779
4		001-122 nǐe	1079 ndIe	4093
5	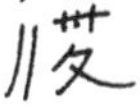	041-064 ndǐě	135̂5 ndI̭e	4130

GLOSS : **CHIUNG** 扃

Middle Chinese : kiweng-
10 NW Chinese : kun̂n

No.	Char.	Nishida	Sofronov	More Pis'men
1	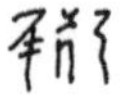	N.L.	N.L.	N.L.
2		N.L.	3379 khI̭u	3262
3		194-062 khĭuɦ	28̂21 khi̭u	0130

GLOSS : **CHO** 捉

Middle Chinese : tṣåk
10 NW Chinese : ċag

No.	Char.	Nishida	Sofronov	More Pis'men
1	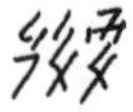	181-123 tšĭor	4258 tśi̭uo	5025
2		255-073 thiɦ	051̂0 thi	0370
3		181-086 thʷiɦ	4309 thwi	0412

GLOSS : **CHO** 濯

Middle Chinese : d̑'åk
10 NW Chinese : c'ag

No.	Char.	Nishida	Sofronov	More Pis'men
1	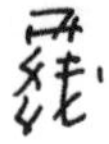	026-095 [illegible]	4980 tśhwôn	1708

GLOSS : **CHOU** 周

Middle Chinese : tś[illegible]u
10 NW Chinese : c[illegible]

No.	Char.	Nishida	Sofronov	More Pis'men
1		018-11b tšĭəw	0188 tśi̭ew	4210

GLOSS : **CH'OU** 醜

Middle Chinese : tś'iə̯u
10 NW Chinese : c'û̂

No.	**Char.**	**Nishida**	**Sofronov**	**More Pis'men**
1		139-072 sɔɦ	1688 so	4298

GLOSS : **CHU** 竹

Middle Chinese : t̑i̭uk
10 NW Chinese : cûg

No.	**Char.**	**Nishida**	**Sofronov**	**More Pis'men**
1		230-062 tI	4743 ti	0367
2		230-092 tšǏu	4737 tsi̭u	3012

GLOSS : **CH'U** 出

Middle Chinese : tś'iuĕt
10 NW Chinese : c'uȓ

No.	**Char.**	**Nishida**	**Sofronov**	**More Pis'men**
1	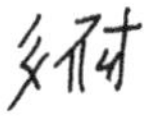	204-06w tšhǏu	3911 tśhi̭ə	0857

GLOSS : **CHÚ** 菊

Middle Chinese : ki̯uk
10 NW Chinese : kûg

No.	Char.	Nishida	Sofronov	More Pis'men
1	[illegible]	N.L.	N.L.	N.L.
2	[illegible]	144-112 kǐụ	3202 ki̯ụ	1800
3	[illegible]	182-122 kǐuɦ	4650 ki̯u	0128

GLOSS : **CHŪ** 鞠

Middle Chinese : ki̯uk
10 NW Chinese : kug

No.	Char.	Nishida	Sofronov	More Pis'men
1	[illegible]	018-084 kǐụ	0236 ki̯ụ	1805

GLOSS :**CH'Ü** 屈

Middle Chinese : k'i̯uət
10 NW Chinese : k'ûr

No.	Char.	Nishida	Sofronov	More Pis'men
1	[illegible]	218-101 khʷɨ	5353 khwI	1099
2	[illegible]	240-063 khʷɨ	4432 khwI	1096
3	[illegible]	078-072 *	2336 khwI	N.L.
4	[illegible]	08 061 ka	5469 kâ	0641
5	[illegible]	058-051 khʷɨ	4795 khwI	1098

GLOSS : **CHÜEH**

Middle Chinese : dz'i̯wät
10 NW Chinese : dzwâr

No	Char.	Nishida	Sofronov	More Pis'men
1		028-101 tsh^{w}aɦ	2596 tshwa	0756

GLOSS : CH'UI 垂

Middle Chinese : źwie̯
10 NW Chinese : źwi̯

No.	Char.	Nishida	Sofronov	More Pis'men
1	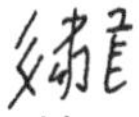	204-121 šǐu	3588 śi̭wu̯	1808
2		N.L.	20̂12 śi̭we	2012
3		156-081 š^{w}ih	46̂82 śi̭we	N.L.

GLOSS : ERH 兒

Middle Chinese : ńźie̯
10 NW Chinese : źi̯

No.	Char.	Nishida	Sofronov	More Pis'men
1	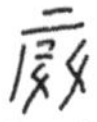	004-081 ňži	N.L.	N.L.
2	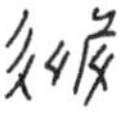	204-08q ňžir	3763 ži̭ə	1147

GLOSS : FEN 豶

Middle Chinese : b̂'i̭uən
10 NW Chinese : b'ûn

No.	Char.	Nishida	Sofronov	More Pis'men
1		028-115 VI̩	N.L.	N.L.

GLOSS : HSI 西

Middle Chinese : siei
10 NW Chinese : sye

No.	Char.	Nishida	Sofronov	More Pis'men
1		017-11d siɦ	0881 si	0392
2		007-132 siɦ	2018 si	3443
3		152-122 tsɨ	2448 sI̭ẹi	2063
4	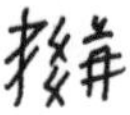	087-121 siɦ	5490 sI̭e	0472

GLOSS : **HSI** 西

Middle Chinese : siei
10 NW Chinese : sye

No	Char.	Nishida	Sofronov	More Pis'men
1		276-041 ʋuh	3635 .wə	0928

GLOSS : **HSI** 息

Middle Chinese : si̯ək
10 NW Chinese : sŷe

No	Char.	Nishida	Sofronov	More Pis'men
1		269-063 siɦ	2308 si	3438
2		204-11w siɦ	3378 si	3440

GLOSS : **HSI** 悉

Middle Chinese : siĕt
10 NW Chinese : sîr

No	Char	Nishida	Sofronov	More Pis'men
1		0[illegible]7-125 sɨ	0770 *	4331
2		204-09r tšhĭẽ	3596 se	N.L.
3	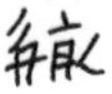	144-075 sI	3268 se	0254
4	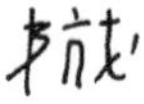	087-091	5480	1073

No.	Char.	Nishida	Sofronov	More Pis'men
		sɨ	sI	
5	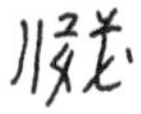	041-113 sɨ	1465 sIeɰ	1512
6	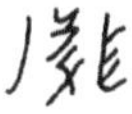	039-092 si̭r	1542 se	3291

GLOSS : **HSIEH** 寫

Middle Chinese : si̭a:
10 NW Chinese : sy̌a

No.	Char.	Nishida	Sofronov	More Pis'men
1	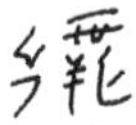	181-101 ɓzɨr	4173 sIn	N.L.
2		116-051 se	4496 sI̭ẹ	0772

GLOSS : **HSIEH** 薛

Middle Chinese : si̭ät
10 NW Chinese : sar

No.	Char.	Nishida	Sofronov	More Pis'men
1		211-067 saɦ	5706 śwê	3343

GLOSS : **HSIEH** 斜

Middle Chinese : si̭ät
10 NW Chinese : sar

No	Char.	Nishida	Sofronov	More Pis'men
1	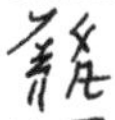	036-121 seɦ	2358 sIn	1285
2	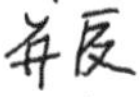	141-001 seɦ	2329 sIn	4042
3		220-052 seɦ	0147 tsi	3434
4	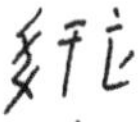	211-064 sǐeɦ	5662 sI̭e	4097
5	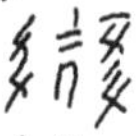	211-131 ʔyɔh	5718 .ôn	4471
6	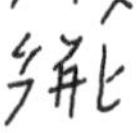	181-072 seɦ	4221 sIn	2121

GLOSS : **HSING** 星

Middle Chinese : sieng
10 NW Chinese : sye

No.	**Char.**	**Nishida**	**Sofronov**	**More Pis'men**
1		017-115 -seɦ	0815 sIn	4045
2	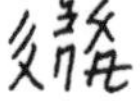	204-12c seɦ	N.L.	N.L.
3		N.L.	N.L.	N.L.

GLOSS :**HSING** 杏

Middle Chinese : ɣɒng
10 NW Chinese : hin

No.	**Char.**	**Nishida**	**Sofronov**	**More Pis'men**
1		017-141 xẽ	0730 xai	4108

GLOSS : **HSÜ**

Middle Chinese : siuĕt
10 NW Chinese : sûr

No.	**Char.**	**Nishida**	**Sofronov**	**More Pis'men**
1		315-081 sǐ"	1327 sIwI	1118
2		109-041 sʷɨ	1Î07 swI	3872
3	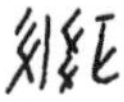	205-093 GǐUɦ	N.L.	N.L.

GLOSS : **HSÜ** 續

Middle Chinese : ziwok
10 NW Chinese : swâg

No.	Char.	Nishida	Sofronov	More Pis'men
1		007-143 sǐuɦ	1966 su	N.L.
2		098-081 sǐuɦ	0659 su	3207

GLOSS : **HSÜAN**

Middle Chinese : ɣiwen
10 NW Chinese : hwan

No	Char.	Nishida	Sofronov	More Pis'men
1		255-042 ti̯	0476 tI̭ẹi	2050
2	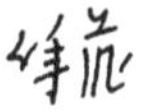	061-073 ti̯	4098 tI̭ẹi	2049

GLOSS : **HSÜEH** 削

Middle Chinese : si̯ak
10 NW Chinese : syag

No.	Char.	Nishida	Sofronov	More Pis'men
1		026-124 sǐu	4919 sI̭wụ	4538

GLOSS : **HUI** 回

Middle Chinese : ɣiweng
10 NW Chinese : hoń

No.	Char.	Nishida	Sofronov	More Pis'men
1		204-09b wǐɔh	3878 wo	4263
2		112-091 wǐɔh	0316 wo	N.L.

GLOSS : I 乙

Middle Chinese : .iě̌t
10 NW Chinese : yīr

No.	Char.	Nishida	Sofronov	More Pis'men
1		026-102 ɣiəw	4905 .êɰ	4238
2		009-117 ɣɨ	1070 .iə	2123
3	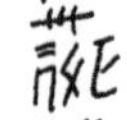	0̂17-11b ɣʉ	0̂682 .i̯ə	2124
4		210-062 li	4003 ldI̯ei	2067
5		017-054 ŋɦuɦ	08̂83 ngI̯u	2256
6		007-092 ŋɦuɦ	2002 ngwu	0208
7		108-101 ɣɨɦ	4341 .iə	0992
8		031-062 ɣiɦ	3978 .iə	4980
9		0̂18-105 ɣiɦ	0244 .iə	0991
10		056-082 ɣɨ	24̂08 .Iə	2478
11		N.L.	08̂75 .i̭ə	0993

GLOSS : I 宜

Middle Chinese : ngjie
10 NW Chinese : 'ji ^

No.	Char.	Nishida	Sofronov	More Pis'men
1		103-092 ŋgiɦ	4350 ngi	0381
2	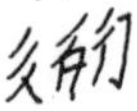	N.L.	N.L.	N.L.
3		171-061 ŋgiɦ	1771 mə	3726

GLOSS : I 衣

Middle Chinese : .jei
10 NW Chinese : 'i^

No.	Char.	Nishida	Sofronov	More Pis'men
1		154-051 ʔir	0444 .i̯e	2321

GLOSS : I 依

Middle Chinese : 'jei
10 NW Chinese : 'i^

No	Char.	Nishida	Sofronov	More Pis'men
1		017-056 ʔiɦ	0928 .i̯ei	5126

GLOSS : I 義

Middle Chinese : ngjie-
10 NW Chinese : 'ji^

No	Char.	Nishida	Sofronov	More Pis'men
1	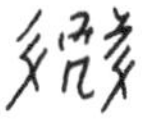	N.L.	3866 .i	0401

GLOSS : I 夷

Middle Chinese : i
10 NW Chinese : i

No	Char.	Nishida	Sofronov	More Pis'men
1		017-162 ʔih	0888 .i	0402
2		297-032 ʔyɨ	5050 .i	3859
3		211-082 ʔyɨ	5691 .I	1078

GLOSS : I 易

Middle Chinese : iäng
10 NW Chinese : oń

No.	Char.	Nishida	Sofronov	More Pis'men
1		099-061 ʔyɨ	2152 .I	3862
2		219-081 ʔyiɦ	1182 .i̭ə	4973
3	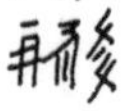	123-111 ʔyiɦ	0380 .i̭ə	4974
4	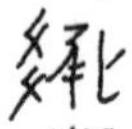	215-071 xiɦ	5770 .i̭e	4868
5		017-056 ʔih	0928 .i̭ei	5126

GLOSS : JAN 染

Middle Chinese : ńźi̭äm:
10 NW Chinese : źyam

No	Char.	Nishida	Sofronov	More Pis'men
1		017-108 liʷõ	N.L.	N.L.
2		041-122 lǐɔɦ	1442 lhi̭o	2830

GLOSS : JOU 柔

Middle Chinese : ńźi̭əu
10 NW Chinese : źyû

No.	Char.	Nishida	Sofronov	More Pis'men
1		017-123 ňžǐew	0681 ngIn	4029
2		211-066 ňžu	5666 źi̭əɰ	1518

GLOSS : **JU** 乳

Middle Chinese : ńźi̯u:
10 NW Chinese : źu

No.	**Char.**	**Nishida**	**Sofronov**	**More Pis'men**
1		181-102 ňžǐu	4290 z̀i̭u	3136

GLOSS : **JU** 汝

Middle Chinese : ńźi̯wo:
10 NW Chinese : źu

No.	**Char.**	**Nishida**	**Sofronov**	**More Pis'men**
1		181-102 ňžǐu	4282 z̀i̭ẹ	N.L.

GLOSS : **KAN** 幹

Middle Chinese : kân-
10 NW Chinese : kan

No.	**Char.**	**Nishida**	**Sofronov**	**More Pis'men**
1		205-043 nạ	N.L.	N.L.
2	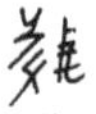	236-058 wạ	2695 wạ	1960
3		017-086 wa	0751 wa	4924
4		179-081 ˀwa	1136 wạ	N.L.

GLOSS : **K'ANG** 康

Middle Chinese : kɒng
10 NW Chinese : kań

No.	**Char.**	**Nishida**	**Sofronov**	**More Pis'men**
1		018-111 kɛ	0226 kẹi	2020
2		123-071 khʷɔ̃	0374 khi̭on	1713

GLOSS : **K'E** 刻

Middle Chinese : k'ɒk
10 NW Chinese : kag

No.	**Char.**	**Nishida**	**Sofronov**	**More Pis'men**
1		010-072 khɨ	4329 khi	3844

GLOSS : **K'E** 剋

Middle Chinese : k'ək
10 NW Chinese : k'eg

No.	**Char.**	**Nishida**	**Sofronov**	**More Pis'men**
1		098-082 khɨɦ	0635 kIə	1173
2		N.L.	N̂.L.	N.L.

GLOSS : **KENG** 更

Middle Chinese : kɒng
10 NW Chinese : keń

No.	**Char.**	**Nishida**	**Sofronov**	**More Pis'men**
1		183-061 kẽ	N.L.	N.L.

GLOSS : **KO** 各

Middle Chinese : kâk
10 NW Chinese : kıɣ

No.	**Char.**	**Nishida**	**Sofronov**	**More Pis'men**
1		261-101 kʉr	0455 kwə̣	2434

GLOSS : KO 葛

Middle Chinese : kât
10 NW Chinese : kar

No.	Char.	Nishida	Sofronov	More Pis'men
1		236-068 kar	2715 kạɰ	2410
2	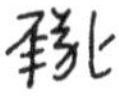	059-071 kaɦ	4819 ka	3544
3		009-112 kaɦ-	4671 ka	3543
4		017-12p kĭah	N.L.	N.L.

GLOSS : KO 箇

Middle Chinese : kâ-
10 NW Chinese : ka

No.	Char.	Nishida	Sofronov	More Pis'men
1		263-001 kɔr	0264 kụo	N.L

GLOSS : KO 閤

Middle Chinese : kạp
10 NW Chinese : kab

No.	Char.	Nishida	Sofronov	More Pis'men
1		107-052 ɣạ	4489 .ạ	4668

GLOSS : KO 割

Middle Chinese : kât
10 NW Chinese : kar

No.	Char.	Nishida	Sofronov	More Pis'men
1		222-051 kaɦ	5389 ka	0562
2		236-068 kar	2715 kạɰ	2410

GLOSS : **K'O** 渴

Middle Chinese : k'ât
10 NW Chinese : kar

No.	Char.	Nishida	Sofronov	More Pis'men
1	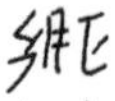	181-073 khaɦ	4199 kha	3628
2		157-071 khaɦ	1738 kha	0570

GLOSS : **K'O** 客

Middle Chinese : kɒk
10 NW Chinese : kag

No.	Char.	Nishida	Sofronov	More Pis'men
1	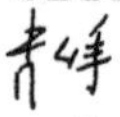	139-061 khI	1701 khê	3341
2	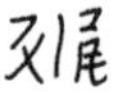	218-062 khI	5350 khê	3340
3		013-062 khɨ	2478 khi̭ə	3880

GLOSS : **KOU** 勾

Middle Chinese : kə̭u-
10 NW Chinese : kâu

No.	Char.	Nishida	Sofronov	More Pis'men
1		N.L.	N.L.	N.L.

GLOSS : **KOU** 苟

Middle Chinese : kə̯u
10 NW Chinese : kau

No.	**Char.**	**Nishida**	**Sofronov**	**More Pis'men**
1		205-052 kĭəw	3548 kêɰ	1482

GLOSS : **KU** 姑

Middle Chinese : kuo
10 NW Chinese : ku

No.	**Char.**	**Nishida**	**Sofronov**	**More Pis'men**
1		033-101 ku	N.L.	N.L.
2		N.L.	N.L.	N.L.
3		211-141 ku-	5761 ku	0178
4		N.L.	4139 ku	0029

GLOSS : **KU** 骨

Middle Chinese : kuət
10 NW Chinese : kur

No.	**Char.**	**Nishida**	**Sofronov**	**More Pis'men**
1		102-051 kʉɦ	0133 kə	0856
2		261-101 kʉr	0455 kwə̣	2434
3		N.L.	N.L.	N.L.

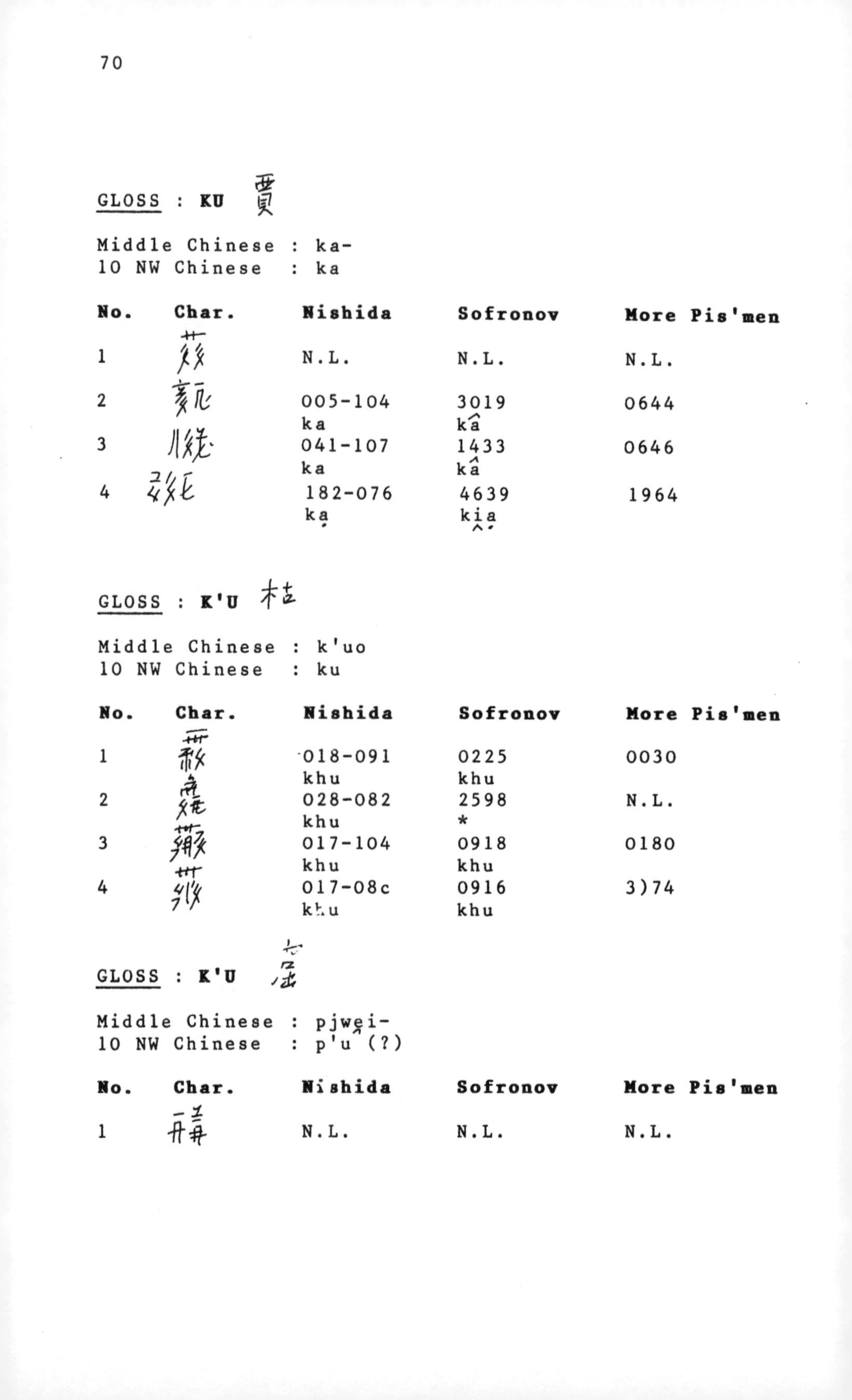

GLOSS : **KU** 賈

Middle Chinese : ka-
10 NW Chinese : ka

No.	Char.	Nishida	Sofronov	More Pis'men
1	[illegible]	N.L.	N.L.	N.L.
2	[illegible]	005-104 ka	3019 kâ	0644
3	[illegible]	041-107 ka	1433 kâ	0646
4	[illegible]	182-076 kạ	4639 ki̭ạ	1964

GLOSS : **K'U** 枯

Middle Chinese : k'uo
10 NW Chinese : ku

No.	Char.	Nishida	Sofronov	More Pis'men
1	[illegible]	018-091 khu	0225 khu	0030
2	[illegible]	028-082 khu	2598 *	N.L.
3	[illegible]	017-104 khu	0918 khu	0180
4	[illegible]	017-08c khu	0916 khu	3)74

GLOSS : **K'U** [illegible]

Middle Chinese : pjwęi-
10 NW Chinese : p'u (?)

No.	Char.	Nishida	Sofronov	More Pis'men
1	[illegible]	N.L.	N.L.	N.L.

GLOSS : **KUA** 刮

Middle Chinese : kwat
10 NW Chinese : kwar

No.	**Char.**	**Nishida**	**Sofronov**	**More Pis'men**
1		185-092 $k^{w}a$	5525 kwạ	N.L

GLOSS : **KUAN** 斡

Middle Chinese : kuân:
10 NW Chinese : kwan

No.	**Char.**	**Nishida**	**Sofronov**	**More Pis'men**
1		261-092 waɦ	0456 wa	4673
2		179-081 ʔwa	N.L.	N.L.

GLOSS : **KUANG** 光

Middle Chinese : kwâng
10 NW Chinese : kwan

No.	**Char.**	**Nishida**	**Sofronov**	**More Pis'men**
1		162-041 kɔr	N.L.	N.L.

GLOSS : **K'UEI** 魁

Middle Chinese : jwe̯i:
10 NW Chinese : 'wei

No.	**Char.**	**Nishida**	**Sofronov**	**More Pis'men**
1	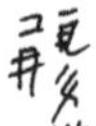	128-091 khʉɦ	4504 khwə	0931
2		211-101 $kh^{w}ɛ$	5660 khwei	3926

GLOSS : **KUO** 郭

Middle Chinese : kwâk
10 NW Chinese : kwag

No.	**Char.**	**Nishida**	**Sofronov**	**More Pis'men**
1		N.L.	N.L.	N.L.
2		181-083 kụ	4196 khụ	4501

GLOSS : **KUO** 果

Middle Chinese : kuâ:
10 NW Chinese : kwa

No.	**Char.**	**Nishida**	**Sofronov**	**More Pis'men**
1		017-171 kɔɦ	0683 ko	1555
2		139-052 kɔɦ	1690 kwo	1579
3		031-063 k^{w}ọ	3971 kọ	2561
4		204-099 kɔɦ	3675 ko	N.L.
5		028-091 kɔɦ	2554 kon	4376

GLOSS : **K'UO** 闊

Middle Chinese : k'uât
10 NW Chinese : kwar

No.	**Char.**	**Nishida**	**Sofronov**	**More Pis'men**
1	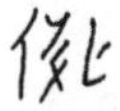	043-071 khaɦ	3103 khwa	3579
2	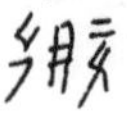	181-087 $kh^{w}a$	4198 khạ	N.L.

GLOSS : **LA** 辣

Middle Chinese : la:
10 NW Chinese : la

No.	Char.	Nishida	Sofronov	More Pis'men
1		009-115 lạ	4696 lI̭ạ	1995
2		204-092 Gar	3663 kạɰ	2409
3		041-067 la	1379 la	0752
4		147-061 lạ	N.L.	N.L.
5		230-075 la	4734 lI̭ạ	1993
6		N.L.	4746 lI̭ạ	5103

GLOSS : **LA** 臈

Middle Chinese : ɣât
10 NW Chinese : ha

No.	Char.	Nishida	Sofronov	More Pis'men
1		039-061 ɬa	1545 ldạ	1957
2	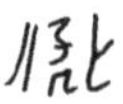	041-077 ɬạ	1485 ldạ	1958

GLOSS : **LAI** 來

Middle Chinese : lậi
10 NW Chinese : lai

No.	Char.	Nishida	Sofronov	More Pis'men
1		105-072 lɛ	2982 lei	3915

GLOSS : LAI 賴

Middle Chinese : lâi-
10 NW Chinese : lai

No.	Char.	Nishida	Sofronov	More Pis'men
1		189-061 lĭɛ̣	2180 lai	4556

GLOSS : LAI 瀨

Middle Chinese : lâi-
10 NW Chinese : lai

No.	Char.	Nishida	Sofronov	More Pis'men
1		139-053 lɛ	1720 ndon	N.L.
2	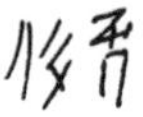	041-095 lĭɛ̣	1443 lậi	0646

GLOSS : LANG 浪

Middle Chinese : lâng
10 NW Chinese : lań

No.	Char.	Nishida	Sofronov	More Pis'men
1	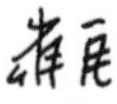	164-061 li	5122 ldIə̣	2159
2	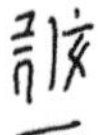	108-061 l·ɦ	4343 la	3568
3		018-08a lo	0203 lo	N.L.
4		054-041 lŏ	5456 lwon	4418
5		018-''1a lč?	0254 ldwon	N.L.
6	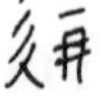	204-056 -lŏ	3400 lwon	4413
7		240-062 *	4429 vieɰ	N.L.
8		144-091 lhɔ	3276 lhọ	2816
9		028-031 lŏ	N.L.	N.L.

GLOSS : **LAO** 牢

Middle Chinese : lâu
10 NW Chinese : lau

No.	**Char.**	**Nishida**	**Sofronov**	**More Pis'men**
1		214-061 ŋgɪ̆uɦ	5168 ndẑi̭on	4376

GLOSS : **LE** 勒

Middle Chinese : lək
10 NW Chinese : leg

No.	**Char.**	**Nishida**	**Sofronov**	**More Pis'men**
1		210-055 ɬI	4023 ldI̭ə	5140
2		058-011 lI	4802 lde	3295
3		204-07f ɬɨr	3565 thI̭oɰ	1644
4	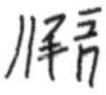	041-112 ɬɨ	1445 lə	N.L.
5		210-061 lɨ	3889 lhI	3864
6		210-086 -VI	4029 we	3305
7		001-131 li	1198 lde	3298
8		204-066 lhɨ	3881 lhə	N.L.
9		204-08c ɬə w	3346 ldeɰ	4179
10		181-062 lʉɦ	4305 ldI̭ə	1182
11		164-041 ɬɨ̣	5126 ldI̭ə̣	2156
12		002-061 lɨ	0286 lə	3104

GLOSS : **LI** 梨

Middle Chinese : lji
10 NW Chinese : lwi

No.	**Char.**	**Nishida**	**Sofronov**	**More Pis'men**
1		N.L.	5592 ma	0726

GLOSS : **LI** 里

Middle Chinese : lji:
10 NW Chinese : lwi

No.	**Char.**	**Nishida**	**Sofronov**	**More Pis'men**
1	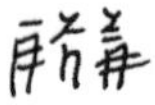	N.L.	N.L.	N.L.

GLOSS : **LENG** 冷

Middle Chinese : lieng:
10 NW Chinese : leń

No.	**Char.**	**Nishida**	**Sofronov**	**More Pis'men**
1		049-091 lǐɛ̣	5263 ldậi	1851

GLOSS : **LI** 力

Middle Chinese : li̯ək
10 NW Chinese : lǐg

No.	**Char.**	**Nishida**	**Sofronov**	**More Pis'men**
1		N.L.	N.L.	N.L.
2	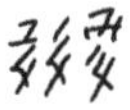	230-112 li	4755 z̀ie	2820
3	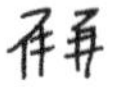	080-051 ḷi	5235 ldÎẹi	N.L.
4		180-086 rir	4114 rîẹ	N.L.
5		269-064 lị	2294 ldI̭ei	N.L.

GLOSS : **LI** 栗

Middle Chinese : li̯ět
10 NW Chinese : lǐr

No.	**Char.**	**Nishida**	**Sofronov**	**More Pis'men**
1		236-063 łɨ̣	2718 ldi̭ə̣	2111

GLOSS : LING 領

Middle Chinese : b'ieng
10 NW Chinese : leń

No.	Char.	Nishida	Sofronov	More Pis'men
1		049-052 ɨe	5270 thIn	5088
2		031-066 rǐẽ	3973 ldI̭e	4147
3		007-088 rir	2020 ri̭ẹ	4876
4		041-108 ɨɛ̣	13̂81 ldI̭e	1906
5		031-067 rǐẽ	397̂7 ldIẹ	N.L.
6		123-064 lɛ	038̂4 ldIe	1907
7	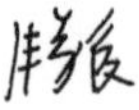	075-111 lǐeń	129̂7 ldI̭e	4100
8	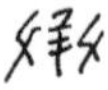	202-082 lǐẹ	5615 riẹ	4795
9		155-043 le-	45̂15 riẹ	4808
10		080-021 rǐẹ	52̂33 riẹ	2225
11		017-08L lǐẽ	09̂21 ldịe	N.L.
12	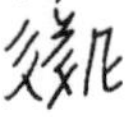	204-096 lhe	36̂90 lhi̭ə	N.L.

GLOSS : LING 嶺

Middle Chinese : b'ieng (?)
10 NW Chinese : len (?)

No.	Char.	Nishida	Sofronov	More Pis'men
1	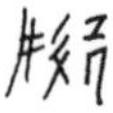	N.L	N.L.	N.L.

GLOSS : **LING** 令

Middle Chinese : li̯äng
10 NW Chinese : leń

No.	Char.	Nishida	Sofronov	More Pis'men
1	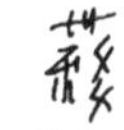	017c-052 le	0971 li̯e̯	4571
2		059-041 leɦ	4815 lIn	4054
3	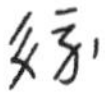	204-05f lǐe	3693 ri̯e̯	4791
4	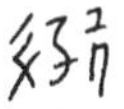	204-071 lǐẽ	N.L.	N.L.
5		047-043 lǐeɦ	2266 li̯e̯	4098
6		147B-041 *	1714 *	N.L.

GLOSS : **LIU** 流

Middle Chinese : li̯əu
10 NW Chinese : lû

No.	Char.	Nishida	Sofronov	More Pis'men
1	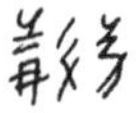	130-101 lǐər	1792 ri̯e̯ɰ	2500

GLOSS : LIU 六

Middle Chinese : li̭uk
10 NW Chinese : lûg

No.	Char.	Nishida	Sofronov	More Pis'men
1		017-114 lǐuɦ	0702 li̭wu	0099
2		018-093 lǐu	0171 lI̭wụ	4549
3		319́-093 lǐuɦ	52̂31́ ldi̭u	0149
4		181-075 Lǐu	418̂4 liwu	3162
5		192-073 lǐụ	29̂05 lI̭wu	4548
6		010̣-051 lǐu	43̂91 lIwụ	4544
7		017́-10g *	06̂87̣ leɰ	4227
8		017-093 lǐu	0722 śi̭wu	3157
9		01́0-102 lǐu	4393 lI̭wu	4547
10		031̇-064 lǐụ	39̂74́ lI̭wụ	4546
11		182̇-111 lǐu	46̂66̇ li̭wu	3160

GLOSS : LO 落

Middle Chinese : lâk
10 NW Chinese : lag

No.	Char.	Nishida	Sofronov	More Pis'men
1		045-121 laɦ	3141 lwa	3586
2		007-142 ɣkǐẹ	1977 .âi	4564

GLOSS : **LO** 羅

Middle Chinese : lâ
10 NW Chinese : la

No.	Char.	Nishida	Sofronov	More Pis'men
1		236-141 -rar	2676 ri̯a	2384
2	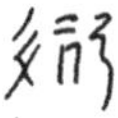	204-07a -rar	3359 ra̦	4911
3		041-104 rar	1466 ri̯a	2383
4		308-071 lɔʀ	0398 ldwon	4425
5		230-102 rar	4711 ri̯ạ	2390

GLOSS : **LOU** 婁

Middle Chinese : li̯u
10 NW Chinese : lû

No.	Char.	Nishida	Sofronov	More Pis'men
1		001-051 ləw	1075 leɰ	1460
2		N.L.	5785 lweɰ	1470
3		122-062 lǐuh?	0367 le	3330
4		170-061 ləw	5087 leɰ	4178

GLOSS : **LU** 魯

Middle Chinese : luo:
10 NW Chinese : lu

No.	Char.	Nishida	Sofronov	More Pis'men
1		236-051 lhu	2712 lhu	2843
2		N.L.	4954 ldu	N.L.

GLOSS : **LU** 路

Middle Chinese : luo-
10 NW Chinese : lug

No.	**Char.**	**Nishida**	**Sofronov**	**More Pis'men**
1		211-101 khʷe	5660 khwei	3926
2		017-124 *	0846 lu	3109
3		086-042 lʉɦ	5473 lwə	3782
4		179-051 lu	1132 lụ	4507
5		006-102 lu	2949 lu	3106

GLOSS : **LU** 盧

Middle Chinese : luo
10 NW Chinese : lu

No.	**Char.**	**Nishida**	**Sofronov**	**More Pis'men**
1		N.L.	N.L.	N.L.
2		026-094 lu	4836 ldu	1777
3		202-092 lụ	5604 ldu	4520

GLOSS : **LÜEH** 略

Middle Chinese : li̯ak
10 NW Chinese : lyag

No.	**Char.**	**Nishida**	**Sofronov**	**More Pis'men**
1		319-093 lĭuɦ	N.L.	N.L.

GLOSS : **LUI** 縲

Middle Chinese : ljwi
10 NW Chinese : lwi

No.	Char.	Nishida	Sofronov	More Pis'men
1		N.L.	0900 ldwẹi	2075

GLOSS : **MA** 馬

Middle Chinese : ma:
10 NW Chinese : ma

No.	Char.	Nishida	Sofronov	More Pis'men
1		187-072 ʔyǐu	0062 .îu	3149
2		N.L.	0746 .i̭u	3155

GLOSS : **MA** 麻

Middle Chinese : ma
10 NW Chinese : ma

No.	Char.	Nishida	Sofronov	More Pis'men
1		026-106 maɦ	4969 ma	0728
2		161-052 ma	5101 ma	0801
3		N.L.	N.L.	N.L.
4		N.L.	N.L.	N.L.
5		269-071 mah	2293 ma	0800
6		018-088 maɦ	0245 ma	0734
7	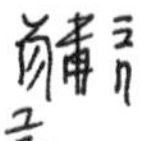	260-121 maɦ	2348 ma	0727
8		236-074 mạ	2776 mI̭ạ	N.L.

GLOSS : **MEI** 每

Middle Chinese : muai
10 NW Chinese : mai

No.	**Char.**	**Nishida**	**Sofronov**	**More Pis'men**
1		044-061 mʷI	3123 me	N.L.
2		080-052 mɛ	5227 mbe̯i	4696
3		044-051 mʷI	3122 me	3281
4		211-031 mʷIɦ	5759 me	3471
5		221-041 ma-	0157 mbâ	N.L.

GLOSS : **MEI** 昧

Middle Chinese : muai-
10 NW Chinese : mai

No.	**Char.**	**Nishida**	**Sofronov**	**More Pis'men**
1	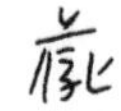	007-087 mɛ	1850 mei	1207
2		017-112 mɛ	1016 mbe	0248

GLOSS : **MENG** 夢

Middle Chinese : mi̯ung-
10 NW Chinese : mêń

No.	**Char.**	**Nishida**	**Sofronov**	**More Pis'men**
1		217-091 mʉɦ	N.L.	N.L.

GLOSS : **MI** 迷

Middle Chinese : miei
10 NW Chinese : mi

No.	Char.	Nishida	Sofronov	More Pis'men
1	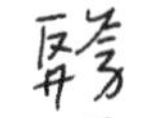	256-072 mbiɦ	0571 mbi	0362
2		255-074 mbiɦ	0488 mbi	3392
3		179-071 mbiɦ	1135 mbi	0385
4	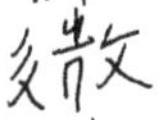	204-107 mbiɦ	3592 mbi	0361
5		N.L.	N.L.	N.L.
6		N.L.	5191 mbi	0359

<u>GLOSS</u> : **MIAO** 藐

Middle Chinese : mi̯ău:
10 NW Chinese : mŷau

No.	Char.	Nishida	Sofronov	More Pis'men
1		204-057 mbǐow	3905 mbô	1587

<u>GLOSS</u> : **MING** 名

Middle Chinese : mi̯āng
10 NW Chinese : mŷeń

No.	Char.	Nishida	Sofronov	More Pis'men
1	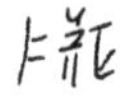	068-091 mIɦ	1257 mIe	0458
2		102-052 meɦ	0̂090 mIn	5078
3		204-08h mĭeɦ	3722 mI̥e	4088
4		010-113 mɛ	43̂36 mbIe	1880
5	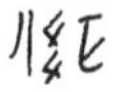	04̇1-081 miɦ	14̂9ı̂ mi	0354
6		114-051 meɦ	3005 mIn	5079
7		205-058 meɦ	3510 mIn	5080
8		208-062 mĭeɦ	2375 mIḙ	1343

9		007-102 miɦ	2062 mi	0356
10	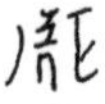	005-071 mǐe	2934 mIẹ	4777
11		N.L.	N.L.	N.L.

GLOSS : **MING** 酩

Middle Chinese : mi̯ăng
10 NW Chinese : myeń

No.	**Char.**	**Nishida**	**Sofronov**	**More Pis'men**
1	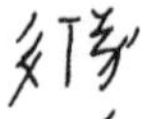	204-08y mǐe	3438 mIẹ	N.L
2	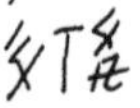	204-o9z mʷɨ	3446 mIẹ	4774
3		051-041 me	1151 mɔ	5039
4		204-08i mǐe	3559 mIe	4775
5	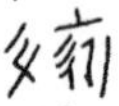	204-08h mǐeɦ	3722 mIẹ	4)88
6	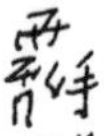	N.L.	N.L.	N.L.
7	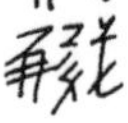	148-101 mIɦ	5298 mIẹ	3491

GLOSS : **MO** 末

Middle Chinese : muât
10 NW Chinese : 'bar

No.	**Char.**	**Nishida**	**Sofronov**	**More Pis'men**
1		047-031 mbar	2267 mbạ	2351
2		008-091 mạ	1831 mbạ	1931
3		N.L.	N.L.	N.L.
4		N.L.	5434 mbe	3285

GLOSS : **MO** 磨

Middle Chinese : muâ
10 NW Chinese : ma

No.	**Char.**	**Nishida**	**Sofronov**	**More Pis'men**
1		211-051 mɔɦ	5671 mo	4260
2		182-112 mɔɦ	4616 mo	4259

GLOSS : **MO** 抹

Middle Chinese : muât
10 NW Chinese : mar

No.	**Char.**	**Nishida**	**Sofronov**	**More Pis'men**
1		211-091 m^{w}a-	N.L.	N.L.

GLOSS : **MO** 麼

Middle Chinese : mua:
10 NW Chinese : ma

No.	**Char.**	**Nishida**	**Sofronov**	**More Pis'men**
1	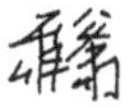	162-092 muɦ	5116 mu	0169
2	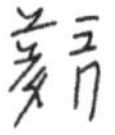	007-10g mɔɦ	1958 mo	4261

GLOSS : **MO** 墨

Middle Chinese : mək
10 NW Chinese : meg

No.	**Char.**	**Nishida**	**Sofronov**	**More Pis'men**
1		211-055 mI	5728 mbe	3283

2		226-032 mI̥	N.L.	N.L.
3	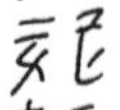	221-043 mʷiɦ	0155 mbe	3468
4	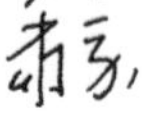	157-051 mI̥	5101 ma	0801

GLOSS : **MO** 魔

Middle Chinese : mua:
10 NW Chinese : ma

No.	**Char.**	**Nishida**	**Sofronov**	**More Pis'men**
1		005-083 mɔɦ	N.L.	N.L.

GLOSS : **MO** 莫

Middle Chinese : muo-
10 NW Chinese : mu

No.	**Char.**	**Nishida**	**Sofronov**	**More Pis'men**
1		204-041 lhe	3420 ldi̭a	3657

GLOSS : **MOU** 謀

Middle Chinese : mi̯ə̯u
10 NW Chinese : mu

No.	**Char.**	**Nishida**	**Sofronov**	**More Pis'men**
1		017-09b mĭUɦ	0961 mbIn	N.L.
2		180-051 mbĭuɦ	4068 mbu	N.L.
3		211-055 mɨr	5764 mbuo	2529
4		144-073 mu	3273 pa̧	N.L.
5		N.L.	N.L.	N.L.

6		031-071 Bur	3972 mbu	N.L.
7	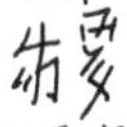	N.L.	3086 mbI̯u	0222
8	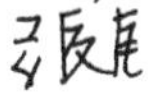	182-104 mbíuɦ	461̂4 mbu	0103
9		020-123 mbǐuɦ	1036 mbu	0106

GLOSS : **MU** 暮

Middle Chinese : muo:
10 NW Chinese : mu

No.	**Char.**	**Nishida**	**Sofronov**	**More Pis'men**
1		204-10d mǐoɦ	3468 mbI̯u	3253
2		159-092 mǐUɦ	30̂86 mbǐu	0̀222
3	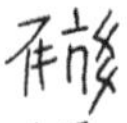	080-091 mǐu	52̂25 mbu	3182
4	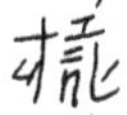	N.L.	0599 *	4815
5		083-041 mǐu	2433 mbu	1783
6	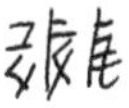	182-104 mbíuɦ	4614 mbu	0103
7	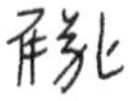	080-064 *	5201 *	N.L.

GLOSS : **MU** 沐

Middle Chinese : muk
10 NW Chinese : mug

No.	**Char.**	**Nishida**	**Sofronov**	**More Pis'men**
1		204-102 mu	3457 mbu	0011

GLOSS : **NA** 捺

Middle Chinese : nâi-
10 NW Chinese : nai

No.	Char.	Nishida	Sofronov	More Pis'men
1		N.L.	1651 na	3626

GLOSS : **NA** 拏

Middle Chinese : ná
10 NW Chinese : na

No.	Char.	Nishida	Sofronov	More Pis'men
1		N.L.	0678 ndẑâ	N.L.
2	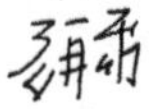	184-111 na	5495 ndźâ	2754
3		N.L.	0786 ndźâ	2991
4	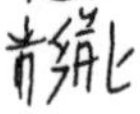	176-091 ndžã̌	1769 tśân	3701
5	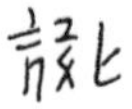	110-071 ndžã̌	2887 ngI̭ẹ	1901

GLOSS : **NA** 納

Middle Chinese : nập
10 NW Chinese : 'dab

No.	Char.	Nishida	Sofronov	More Pis'men
1	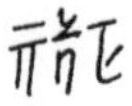	102-084 nạ	N.L.	N.L.
2		081-041 na	5251 ndạ	4654
3		230-083 nạ	4777 ndạ	N.L.

GLOSS : **NA** 那

Middle Chinese : nâ
10 NW Chinese : na

No.	Char.	Nishida	Sofronov	More Pis'men
1		026-093 na	N.L.	N.L.
2		204-077 naɦ	3456 na	0547
3		007-116 naɦ	2055 na	0554
4		N.L.	N.L.	N.L.
5		018-08b nɔɦ	0240 no	4277
6	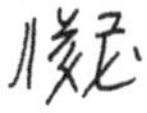	007-104 naw	1790 naɰ	3661
7	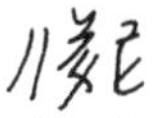	041-102 now	1403 no	1550
8	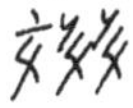	233-102 nɔw	N.L.	N.L.
9	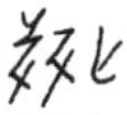	235-064 na	2114 ndo	4289
10	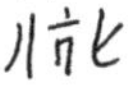	041-066 nɨ	N.L.	N.L.
11	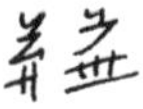	N.L.	N.L.	N.L.
12	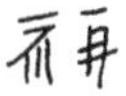	051-052 nõ	1141 ndon	1662

GLOSS : **NAI** 奈

Middle Chinese : nâi-
10 NW Chinese : nai

No.	Char.	Nishida	Sofronov	More Pis'men
1	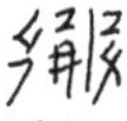	181-122 nɛ̌	4273 nI̥	4603
2		147-041 ²yǐu	N.L.	N.L.

GLOSS : **NAI** 乃

Middle Chinese : nậi:
10 NW Chinese : nei

No.	**Char.**	**Nishida**	**Sofronov**	**More Pis'men**
1		018-095 nɛ	0230 nei	3904
2		017-102 nɛ	0860 nại	4551
3		181-091 nɛ	4209 nei	3907
4		189-021 nɛ	N.L.	N.L.
5	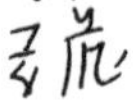	182-074 nhe	N.L.	N.L.
6	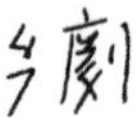	181-112 nẹ	N.L.	N.L.

GLOSS : **NEI** 内

Middle Chinese : nập
10 NW Chinese : 'dei

No.	**Char.**	**Nishida**	**Sofronov**	**More Pis'men**
1		098-061 pɛ̃	0643 pI̭	4606

GLOSS : **NENG** 能

Middle Chinese : nəng
10 NW Chinese : niṅ

No.	**Char.**	**Nishida**	**Sofronov**	**More Pis'men**
1	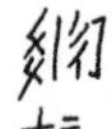	211-063 nɛ̃	5678 nə	N.L.
2	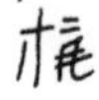	100-062 nhɨ	0590 nI̭ə	1172
3	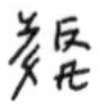	236-077 nɨ	2647 nI̭wə̣	N.L.
4		017-11L nɛ̃	0848 nẹ	N.L.
5		039-051	1539	4937

		nɨ̃	tə̣	
6		246-043 nɨ?	2959 nI	1041
7		007-093 ndɨ	1819 ndI	3840
8		N.L	N.L.	N.L.
9		041-066 nɨ	1420 nwə	0928
10	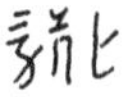	187-071 nɨ	0059 nI	1039
11		N.L.	4632 ndÎə̣	2138
12		026-062 ndɨ	4925 ndI	0779

GLOSS : **NI** 溺

Middle Chinese : niɛk
10 NW Chinese : nig

No.	**Char.**	**Nishida**	**Sofronov**	**More Pis'men**
1		181-052 nrǐu	4150 mu	N.L.
2		026-064 *	4895 z̀i̭wu	3170
3		005-102 nị	N.L.	N.L.

GLOSS : **NI** 你

Middle Chinese : ngie̯-
10 NW Chinese : ni

No.	**Char.**	**Nishida**	**Sofronov**	**More Pis'men**
1	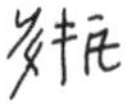	208-063 neɦ	2370 nIn	4065
2		211-073 neɦ	5673 nIn	4005
3		096-064 nǐẹ	0625 nIẹ	2215
4		269-065 nIɦ	22̂97 nIe	3501
5		230-084 naɦ	4̂760 ni	4784
6		N.L.	1235 nIn	5093

No.	Char.	Nishida	Sofronov	More Pis'men
7		017-135 ni	N.L.	N.L.
8		017-132 neɦ-	0861 nIn	4014
9		007-065 niɦ	2104 ni	3405
10	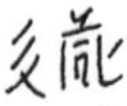	204-09c niɦ	3605 ni	3407
11	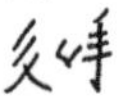	N.L.	3769 nI̭e	1346
12		110-053 neɦ	2875 nIn	4011
13		123-062 nǐe	0331 ni	N.L.

GLOSS : **NI** 泥

Middle Chinese : niei
10 NW Chinese : 'de

No.	Char.	Nishida	Sofronov	More Pis'men
1	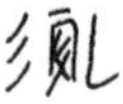	201-081 ndiɦ	3309 ndi	3413

GLOSS : **NI** 尼

Middle Chinese : ni
10 NW Chinese : 'di

No.	Char.	Nishida	Sofronov	More Pis'men
1		N.L.	N.L.	N.L.
2		177-[illegible]1 ni	N.L.	N.L.
3		244-071 ňi	2195 ndźi̭ẹi	2703

GLOSS : NIANG 娘

Middle Chinese : niăng:
10 NW Chinese : nyaṅ

No.	Char.	Nishida	Sofronov	More Pis'men
1		N.L.	N.L.	N.L.
2	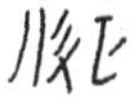	041-071 nɔɦ	1427 nI̭uo	1756
3		243-072 na	N.L.	N.L.

GLOSS : NIEH 聶

Middle Chinese : ńi̭äp
10 NW Chinese : 'ḋyab

No.	Char.	Nishida	Sofronov	More Pis'men
1		003-122 ňɛɦ	0044 ndźi̭a	N.L.
2	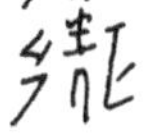	181-09g ňɪ̌ɛ	4211 ndźi̭a	N.L.

GLOSS : NING 寧

Middle Chinese : nieng
10 NW Chinese : neṅ

No.	Char.	Nishida	Sofronov	More Pis'men
1	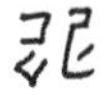	182-043 neɦ	4652 nIn	4069
2		006-101 nreɦ	2930 nIn	4063
3		205-065 ndɪ̌ẽ	3341 mI̭e	1421
4		098-072 nʷeɦ	0651 nwIn	1308
5		204-06e nɪ̌eɦ	3769 nI̭e	1346
6	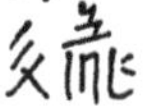	N.L.	N.L.	N.L.

GLOSS : **NING** 寧

Middle Chinese : ńieng
10 NW Chinese : 'deṅ

No.	Char.	Nishida	Sofronov	More Pis'men
1	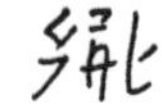	181-084 nε	N.L.	N.L.
2		183-041 neɦ	5816 ndIn	5100
3		041-064 ndǐẽ	1355 ndI̭e	4130

GLOSS : **NING** 獰

Middle Chinese : ńieng
10 NW Chinese : 'deṅ

No.	Char.	Nishida	Sofronov	More Pis'men
1		N.L.	N.L.	N.L.

GLOSS : **NO** 諾

Middle Chinese : nâk
10 NW Chinese : nag

No.	Char.	Nishida	Sofronov	More Pis'men
1		017-041 nɔɦ	0975 ndo	N.L.

GLOSS : **NU** 奴

Middle Chinese : nuo
10 NW Chinese : nu

No.	Char.	Nishida	Sofronov	More Pis'men
1	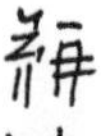	056-051 nU	2410 ndu	N.L.
2		135-052 nuɦ	1300 ndu	0173

3		192-091 nuɦ	4423 ndu	3225
4		186-041 mʷI	1164 *	N.L.

GLOSS : **NU** 怒

Middle Chinese : nuo=
10 NW Chinese : nu

No.	Char.	Nishida	Sofronov	More Pis'men
1		017-11h ʔaɦ	0708 .a	3559

GLOSS : **NŰ** 女

Middle Chinese : ńi̯wo=
10 NW Chinese : 'ĵi

No.	Char.	Nishida	Sofronov	More Pis'men
1	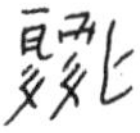	305-091 ňǐu	0427 ndźi̭u	2996

GLOSS : **O** 餓

Middle Chinese : ngâ-
10 NW Chinese : 'ga

No.	Char.	Nishida	Sofronov	More Pis'men
1		204-05b ŋǐõ	3915 ngôn	4451
2	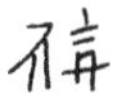	049-062 ŋǐõ	5280 ngôn	4452
3		017-062 ŋǐõ	0977 ngôn	4454
4		211-052 ŋoɦ	5714 ngọ	N.L.
5	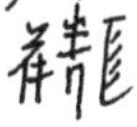	083-121 ŋǐõ	2437 ngon	4457

GLOSS : O 訛

Middle Chinese : ngua
10 NW Chinese : 'gua

No.	Char.	Nishida	Sofronov	More Pis'men
1		241-055 -ɣɔɦ	2210 .o	N.L.
2		001-101 vor	N.L.	N.L.
3		218-101 khʷi	5353 khwi	1099
4		192-051 ɣɔɦ	2903 .0	1569
5		315-053 ɣọ̃	1329 .wo	2191
6		260-031 ɣọ	2350 .won	2190
7		208-041 ɣɔɦ	2386 .o	1570
8		181-051 ɣɔɦ	4176 .o	4305
9		017-095 ɣọ	0792 .wa	N.L.
10		204-044 vor	3367 wụo	2513
11		218-091 vaɦ	5361 wa	0606

GLOSS : O 遏

Middle Chinese : .ât
10 NW Chinese : ʔar

No.	Char.	Nishida	Sofronov	More Pis'men
1		N.L.	5162 nga	0741
2		255-093 ŋha	0536 *	4687

GLOSS : **PA** 巴

Middle Chinese : pa
10 NW Chinese : pa

No.	Char.	Nishida	Sofronov	More Pis'men
1		235-041 pạ	2629 pạ	1973

GLOSS : **PA** 芭

Middle Chinese : pa
10 NW Chinese : pa

No.	Char.	Nishida	Sofronov	More Pis'men
1		159-091 paɦ-	3090 pa	0712

GLOSS : **PAI** 擺

Middle Chinese : pjie̯
10 NW Chinese : pwi

No.	Char.	Nishida	Sofronov	More Pis'men
1		275-041 pɛ	5583 pại	4755

GLOSS : **PAI** 敗

Middle Chinese : b'wai
10 NW Chinese : bwai

No.	Char.	Nishida	Sofronov	More Pis'men
1		144-084 pĭɛ	3264 *	3518

GLOSS : PAI 白

Middle Chinese : -pɒk
10 NW Chinese : peg

No.	Char.	Nishida	Sofronov	More Pis'men
1		139-101 pIĕ	1693 pê	0283
2		297-094 pi̥ĕ	5053 pê̥i	2016

GLOSS : PAI 柏

Middle Chinese : pɒk
10 NW Chinese : peg

No.	Char.	Nishida	Sofronov	More Pis'men
1	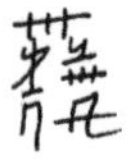	017-161 pIĕ	0759 pê	0284

GLOSS : PAN 板

Middle Chinese : pwan=
10 NW Chinese : ban

No.	Char.	Nishida	Sofronov	More Pis'men
1		098-111 paɦ	0646 pa	0710

GLOSS : P'AN 盤

Middle Chinese : p'uan
10 NW Chinese : p'an

No.	Char.	Nishida	Sofronov	More Pis'men
1		018-08b nɔɦ	0240 no	4277
2	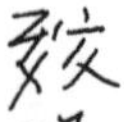	239-052 nɔw	5138 ndoɰ	4374
3		N.L.	N.L.	N.L.

GLOSS : **P'ANG** 旁

Middle Chinese : b'wâng
10 NW Chinese : bo

No.	**Char.**	**Nishida**	**Sofronov**	**More Pis'men**
1	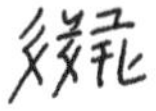	204-129 phõ	3688 phon	1649

GLOSS : **P'ANG** 傍

Middle Chinese : b'wâng
10 NW Chinese : bo

No.	**Char.**	**Nishida**	**Sofronov**	**More Pis'men**
1		N.L.	3324 phon	1654

GLOSS : **PEI** 盃

Middle Chinese : puậi
10 NW Chinese : pai

No.	**Char.**	**Nishida**	**Sofronov**	**More Pis'men**
1		154-021 p^{w}ɨ	0439 pI	1015

GLOSS : **PEI** 北

Middle Chinese : pək
10 NW Chinese : pug

No.	**Char.**	**Nishida**	**Sofronov**	**More Pis'men**
1		N.L.	N.L.	N.L.
2		017-081 BI	0993 pu	3171

GLOSS : P'EI 裴

Middle Chinese : pjweí
10 NW Chinese : p'u

No.	Char.	Nishida	Sofronov	More Pis'men
1	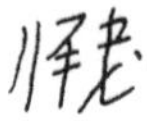	041-09b pʷi	1470 phei	1204

GLOSS : PENG 崩

Middle Chinese : pəng
10 NW Chinese : peṅ

No.	Char.	Nishida	Sofronov	More Pis'men
1	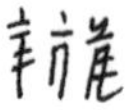	N.L.	N.L.	N.L.

GLOSS : P'I 皮

Middle Chinese : b'ji̯e
10 NW Chinese : b'wi̯

No.	Char.	Nishida	Sofronov	More Pis'men
1		039-081 phi	1614 phi	0353
2		305-053 phIɦ	0428 phIe	0456
3	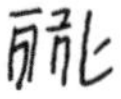	154-061 phiɦ	0447 phi	0351

GLOSS : PING 兵

Middle Chinese : pi̯wɒng
10 NW Chinese : pe

No.	Char.	Nishida	Sofronov	More Pis'men
1		204-10j pẽ	3600 pIe	1921

GLOSS : PO 播

Middle Chinese : puâ-
10 NW Chinese : pwa

No.	Char.	Nishida	Sofronov	More Pis'men
1		098-161 pɔɦ	0640 po	1537

GLOSS : PO 波

Middle Chinese : puâ
10 NW Chinese : pa

No.	Char.	Nishida	Sofronov	More Pis'men
1		205-06a pɔɦ	3336 po	1536

GLOSS : PO 孛

Middle Chinese : b'uət
10 NW Chinese : b'ur

No.	Char.	Nishida	Sofronov	More Pis'men
1		297-084 khɨ	2734 *	N.L.
2	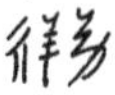	N.L.	N.L.	N.L.
3	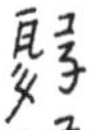	N.L.	N.L.	N.L.
4	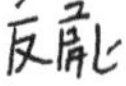	255-111 pʉɦ	0540 phə	3717
5		007-054 pʉɦ	2088 phə	3719
6		007-112 phʉɦ	2094 phə	3724
7		305-041 phuɦ	0422 phI̭oɰ	4384

GLOSS : **P'O** 拍

Middle Chinese : p'ɒk
10 NW Chinese : p'ag

No.	**Char.**	**Nishida**	**Sofronov**	**More Pis'men**
1		236-053 phe	2804 phe	3332

GLOSS : **P'O** 破

Middle Chinese : p'uâ-
10 NW Chinese : pa

No.	**Char.**	**Nishida**	**Sofronov**	**More Pis'men**
1	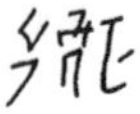	181-096 ɣɔɦ	N.L.	N.L.

GLOSS : **PU** 不

Middle Chinese : pi̯ə̯u=
10 NW Chinese : pu

No.	**Char.**	**Nishida**	**Sofronov**	**More Pis'men**
1		246-031 pʉɦ	0596 pə	0876
2		032-061 pʷɨ	5568 pI	1014

GLOSS : **PU** 布

Middle Chinese : puo-
10 NW Chinese : pu

No.	**Char.**	**Nishida**	**Sofronov**	**More Pis'men**
1	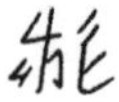	. 159-041 xar	3072 .ạ	2335

GLOSS : **P'U** 普

Middle Chinese : p'uo
10 NW Chinese : po

No.	**Char.**	**Nishida**	**Sofronov**	**More Pis'men**
1	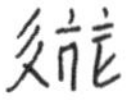	204-09j phu	3709 phu	3174
2		146-001 phu	1664 phu	3065
3		110-051 phu	2879 phu	0006

GLOSS :**SA** 薩

Middle Chinese : ṣân (?)
10 NW Chinese : sar (?)

No.	**Char.**	**Nishida**	**Sofronov**	**More Pis'men**
1		017-096 saɦ	0981 sa	0748
2		182-06b saɦ	4646 sa	3557

GLOSS70·**SAI** 塞

Middle Chinese : sậi-
10 NW Chinese : sa

No.	**Char.**	**Nishida**	**Sofronov**	**More Pis'men**
1		N.L.	N.L.	N.L.

GLOSS : **SAI** 腮

Middle Chinese : sậi
10 NW Chinese : se

No.	**Char.**	**Nishida**	**Sofronov**	**More Pis'men**
1		007-105 sɛ	1855 sei	1195

GLOSS : SANG 桑

Middle Chinese : sâng
10 NW Chinese : saṅ

No.	Char.	Nishida	Sofronov	More Pis'men
1		204-08r sɔɦ	3441 so	4295
2		140-041 *	1718 so	2678
3		119-051 sɔɦ	2896 so	N.L.
4		211-062 -sɔɦ	5721 so	4294

GLOSS : SE 色

Middle Chinese : si k
10 NW Chinese : ceg

No.	Char.	Nishida	Sofronov	More Pis'men
1		N.L.	0161 si̭ə	3881

GLOSS : SHANG 尚

Middle Chinese : źi̯ang-
10 NW Chinese : zŷaṅ

No.	Char.	Nishida	Sofronov	More Pis'men
1		028-093 šǐwõ	2599 śi̯on	1726
2		181-υ71 šǐɔɦ	4304 śi̭o	4338

GLOSS : **SHE** 捨

Middle Chinese : śi̯a
10 NW Chinese : çâ

No.	**Char.**	**Nishida**	**Sofronov**	**More Pis'men**
1		144-092 šɛɦ	3232 śi̭ei	5059
2		017-08a šǐẽ	0675 śi̭e	4114

GLOSS : **SHENG** 聖

Middle Chinese : śi̯äng-
10 NW Chinese : çên

No.	**Char.**	**Nishida**	**Sofronov**	**More Pis'men**
1		205-001 šǐẽ	3301 śi̭e	4113

GLOSS : **SHIH** 史

Middle Chinese : ṣi=
10 NW Chinese : çi

No.	**Char.**	**Nishida**	**Sofronov**	**More Pis'men**
1		239-041 šʉ	5140 śə̑	0951

GLOSS : **SHIH** 使

Middle Chinese : ṣi=
10 NW Chinese : çi

No.	**Char.**	**Nishida**	**Sofronov**	**More Pis'men**
1		182-062 šǐẽ	4594 śi̭ə	0987

GLOSS : **SHIH** 石

Middle Chinese : źi̯äk
10 NW Chinese : çîg

No.	Char.	Nishida	Sofronov	More Pis'men
1	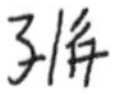	185-064 ši	5516 śi̭ə	N.L.

GLOSS : **SHIH** 士

Middle Chinese : dẓ'i
10 NW Chinese : çi

No.	Char.	Nishida	Sofronov	More Pis'men
1		072-041 tshliɦ	5333 tshI	1179

GLOSS : **SHIH** 食

Middle Chinese : dz'i̯ək
10 NW Chinese : çig

No.	Char.	Nishida	Sofronov	More Pis'men
1		139-062 šiɦ	1708 śi̭e	5010

GLOSS : **SHIH** 試

Middle Chinese : śi̯ '.
10 NW Chinese : çîg

No.	Char.	Nishida	Sofronov	More Pis'men
1		139-062 šiɦ	1708 śi̯ə	3364
2	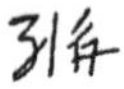	185-064 ši	55̂16 śi̭ə	N.L.

GLOSS : **SHUAI** 率

Middle Chinese : śiuĕt
10 NW Chinese : çwar

No.	**Char.**	**Nishida**	**Sofronov**	**More Pis'men**
1		181-099 šwi	4244 śwê	0302
2		144-064 ~~šʉ~~	3294 śwə̂	0964

GLOSS : **SHUO** 說

Middle Chinese : śi̯wät
10 NW Chinese : çŵar

No.	**Char.**	**Nishida**	**Sofronov**	**More Pis'men**
1	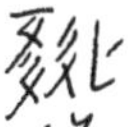	226-071 tšhĭə̃	1213 tśhên	0508
2		269-066 BĬɛ	2298 śi̯wa	0774
3		017-09a šĭa	0̂909 śi̭a	3607

GLOSS : **SHOU** 手

Middle Chinese : śi̭ə̭u=
10 NW Chinese : çeu

No.	**Char.**	**Nishida**	**Sofronov**	**More Pis'men**
1		269-093 šĭəw	2276 śi̭eɰ	4214

GLOSS 76. **SO** 娑

Middle Chinese : sâ
10 NW Chinese : sa

No.	**Char.**	**Nishida**	**Sofronov**	**More Pis'men**
1		134-051 sʷaɦ	1285 swa	N.L.

GLOSS : **SU** 宿

Middle Chinese : si̯uk
10 NW Chinese : ɕûg

No.	Char.	Nishida	Sofronov	More Pis'men
1		098-074 ʔyɣ̆əw	0659 su	3207

GLOSS : **SUI** 碎

Middle Chinese : sua̯i-
10 NW Chinese : sai

No.	Char.	Nishida	Sofronov	More Pis'men
1		005-082 sɛ̣̃	3021 swI̱	1920

GLOSS : **TA** 達

Middle Chinese : t'a
10 NW Chinese : ta

No.	Char.	Nishida	Sofronov	More Pis'men
1	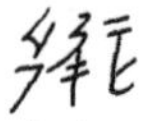	181-093 thaɦ	4310 tha	0737
2		2[illegible]4-042 thaɦ	3464 tha	0544

GLOSS : **TA** 他

Middle Chinese : t'a
10 NW Chinese : ta

No.	Char.	Nishida	Sofronov	More Pis'men
1		204-042 thaɦ	3464 tha	0544

GLOSS : **TA** 怛

Middle Chinese : tât
10 NW Chinese : tar

No.	**Char.**	**Nishida**	**Sofronov**	**More Pis'men**
1	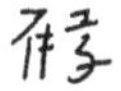	080-055 tạ	5238 tIạ	1984
2	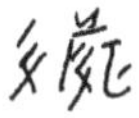	204-125 taɦ	3612 ta	0735
3		236-081 tạ	2782 tạ	4683

GLOSS : **TANG** 當

Middle Chinese : tâng
10 NW Chinese : taṅ

No.	**Char.**	**Nishida**	**Sofronov**	**More Pis'men**
1		008-084 tɔɦ	1842 to	4269

GLOSS : **TA** 打

Middle Chinese : t'a
10 NW Chinese : ta

No.	**Char.**	**Nishida**	**Sofronov**	**More Pis'men**
1		157-052 taɦ	1759 ta	0542

GLOSS : **TANG** 黨

Middle Chinese : tâng=
10 NW Chinese : taṅ

No.	**Char.**	**Nishida**	**Sofronov**	**More Pis'men**
1		204-08j tɔɦ	3667 tôn	4265
2		N.L.	N.L.	N.L.

GLOSS : **TANG** 党

Middle Chinese : tâng
10 NW Chinese : taṅ

No.	**Char.**	**Nishida**	**Sofronov**	**More Pis'men**
1		167-001 tõ	5096 ton	1656

GLOSS : **T'ANG** 湯

Middle Chinese : t'âng
10 NW Chinese : t'aṅ

No.	**Char.**	**Nishida**	**Sofronov**	**More Pis'men**
1		105-102 th h	2996 tho	4273

GLOSS : **T'ANG** 唐

Middle Chinese : d'âng
10 NW Chinese : daṅ

No.	**Char.**	**Nishida**	**Sofronov**	**More Pis'men**
1	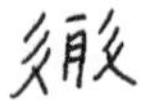	204-09h toĥ	3405 thọ	4712

GLOSS : **T'E** 特

Middle Chinese : d'ək
10 NW Chinese : deg

No.	**Char.**	**Nishida**	**Sofronov**	**More Pis'men**
1		026-117 thʉĥ	4900 thɔ	0897
2	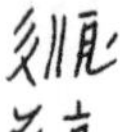	204-08w thɨ	3520 thIə̣	2137
3	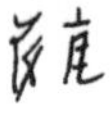	241-061 thɨ	221̂4 thI	3827

GLOSS : **TI** 底

Middle Chinese : tiei
10 NW Chinese : tei

No.	Char.	Nishida	Sofronov	More Pis'men
1		255-042 tị	0476 tÎẹi	2050
2		230-062 tI	4743 ti	0367

GLOSS : **T'IEN** 田

Middle Chinese : d'ien
10 NW Chinese : dyań

No.	Char.	Nishida	Sofronov	More Pis'men
1		230-031 thẽ	4775 thI̭e	1418

GLOSS : **TING** 頂

Middle Chinese : tieng
10 NW Chinese : tyeń

No.	Char.	Nishida	Sofronov	More Pis'men
1		041-099 tɛ̣̃	1365 tỊ	1437

GLOSS : **TING** 丁

Middle Chinese : tieng
10 NW Chinese : tyeń

No.	Char.	Nishida	Sofronov	More Pis'men
1	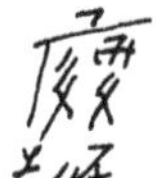	009-124 -teɦ	4461 tIn	3989
2	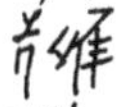	106-061 teɦ	1915 tIn	3988
3		184-081 teɦ	5500 tIe	1307
4		031-091 tɛ̣̃	3976 tỊ	1976

GLOSS : **TO** 多

Middle Chinese : tâ
10 NW Chinese : ta

No.	**Char.**	**Nishida**	**Sofronov**	**More Pis'men**
1		051-051 tụ	1152 twụ	1768
2		N.L.	N.L.	N.L.

GLOSS : **T'O** 托

Middle Chinese : t"âk
10 NW Chinese : tag

No.	**Char.**	**Nishida**	**Sofronov**	**More Pis'men**
1		204-06b thU	3565 thI̭oɰ	1644
2		181-092 thU	4231 thwu	3803
3		194-041 thU	2834 *	0207

GLOSS : **TS'A** 擦

Middle Chinese : tṣ'ât (?)
10 NW Chinese : ç'ar (?)

No.	**Char.**	**Nishida**	**Sofronov**	**More Pis'men**
1		236-082 na	2812 nI̭ạ	4685

GLOSS : **TSAI** 栽

Middle Chinese : tsậi
10 NW Chinese : tsa

No.	**Char.**	**Nishida**	**Sofronov**	**More Pis'men**
1		204-05c sǐe	3584 tsai	1374

GLOSS : **TSAI** 宰

Middle Chinese : tsậi=
10 NW Chinese : tsai

No.	Char.	Nishida	Sofronov	More Pis'men
1		110-082 tse-	2873 tsai	4395

GLOSS : **TS'ANG** 蒼

Middle Chinese : ts'âng
10 NW Chinese : ts'aṅ

No.	Char.	Nishida	Sofronov	More Pis'men
1		259-041 tshõ	1636 tshọ	4718
2		028-123 tshõ	2583 tshon	4403

GLOSS : **TSE** 則

Middle Chinese : tsək
10 NW Chinese : tsig

No.	Char.	Nishida	Sofronov	More Pis'men
1	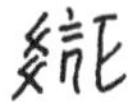	211-085 tsIr	5716 tsẹ	2284
2		211-103 tsʉ	5681 tsə̣	2103

3		008-082 tsiər	1879 tsəɰ	N.L.
4		098-091 tsIr	0626 tsẹ	2285
5		008-083 tsɨ	1830 tsI	1064
6		017-064 šĭu	0807 tsI̭ẹ	2543
7	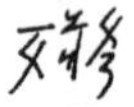	219-101 tsəw	N.L.	N.L.
8	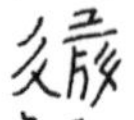	204-104 tsʉ̣	3797 tsə̣	2101
9	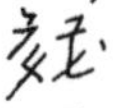	236-057 tị	2767 śi̭a	0691
10		026-111 -tsʉɦ	4984 tse	N.L.
11	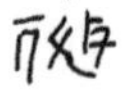	103-074 tsǐor	0299 *	4997
12		017-151 tsʉ	1012 tsə̣	2104
13	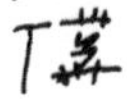	040-111 tsǐor	4315 *	4998

<u>GLOSS</u> : **TSE** 賊

Middle Chinese : dz'ək
10 NW Chinese : dzeg

No.	Char.	Nishida	Sofronov	More Pis'men
1	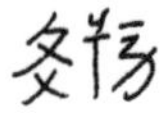	211-086 tshɨ	5693 tshI	1068
2		072-041 tshliɦ	5333 tshI̭ə	1179
3		N.L.	N.L.	N.L.
4	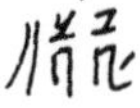	N.L.	N.L.	N.L.
5		080-072 tsǐə̣r	5206 tsheɰ	4062

GLOSS : **TSU** 足

Middle Chinese : tsi̭wok
10 NW Chinese : tsûg

No.	**Char.**	**Nishida**	**Sofronov**	**More Pis'men**
1		155-041 tsǐụ	4516 tsI̭wu	1827

GLOSS : **TS'U** 粗

Middle Chinese : dz'uo
10 NW Chinese : dzu

No.	**Char.**	**Nishida**	**Sofronov**	**More Pis'men**
1	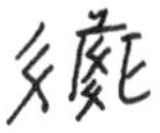	204-125 taɦ	3612 ta	0735

GLOSS : **TS'UN** 寸

Middle Chinese : ts'uən-
10 NW Chinese : tsun

No.	**Char.**	**Nishida**	**Sofronov**	**More Pis'men**
1		039-052 tshǐə̌	1598 tshI̭wen	0523

GLOSS : **TU** 瀆

Middle Chinese : d'uk
10 NW Chinese : dog

No.	Char.	Nishida	Sofronov	More Pis'men
1	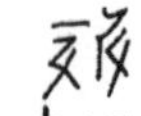	221-063 tI̤	0148 thei	2005
2	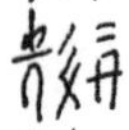	139-091 təw	1699 ndwu	3113
3	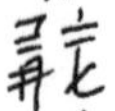	132-041 rạ	4367 lha	2824
4	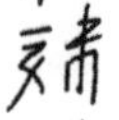	221-065 tI̤	0149 thẹi	2487
5	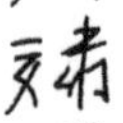	220-052 seɦ	0147 tsi	3434
6		N.L.	N.L.	N.L.
7		N.L.	N.L.	N.L.

GLOSS : TU 肚

Middle Chinese : d'uo=
10 NW Chinese : du

No.	Char.	Nishida	Sofronov	More Pis'men
1		204-11c thu	3376 .wei	1230

GLOSS : TU 都

Middle Chinese : tuo=
10 NW Chinese : tu

No.	Char.	Nishida	Sofronov	More Pis'men
1	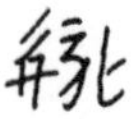	144-052 tụ	3292 tụ	1759
2		110-051 phu	2879 phu	0006
3		219-052 tụ	1186 tI̭oɰ	1643

GLOSS : **T'UI** 推

Middle Chinese : t'uậi
10 NW Chinese : t'ai

No.	**Char.**	**Nishida**	**Sofronov**	**More Pis'men**
1		N.L.	N.L.	N.L.

GLOSS : **TZU** 滓

Middle Chinese : dz'i
10 NW Chinese : dzi

No.	**Char.**	**Nishida**	**Sofronov**	**More Pis'men**
1		017-021 kʉɦ	0748 kə	N.L.

GLOSS : **WA** 韈

Middle Chinese : miwɒt
10 NW Chinese : 'b̂ar

No.	**Char.**	**Nishida**	**Sofronov**	**More Pis'men**
1		007-123 ɱvĭa	1999 vi̭a	0672

GLOSS : **WAI** 外

Middle Chinese : ngwâi-
10 NW Chinese : gwe

No.	**Char.**	**Nishida**	**Sofronov**	**More Pis'men**
1		098-071 VI	0645 we	3308
2		181-094 ɱvɛ	4279 wẹ	4860

GLOSS : WEI 韋

Middle Chinese : jwḙi
10 NW Chinese : 'wî

No.	Char.	Nishida	Sofronov	More Pis'men
1		085-051 wi̭	0606 vi̭ẹi	2026
2	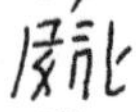	039-114 wi	1605 vi̭e	0309
3		N.L.	N.L.	N.L.
4		208-061 wi̭	N.L.	N.L.

GLOSS : WEI 蔚

Middle Chinese : ·jwḙi
10 NW Chinese : ywî

No.	Char.	Nishida	Sofronov	More Pis'men
1		007-061 ʔwɨr	1955 .i̭wə̣	4989

GLOSS : WEI 嵬

Middle Chinese : nguậi
10 NW Chinese : 'gai

No.	Char.	Nishida	Sofronov	More Pis'men
1		018-092 VI	0179 we	5031
2		111 [illegible] VI	2483 we	0259
3	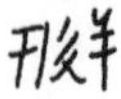	098-101 VI	0624 we	3310
4		191-041 VI̭	N.L.	N.L.
5		098-071 VI	0645 we	3308
6		050-051 VI	5286 5286	3314 3314
7	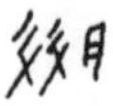	N.L.	N.L.	N.L.

8		N.L.	N.L.	N.L.
9		204-10f mvI	3384 we	3302
10		194-071 vẹ	2840 wai	2210
11		007-11b ɣʷɛ	1774 .wại	4762
12	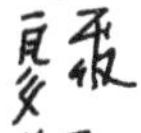	305-081 vỊr	0425 we	4861
13		194-051 nʷɨ	2838 nwI	1092
14	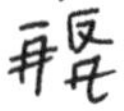	123-072 VI	0327 we	0265

GLOSS : **WEI** 為

Middle Chinese : jwie
10 NW Chinese : wu

No.	**Char.**	**Nishida**	**Sofronov**	**More Pis'men**
1		009-081 wi	4536 nâi	4104
2		056-061 wi	2413 vie	0305
3		204-069 khiɦ	3666 vio	1595
4		056-043 wi	2409 vie	0308
5		090-041 wi	3070 viei	3954
6		234-061 wɛɦ	0045 viei	1265
7		301-051 wị	4996 viẹi	5136
8	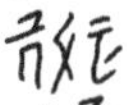	107-072 ʔwiɦ	4479 nIa	0770
9		269-103 wị	2317 viẹi	2031

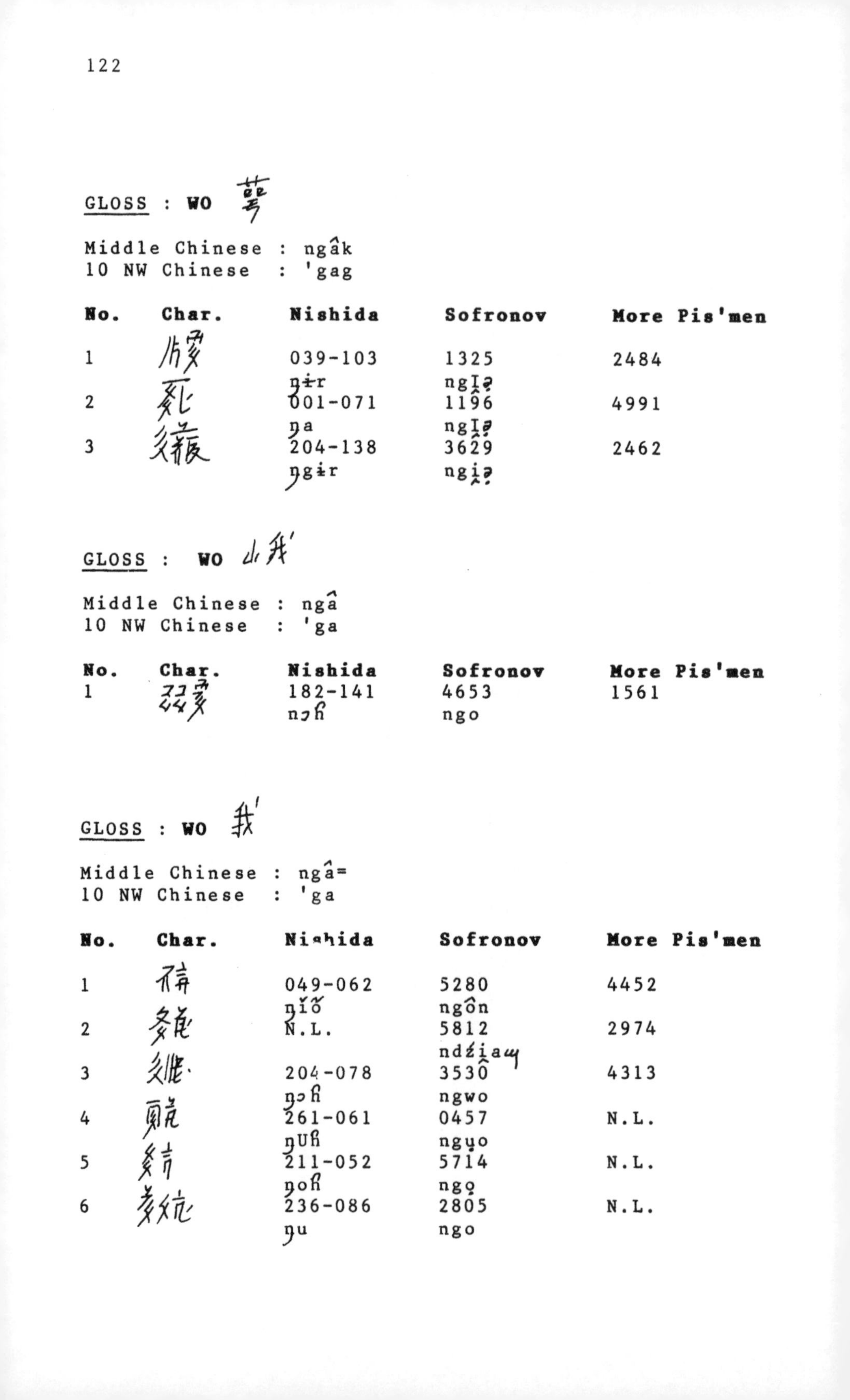

GLOSS : **WO** 萼

Middle Chinese : ngâk
10 NW Chinese : 'gag

No.	**Char.**	**Nishida**	**Sofronov**	**More Pis'men**
1	[illegible]	039-103 ŋɨr	1325 ngI̯ə	2484
2	[illegible]	001-071 ŋa	1196 ngI̯ə	4991
3	[illegible]	204-138 ŋgɨr	3629 ngi̯ə	2462

GLOSS : **WO** 峨

Middle Chinese : ngâ
10 NW Chinese : 'ga

No.	**Char.**	**Nishida**	**Sofronov**	**More Pis'men**
1	[illegible]	182-141 nɔɦ	4653 ngo	1561

GLOSS : **WO** 我

Middle Chinese : ngâ=
10 NW Chinese : 'ga

No.	**Char.**	**Nishida**	**Sofronov**	**More Pis'men**
1	[illegible]	049-062 ŋɨ̌ǒ	5280 ngôn	4452
2	[illegible]	N.L.	5812 ndźi̯aɰ	2974
3	[illegible]	204-078 ŋɔɦ	3530 ngwo	4313
4	[illegible]	261-061 ŋUɦ	0457 ngu̯o	N.L.
5	[illegible]	211-052 ŋoɦ	5714 ngọ	N.L.
6	[illegible]	236-086 ŋu	2805 ngo	N.L.

GLOSS : **WU** 惡

Middle Chinese : .âk
10 NW Chinese : yag

No.	Char.	Nishida	Sofronov	More Pis'men
1		249-071 ʔu	4523 .wu	4515
2		204-10e ɣuɦ	3868 .u	N.L.

GLOSS : **WU** 悟

Middle Chinese : nguo-
10 NW Chinese : 'go

No.	Char.	Nishida	Sofronov	More Pis'men
1		080-083 ŋgu	5232 ngu	3078
2		017-12d ŋgu	0867 ngu	3075
3		N.L.	N.L.	N.L.

GLOSS : **WU** 五

Middle Chinese : nguo=
10 NW Chinese : 'go

No.	Char.	Nishida	Sofronov	More Pis'men
1		007-122 ɣu	1968 .u	4506
2		041-065 ʔu	1454 .u	3086

GLOSS : **WU** 吾

Middle Chinese : nguo
10 NW Chinese : 'go

No	Char.	Nishida	Sofronov	More Pis'men
1	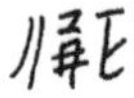	041-09a -ʔu	1456 .u	3088
2		204-10c ɣuɦ	3868 .u	N.L.

GLOSS : **WU** 吴

Middle Chinese : nguo
10 NW Chinese : 'go

No.	Char.	Nishida	Sofronov	More Pis'men
1		204-113 ɣuɦ	3625 .u	0183
2		N.L.	N.L.	N.L.
3	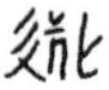	204-09g ɣuɦ	3619 .u	0181
4		204-10c ɣuɦ	3868 .u	N.L.

GLOSS : **WU** 午

Middle Chinese : nguo=
10 NW Chinese : 'go

No.	Char.	Nishida	Sofronov	More Pis'men
1		249-071 ʔụ	4523 .wụ	4515

GLOSS : **WU** 無

Middle Chinese : mi̭u
10 NW Chinese : 'bu

No.	**Char.**	**Nishida**	**Sofronov**	**More Pis'men**
1		236-071 ɱvǐụ	2731 vi̭ụ	1791

GLOSS : **WU** 勿

Middle Chinese : mi̭uət
10 NW Chinese : mur

No.	**Char.**	**Nishida**	**Sofronov**	**More Pis'men**
1		208-053 ɱvɨ	2371 vi̭ə	2115
2		085-052 ɱvʉr	0616 wə̣	4954
3	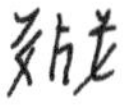	208-092 ɱvɨ	2377 vi̭ə	N.L.
4	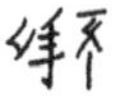	061-051 ɱvɨɦ	4095 wə	1134
5		085-071 ɱvʉr	0613 wə̣	4955
6		181-09a ɱvɨɦ	4242 viə	3801
7	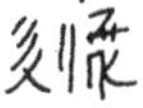	206-111 ɱvǐuɦ	3960 vi̭u	0072

GLOSS : **YA** 牙

Middle Chinese : nga
10 NW Chinese :'ga

No.	**Char.**	**Nishida**	**Sofronov**	**More Pis'men**
1		N.L.	N.L.	N.L.

GLOSS : **YANG** 養

Middle Chinese : i̯ang=
10 NW Chinese : yaṅ

NO.	Char.	Nishida	Sofronov	More Pis'men
1	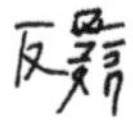	255-143 ʔyɔɦ	0491 .ôn	4474

GLOSS : **YAO** 要

Middle Chinese : .i̯äu
10 NW Chinese : yau

No.	Char.	Nishida	Sofronov	More Pis'men
1		293-021 xiɦ	N.L.	N.L.
2	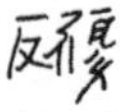	255-131 ʔyaɦ	0557 .i̭aɯ	4934
3	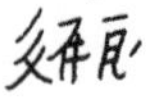	N.L.	N.L.	N.L.

GLOSS : **YAO** 藥

Middle Chinese : i̭ak
10 NW Chinese : yag

No.	Char.	Nishida	Sofronov	More Pis'men
1		181-042 ʔyĭuɦ	4197 .i̭u	0145
2		202-111 ʔyǐu	5574 .u	N.L.
3		187-∪,2 ʔyìu	0062 .i̭u	3149

GLOSS : **YEH** 耶

Middle Chinese : i̯a
10 NW Chinese : ya

No.	Char.	Nishida	Sofronov	More Pis'men
1		259-001 ʔyar	1632 .i̯a	2377
2	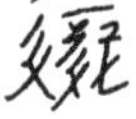	204-09c ʔyǐeɦ	3483 .i̯we	1362

GLOSS : **YEH** 野

Middle Chinese : i̯a=
10 NW Chinese : ya

No.	Char.	Nishida	Sofronov	More Pis'men
1	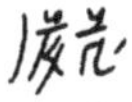	039-131 ʔyeɦ	1512 .In	4049
2	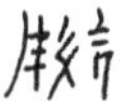	075-091 ʔyǐẽ	1279 .i̯e	4115
3	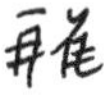	122-061 ʔyǐẽ	0343 .i̯e	4116

GLOSS : **YEH** 頁

Middle Chinese : i̯a=
10 NW Chinese : ya

No.	Char.	Nishida	Sofronov	More Pis'men
1	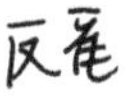	255-06b mbiɦ	0488 mbi	3392

GLOSS : **YEH** 耶

Middle Chinese : i̯a
10 NW Chinese : ya

No.	Char.	Nishida	Sofronov	More Pis'men
1		204-09c ʔyǐeɦ	3483 .i̯we	1362
2		049-061 ʔyeɦ	5283 .In	1296

GLOSS : **YEN** 彥

Middle Chinese : ngi̯ăn
10 NW Chinese : 'gy̑an

No.	Char.	Nishida	Sofronov	More Pis'men
1		123-041 ŋẽ	0369 ngên	0506

GLOSS : **YI** 逆

Middle Chinese : ngi̯ɒk
10 NW Chinese : 'gyag

No.	Char.	Nishida	Sofronov	More Pis'men
1	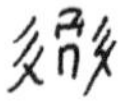	N.L.	N.L.	N.L.

GLOSS : **YING** 迎

Middle Chinese : ngi̯ɒng
10 NW Chinese : 'gyoń

No.	Char.	Nishida	Sofronov	More Pis'men
1		018-123 ŋoṣ	0207 ngI̭ẹ	1902
2		262-081 ŋeĥ	0467 ngIn	4036
3	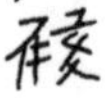	080-071 ŋeĥ	5240 ngIn	1275
4		105-051 ŋ·eĥ	2978 ngIn	4033
5		070-061 ŋeĥ	5337 ngIn	4032
6		N.L.	N.L.	N.L.
7		306-061 ŋgɛ	0396 ngI̭ẹ	1899

GLOSS : **YU** 疣

Middle Chinese :
10 NW Chinese :

No.	Char.	Nishida	Sofronov	More Pis'men
1		001-083 phǐow	0075 pho	4321
2		054-061 phǐõ	5461 phôn	1700
3		205-053 Fǐẹ	3428 phô	4319
4		072-091 tshliɦ	5330 tshI̭ə	N.L.

GLOSS : **YU** 由

Middle Chinese : i̯ə̯u
10 NW Chinese : y̯u

No.	Char.	Nishida	Sofronov	More Pis'men
1		N.L.	3525 .êɰ	N.L
2	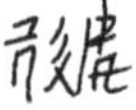	107-111 ʔyǐəw	4483 .êɰ	4222

GLOSS : **YÜ** 餘

Middle Chinese : i̭wo
10 NW Chinese : yu

No.	Char.	Nishida	Sofronov	More Pis'men
1		045-072 ʔyur	3142 .i̯u	0092
2		211-081 ʔyǐuɦ	5712 .i̭u	0147
3		181-104 ʔyǐur	4230 ži̭ẹ	N.L.

GLOSS : YÜ 余

Middle Chinese : i̭wo
10 NW Chinese : yu

No.	Char.	Nishida	Sofronov	More Pis'men
1		017-152 ʔyĭur	0927 .i̭u	2263
2	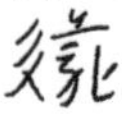	204-09a ʔyĭuɦ	3598 .I̭u	0238

GLOSS : YÜ 玉

Middle Chinese : ngi̭wok
10 NW Chinese : 'gûg

No.	Char.	Nishida	Sofronov	More Pis'men
1		033-071 ŋgĭuɦ	5791 ngi̭u	3204
2		N.L.	N.L.	N.L.
3		242-041 ŋĭuɦ	2189 ngi̭u	0134
4		041-084 ŋgĭuɦ	1464 ngi̭u	3202
5		N.L.	3020 ngi̭u	3203
6		N.L.	2186 ngi̭u	3199
7	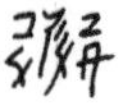	182-123 ŋĭuɦ	4623 ngi̭u	0131

GLOSS : YÜAN

Middle Chinese : li̭wok
10 NW Chinese : lôg

No.	Char.	Nishida	Sofronov	More Pis'men
1		N.L.	4756 ʑi̭ə	1160
2		N.L.	4877 ldi̭u	N.L.

GLOSS : **YÜEH**

Middle Chinese : i̯wät
10 NW Chinese : w̑ar

No.	**Char.**	**Nishida**	**Sofronov**	**More Pis'men**
1		156-051 śʷiɦ	4684 śi̭we	0334

GLOSS : **YÜEH** 月

Middle Chinese : ngi̭wɒt
10 NW Chinese : 'gar

No.	**Char.**	**Nishida**	**Sofronov**	**More Pis'men**
1		044-091 ^{2}wɨr	3125 .I̭ə	1156

GLOSS : **YUNG** 永

Middle Chinese : ji̭wɒng
10 NW Chinese : wań

No.	**Char.**	**Nishida**	**Sofronov**	**More Pis'men**
1		N.L.	N.L.	N.L.
2		006-091 wɛ̣	2926 vi̭ẹ	4567

POLYSYLLABIC GLOSSES

GLOSS : **CHI-CHIA** 極枷

Middle Chinese : g'i̯ək - ka
10 NW Chinese : çiĝ - ka

No.	Char.	Nishida	Sofronov	More Pis'men
1		007-133 khĭaĥ	1851 kâ	2360

GLOSS : CH'I - CHIA 其賈

Middle Chinese : kji - ka-
10 NW Chinese : gi - ka

No.	Char.	Nishida	Sofronov	More Pis'men
1	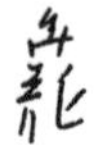	028-094 kha	2573 khâ	3594

GLOSS : **HSI - CH'ING** 西頃

Middle Chinese : siei - k'i̯wäng
10 NW Chinese : sye - k'waṅ

No	Char.	Nishida	Sofronov	More Pis'men
1	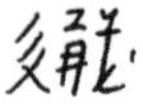	N.L.	3831 tśi̭on	1715
2		138-081 stshĭẽ	1320 sI̭e	1430

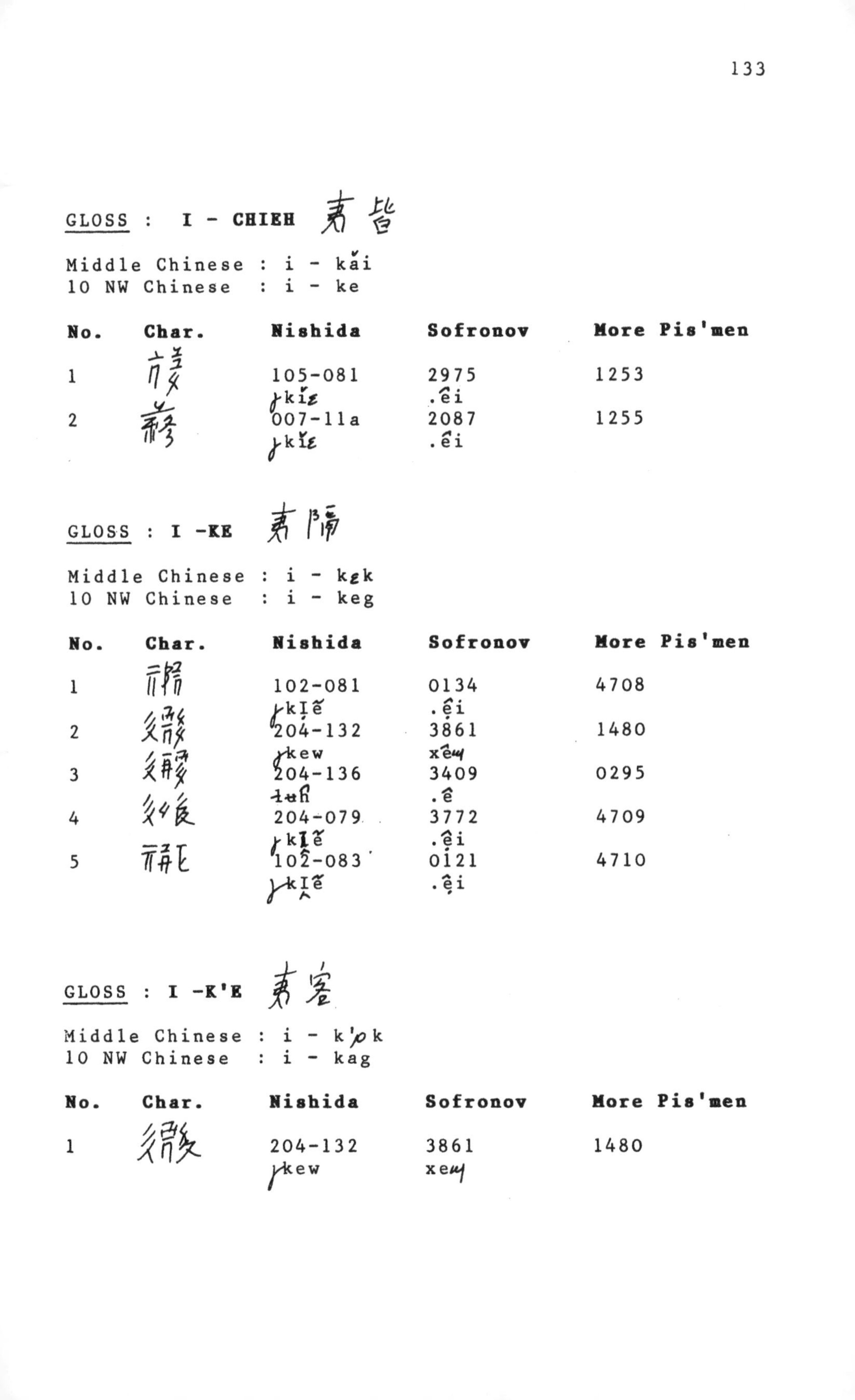

GLOSS : I - CHIEH 夷皆

Middle Chinese : i - kǎi
10 NW Chinese : i - ke

No.	Char.	Nishida	Sofronov	More Pis'men
1	[illegible]	105-081 ɣkǐɛ	2975 .êi	1253
2	[illegible]	007-11a ɣkǐɛ	2087 .êi	1255

GLOSS : I -KE 夷隔

Middle Chinese : i - kɛk
10 NW Chinese : i - keg

No.	Char.	Nishida	Sofronov	More Pis'men
1	[illegible]	102-081 ɣkɪ̣ĕ	0134 .ệi	4708
2	[illegible]	204-132 ɣkew	3861 xêɰ	1480
3	[illegible]	204-136 ɨʉñ	3409 .ê	0295
4	[illegible]	204-079 ɣkɪ̣ĕ	3772 .ệi	4709
5	[illegible]	102-083 ɣkɪ̣ĕ	0121 .ệi	4710

GLOSS : I -K'E 夷客

Middle Chinese : i - k'ɒk
10 NW Chinese : i - kag

No.	Char.	Nishida	Sofronov	More Pis'men
1	[illegible]	204-132 ɣkew	3861 xêɰ	1480

GLOSS : **I - KENG** 夷耿

Middle Chinese : i - kɛng:
10 NW Chinese : i - keń

No.	Char.	Nishida	Sofronov	More Pis'men
1		007-142 ɣkĭɛ	1977 .ậi	4564

GLOSS : **I - KO** 夷格

Middle Chinese : i - kɒk
10 NW Chinese : i - kag

No.	Char.	Nishida	Sofronov	More Pis'men
1	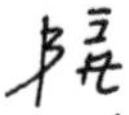	087-063 ɣkīẽr	5476 .ie̥	2305
2	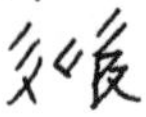	204-079 ɣkiẽ̥	3772 .ệi	4709

GLOSS : **I - CH'ING** 繹輕

Middle Chinese : i̯äk - k'i̯äng
10 NW Chinese : îg - kye

No.	Char.	Nishida	Sofronov	More Pis'men
1		1[illegible]9-102 lʷi	1686 lwi	0430

GLOSS : **I - HUI** 宜會

Middle Chinese : ngjie̥ - ɣwâi-
10 NW Chinese : 'ji - hwa

No.	Char.	Nishida	Sofronov	More Pis'men
1		230-074 ŋɣɛ	4718 nge̥	4863
2	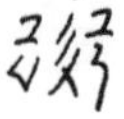	182-081 ŋɣɛ	4640 ngwei	3927

GLOSS : **I - KUA** 宜刮

Middle Chinese : ngjię - kwat
10 NW Chinese : 'ji - kar

No.	**Char.**	**Nishida**	**Sofronov**	**More Pis'men**
1	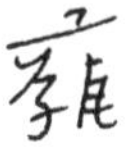	009-101 ŋʑĩã	4540 ngi̭wan	3712

GLOSS : **I - TSE** 宜則

Middle Chinese : ngjię - tsək
10 NW Chinese : 'ji - tsig

No.	**Char.**	**Nishida**	**Sofronov**	**More Pis'men**
1		030-031 ŋzʉr	2856 ngə̣	2421
2	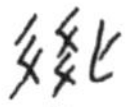	204-06d ŋzĩə r	3936 rIə̣	2483
3		028-121 ŋzʉr	2574 ngIu̯	2255
4		213-081 ŋzĩə r	N.L.	N.L.
5		028-101 tshʷaɦ	2596 tshwa	0756
6	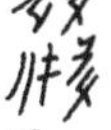	041-097 ŋzĩə r	1352 ngəɰ	2493
7		287-041 ŋzĩə r	4917 ndIu̯	1825
8		017-054 ŋzur	0883 ngIu̯	2256
9		026-104 ŋzur	4949 mgIu̯	2252
10		028-095 ŋzʉr	2576 ngə̣	2422

GLOSS : **I-TSE** 口移則

Middle Chinese : iḙ - tsək
10 NW Chinese : î - tsig

No.	**Char.**	**Nishida**	**Sofronov**	**More Pis'men**
1	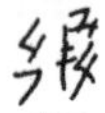	181-108 ɓzIě	4282 żi̭e̯	N.L.
2		017-062 ɓzəw	0821 żeɰ	4184
3		259-031 ɓzɨɦ	1647 żə̣̂	4948
4		009-102 ɓzɨ	4387 *	N.L.
5		008-072 ɓzɨr	1876 żiə	1058
6		017-09d ɓzɨɦ	0759 żə̣̂	4950
7		236-06d *	2732 *	3615
8		169-041 ɓzɨr	5081 nI	1040
9		299-061 ɓzɨ	2618 żə̣̂	4988
10		N.L.	5200 żeɰ	5002
11		017-11j ɓzoɦ	0980 żəɰ	4255
12		208-091 ɓzɨɦ	2385 żẹɰ	5005

GLOSS : **I-TSO** 口移作

Middle Chinese : ie tsâk
10 NW Chinese : î - tsag

No.	**Char.**	**Nishida**	**Sofronov**	**More Pis'men**
1		017-098 ɓzɔr	0944 żwon	4432

GLOSS : **I-TSU** 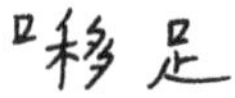

Middle Chinese : ie̯ - tsi̯wok
10 NW Chinese : i͡ - tswâg

No.	**Char.**	**Nishida**	**Sofronov**	**More Pis'men**
1		144-041 ɓzǐu	3207 *	4833
2		256-112 ɓzǐu	0567 *	4834

GLOSS : **JIH-SHUAI** 日率.

Middle Chinese : n̋źi̯ět - ṣiuět
10 NW Chinese : źyâr - ç̡war

No.	**Char.**	**Nishida**	**Sofronov**	**More Pis'men**
1		N.L.	N.L.	N.L.

GLOSS : **JIH-TSE** 日責

Middle Chinese : n̋źi̯ět-tṣɛ̣k
10 NW Chinese : źyâr-ç̡eg

No.	**Char.**	**Nishida**	**Sofronov**	**More Pis'men**
1	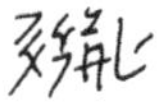	N.L.	N.L.	N.L.

GLOSS : **KU-YU** 骨魚

Middle Chinese : kuɔt-ngi̯wo
10 NW Chinese : kur-'gû

No.	Char.	Nishida	Sofronov	More Pis'men
1	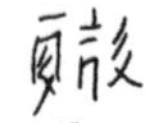	261-091 ŋɣɐr	0460 ngwə̣	2436
2		044-071 ŋɣɐñ	3118 ngwə	0935
3		073-061 ŋɣɐr	5407 ngwə̣	2439
4		017-11f ŋɣɐr	0863 ngwə̣	2437
5		002-062 ŋɣu	0292 ngu	3119

GLOSS : **LI-CH'ING** 力頃

Middle Chinese : liək-k"iwäng
10 NW Chinese : lig-k'wañ

No.	Char.	Nishida	Sofronov	More Pis'men
1	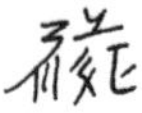	054-101 lʷẹ	5454 lÎwe	4598

GLOSS : **LI-CHIUNG** 力扃

Middle Chinese : liək-kiweng
10 NW Chinese : lig-kuñ

No.	Char.	Nishida	Sofronov	More Pis'men
1		2?0-021 *	4761 lhiwe	2835

GLOSS : **LIU-TING** 六丁

Middle Chinese : liuk-tieng
10 NW Chinese : lug-teñ

No.	Char.	Nishida	Sofronov	More Pis'men
1	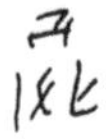	026-061 rɣur	4876 riụ	2266

GLOSS : **NI-CHAN** 尼盞

Middle Chinese : ńi-tsǎn=
10 NW Chinese : 'di-ċ'añ

No.	Char.	Nishida	Sofronov	More Pis'men
1	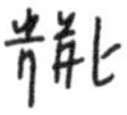	N.L.	N.L.	N.L.

GLOSS : **NI-CH'ANG** 尼長

Middle Chinese : ńi-t̂'i̯ang
10 NW Chinese : 'di-ċ'yañ

No.	Char.	Nishida	Sofronov	More Pis'men
1		N.L.	N.L.	N.L.
2		162-032 ⁿdžǐɔɦ	5109 ndźi̯o	2734
3		017-094 ⁿdžo	0783 ndzion	2990
4		204-11x ⁿdžoɦ	3719 ndźi̯won	2748
5	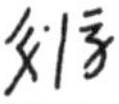	210-064 ⁿdžǐwõ	3991 ndźi̯o	2960
6		291-051 ⁿdžoɦ	N.L.	N.L.

GLOSS : **NI-CHENG** 尼正

Middle Chinese : ńi-ts'ịäng
10 NW Chinese : 'di-cêñ

No.	Char.	Nishida	Sofronov	More Pis'men
1		105-063 ⁿdžẽ	2973 ndźi̯ẹ	4395
2		247B-041 ⁿdže	2942 ndźi̯ei	2718
3		211-122 ⁿdžǐwo	5753 ndźi̯ei	2947
4		220-053 ⁿdžǐwõ	5378 ndźi̯e	N.L.

GLOSS : NI-CHI 尼積

Middle Chinese : ńi-tsi̯äk
10 NW Chinese : 'di-tŝig

No.	Char.	Nishida	Sofronov	More Pis'men
1	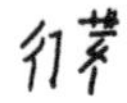	045-091 ^{n}dziɦ	3132 ndzI̭ei	2870
2		017-12b ^{n}dziɦ	0738 ndzI̭ẹi	2865
3		315-041 ^{n}dziɦ	1337 ndzI̭ẹi	2863
4	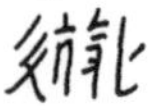	204-137 ^{n}dziɦ	3617 ndzI̭ẹi	2862
5	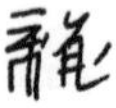	179-072 ^{n}dzẽ	1133 ndzI̭e	2653

GLOSS : NI-CHIEH 尼節

Middle Chinese : ńi-tsiɛt
10 NW Chinese : 'di-tser

No.	Char.	Nishida	Sofronov	More Pis'men
1	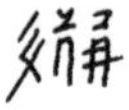	204-115 ^{n}dzaɦ	3621 ndzI̭ə	2639

GLOSS : NI-CHING 尼井

Middle Chinese : ńi-tsi̯äng
10 NW Chinese : 'di-tŝeń

No.	Char.	Nishida	Sofronov	More Pis'men
1		146-053 ^{n}dzẽ	N.L.	N.L.

GLOSS : **NI-CH'ING** 尼精

Middle Chinese : ńi-tsi̯äng
10 NW Chinese : 'di-tsiń

No.	**Char.**	**Nishida**	**Sofronov**	**More Pis'men**
1		N.L.	N.L.	N.L.
2		211-121 ^{n}dzẽ̆	5676 ndzI̭e	2655
3		179-072 ^{n}dzẽ̆	1133 ndzI̭e	2653
4	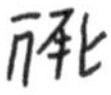	103-061 ^{n}dzĭẽ̆	0303 ndzI̭e	2880

GLOSS : **NI-CH'ING** 尼頃

Middle Chinese : ńi-k'i̯wăng
10 NW Chinese : 'di-k'wań

No.	**Char.**	**Nishida**	**Sofronov**	**More Pis'men**
1		018-051 ^{n}tśhiẽ̆	0241 ndźi̭we	2982
2		018-112 ^{n}tšhiẽ̆	0292 ndźi̭we	N.L.
3		026-113 ŋaĥ	5175 ndźi̭we	1215

GLOSS : **NI-CHO** 尼卓

Middle Chinese : ńi-tâk
10 NW Chinese : 'di-cag

No.	**Char.**	**Nishida**	**Sofronov**	**More Pis'men**
1	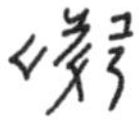	180-108 ^{n}džĭow	4091 nôn	4437

GLOSS : **NI-CHOU** 尼周

Middle Chinese : ńi-tśi̯əu
10 NW Chinese : 'di-cû

No.	**Char.**	**Nishida**	**Sofronov**	**More Pis'men**
1		211-001 ⁿdžu?	5649 ndźi̭eu̯	2745

GLOSS : **NI-CHUAN** 尼專

Middle Chinese : ńi-d̂'i̯wän
10 NW Chinese : 'di-jŵań

No.	**Char.**	**Nishida**	**Sofronov**	**More Pis'men**
1		017-052 ⁿdží̃ẵ	0762 tśi̭wan	0861

GLOSS : **NI-CHUI** 尼追

Middle Chinese : ńi-t̂wi
10 NW Chinese : 'di-twi

No.	**Char.**	**Nishida**	**Sofronov**	**More Pis'men**
1		236-049 Gĭẽ̆	2762 tI	N.L.
2		ɔ 9-101 *	3749 ndzu	2895
3		299-021 ⁿdžwɪɦ	2617 ndźi̭ei	2758
4		N.L.	N.L.	N.L.

GLOSS : **NI-CHUN** 尼准

Middle Chinese : ńi-tśi̯uĕn=
10 NW Chinese : 'di-cʕuń

No.	Char.	Nishida	Sofronov	More Pis'men
1		144-081 ^{n}džǐuɦ	3197 tśi̭wan	3710

GLOSS : **NI-HSI** 尼習

Middle Chinese : ńi-zi̭əp
10 NW Chinese : 'di-ŝyap

No.	Char.	Nishida	Sofronov	More Pis'men
1		290-061 si	4867 ndzI̭ə	1934

GLOSS : **NI-HSIANG** 尼相

Middle Chinese : ńi-si̭ang
10 NW Chinese : 'di-ŝyo

No.	Char.	Nishida	Sofronov	More Pis'men
1		319-081 ^{n}dzu	3749 ndzu	2895

GLOSS : **NI-KOU** 尼苟

Middle Chinese : ńi-kə̣u
10 NW Chinese : 'di-kau

No.	Char.	Nishida	Sofronov	More Pis'men
1		233-081 ^{n}džị̵	N.L.	N.L.
2		N.L.	N.L.	N.L.

GLOSS : **NI-KU** 泥骨

Middle Chinese : ńi-kuət
10 NW Chinese : 'di-kur

No.	Char.	Nishida	Sofronov	More Pis'men
1	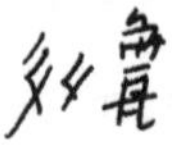	204-134 nrʉɦ	3766 ndwe̩ɰ	N.L.

GLOSS : **NI-LANG** 泥浪

Middle Chinese : ńi-lâng
10 NW Chinese : 'di-lań

No.	Char.	Nishida	Sofronov	More Pis'men
1		075-081 nɨɔɦ	1270 ndI̭o̩n	4743

GLOSS : **NI-LIU** 泥六

Middle Chinese : ńi-li̯uk
10 NW Chinese : 'di-l̂ug

No.	Char.	Nishida	Sofronov	More Pis'men
1		**008-051** **nrǐu̇**	**1832** **niu**	**0119**
2		**041-091** **nriuɦ**	**1354** **ndi̭u**	**0126**

GLOSS : **NI-SHA** 尼耜

Middle Chinese : ṅi-zi=
10 NW Chinese : 'di-si

No.	Char.	Nishida	Sofronov	More Pis'men
1	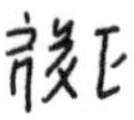	109-081 *	1104 *	4484

GLOSS : **NI-SHUAI** 尼率

Middle Chinese : ńi-ṣiuĕt
10 NW Chinese : 'di-ḉwar

No.	**Char.**	**Nishida**	**Sofronov**	**More Pis'men**
1		026-132 ⁿdžɨr	N.L.	N.L.

GLOSS : **NI-SHUO** 尼說

Middle Chinese : ńi-śiwät
10 NW Chinese : 'di-ç̂war

No.	**Char.**	**Nishida**	**Sofronov**	**More Pis'men**
1		056-081 ⁿdzɨ	2417 ndźi̭wa	2728

GLOSS : **NI-T'AI** 泥台

Middle Chinese : ni-t'âi
10 NW Chinese : 'di-t'ai

No.	**Char.**	**Nishida**	**Sofronov**	**More Pis'men**
1		123B-061 thǐe	0433 ndai	1322

GLOSS : **NI-TE** 尼得

Middle Chinese : ńi-d'ậi
10 NW Chinese : 'di-tig

No.	**Char.**	**Nishida**	**Sofronov**	**More Pis'men**
1	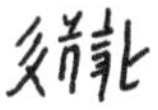	204-137 ⁿdziɦ	3617 ndzI̭ẹi	2862

GLOSS : NI-TSAI 尼栽

Middle Chinese : ńi-tsâi
10 NW Chinese : 'di-tṡa

No.	Char.	Nishida	Sofronov	More Pis'men
1		185-063 ndzɛ	5509 ndzai	2652

GLOSS : NI-TS'ANG 尼倉

Middle Chinese : ńi-ts'âng
10 NW Chinese : 'di-ts'aṅ

No.	Char.	Nishida	Sofronov	More Pis'men
1		017-119 tshoṅ	0780 ndzon	0317

GLOSS : NI-TSE 尼窄

Middle Chinese : ni-tṣɐk
10 NW Chinese : 'di-ćag

No.	Char.	Nishida	Sofronov	More Pis'men
1		218-051 ndžIĕ	5356 ndźə̂	2752

GLOSS : NI-TSE 尼則

Middle Chinese : ńi-tsək
10 NW Chinese : 'di-tsig

No.	Char.	Nishida	Sofronov	More Pis'men
1		204-034 ndzɨ	3484 ndzÎeɯ	2597
2		204-09p' ndu?	3802 ndze	2636
3		N.L.	N.L.	N.L.

No.	Char.	Nishida	Sofronov	More Pis'men
4		026-098 ndzʉɦ	4882 ndzI	2617
5		007-071 ndziɦ	1849 ndzI̭ʔ	N.L.
6	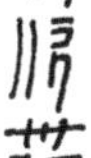	041-051 ndzɨ	1366 ndzI̭ʔ	2927
7		017-072 ndzu	0986 ndze	2899

GLOSS : **NI-TSE** 尼責

Middle Chinese : ńi-tṣɛk
10 NW Chinese : 'di-ceg

No.	Char.	Nishida	Sofronov	More Pis'men
1	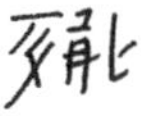	N.L.	N.L.	N.L.
2		298-041 ndžiɦ	2543 ndźêi	N.L.
3	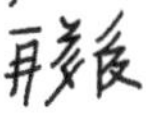	123-123 ndžɨɦ	0349 ndźə̂	2759
4		026-098 ndzʉɦ	4882 ndzI	2617
5	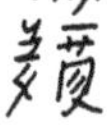	238-111 ndzɨɦ	2517 ndźêi	N.L.
6	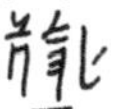	106-081 ndzi̯	N.L.	N.L.
7		297-001 ndźi?	4990 ndzI	2706
8		N.L.	N.L.	N.L.

GLOSS : **NI-TSU** 尼卒

Middle Chinese : ńi-tsuət
10 NW Chinese : 'di-tsur

No.	Char.	Nishida	Sofronov	More Pis'men
1		061-041 ndzʉɦ	4105 ndzI̭wo	2918
2	 8.-	007-108 ndzoɦ	2064 ndzwI	N.L.

GLOSS : **NI-TSU** 尼祖

Middle Chinese : ńi-tsuo=
10 NW Chinese : 'di-tsu

No.	**Char.**	**Nishida**	**Sofronov**	**More Pis'men**
1		010-091 ^{n}dzǐu	4394 ndzu	2656
2		319-081 ^{n}dzu	3749 ndzu	2895

GLOSS : **NI-TSU** 尼足

Middle Chinese : ńi-tsi̯wok
10 NW Chinese : 'di-tŝwag

No.	**Char.**	**Nishida**	**Sofronov**	**More Pis'men**
1		205-111 ^{n}dzǐụ	3330 ndzI̭ụ	2887
2	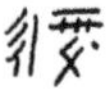	205-092 ^{n}dzǐụ	3315 ndzI̭u	2888
4		204-081 ^{n}dzǐu	3947 ndzu	2875
5	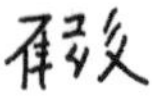	081-081 ^{n}dzǐu	5250 ndzI̭u	2590

GLOSS : **SHUO-NI** 說尼

Middle Chinese : ´i̯wät-ńi
10 NW Chinese : çwar-'di

No.	**Char.**	**Nishida**	**Sofronov**	**More Pis'men**
1		056-061 ^{n}dzɨ	2417 ndźi̯wa	2728
2	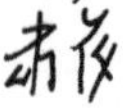	157-063 ň̌dzɨ̌	5341 ndźi̭wa	2726

GLOSS : TING-KU 丁谷

Middle Chinese : tieng-kuk
10 NW Chinese : tyeṅ-kug

No.	Char.	Nishida	Sofronov	More Pis'men
1		205-068 ko	3537 twI	1087

GLOSS : YÜ-KO 魚各

Middle Chinese : ngi̯wo-kâk
10 NW Chinese : 'gu-kag

No.	Char.	Nishida	Sofronov	More Pis'men
1		204-07v ŋgǐeĥ	3912 ngwə	1140

GLOSS : YÜ-TSENG 魚

Middle Chinese : ngi̯wo-tsəng
10 NW Chinese : 'gu-tseń

No.	Char.	Nishida	Sofronov	More Pis'men
1		182-081 ŋɣɛ	4640 ngwei	3927

DIACRITIC HO 合

GLOSS : **CHI**$_{\text{HO}}$ 濟$_{合}$

Middle Chinese : dz'iei$_{\text{ɣa̤p}}$

10 NW Chinese : dzei$_{\text{hab}}$

No.	Char.	Nishida	Sofronov	More Pis'men
1		007-094 tshl^{w}iɦ	2014 tshweɯ	1465

GLOSS : **CHOU**$_{\text{HO}}$ 周$_{合}$

Middle Chinese : tsi̯ə̯u$_{\text{ɣa̤p}}$

10 NW Chinese : cu$_{\text{hab}}$

No.	Char.	Nishida	Sofronov	More Pis'men
1		N.L.	5654 tsi̭weɯ	4230

GLOSS : **CH'OU**$_{\text{HO}}$ 抽$_{合}$

Middle Chinese : t̂'i̯ə̯u$_{\text{ɣa̤p}}$

10 NW Chinese : c'u$_{\text{hab}}$

No.	Char.	Nishida	Sofronov	More Pis'men
1		028-086 *	2534 tśhi̭weɯ	N.L.
2	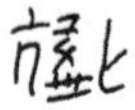	105-171 *	2998 thwo	1578

GLOSS : **HSIANG$_{HO}$** 相合

Middle Chinese : si̯ang-ɣạp

10 NW Chinese : syo$_{hab}$

No.	**Char.**	**Nishida**	**Sofronov**	**More Pis'men**
1		017-133 stshĭɔɦ	0784 sIwo	1620
2		236-04c kiɦ	2̂644 ki	0421

GLOSS : **HSIEH$_{HO}$** 斜合

Middle Chinese : si̯ät ɣạp

10 NW Chinese : sar$_{hab}$

No.	**Char.**	**Nishida**	**Sofronov**	**More Pis'men**
1	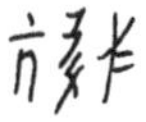	105-101 stshĭẽ	2991 sÎe	4132

GLOSS : **LE$_{HO}$** 勒合

Middle Chinese : lək ɣạp
10 NW Chinese : leg$_{hab}$

No.	**Char.**	**Nishida**	**Sofronov**	**More Pis'men**
1		297-072 lʷɨ	5005 lhe	5003

GLOSS : **LING$_{HO}$** 令合

Middle Chinese : li̯äng ɣạp
10 NW Chinese : leñ$_{hab}$

No.	**Char.**	**Nishida**	**Sofronov**	**More Pis'men**
1		007-101 lʷẹ	2106 lÎwe	1912

GLOSS : **LIU$_{HO}$** 六合

Middle Chinese : li̯uk ɣap
10 NW Chinese : lug hab

No.	Char.	Nishida	Sofronov	More Pis'men
1		017-09c -lǐu	0745 lÎwu	1831
2	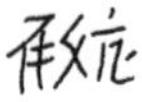	080-082 lǐuɦ	5244 li̭wu	0168

GLOSS : **LOU$_{HO}$** 婁合

Middle Chinese : li̯u ɣạp
10 NW Chinese : lu hab

No.	Char.	Nishida	Sofronov	More Pis'men
1		216-051 lǝw	5785 lweɰ	1470

GLOSS : **MA$_{HO}$** 馬合

Middle Chinese : ma: ɣạp
10 NW Chinese : ma hab

No.	Char.	Nishida	Sofronov	More Pis'men
1	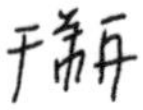	098-112 ˀyǐwo	0638 .i̭uo	1755

GLOSS : **NENG$_{HO}$** 能

Middle Chinese : nǝęng ɣạp
10 NW Chinese : niń hab

No.	Char.	Nishida	Sofronov	More Pis'men
1	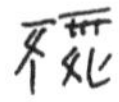	252-101 nʷɨ	1224 nI̭wI	3876
2		017-12g *	0787 nwi	1089
3		205-041 nʷɨ	3516 nI̭wI	1113
4		N.L.	N.L.	N.L.

GLOSS : **NI$_{HO}$** 你合

Middle Chinese : ngie̯-ɣa̭p
10 NW Chinese : ni$_{hab}$

No.	Char.	Nishida	Sofronov	More Pis'men
1		204-10i Tiĥ	3838 nI̭wi	3460

GLOSS : **NI$_{HOTE}$** 泥合得

Middle Chinese : ńi$_{ɣa̭p}$d'ậi=

10 NW Chinese : 'di$_{hab}$tig

No.	Char.	Nishida	Sofronov	More Pis'men
1	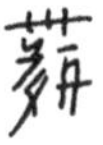	017-10a -təw	0816 ndwu	3115

GLOSS : **NI$_{HOTSE}$** 尼合則

Middle Chinese : ńi$_{ɣa̭p}$tsək

10 NW Chinese : 'di$_{had}$tsig

No.	Char.	Nishida	Sofronov	More Pis'men
1		028-131 ⁿdzʷɨ	2575 ndzwə	2664
2		065-051 ⁿdzʷɨ	4448 ndzeɰ	2682

GLOSS : **SHANG$_{HO}$** 尚合

Middle Chinese : źi̯ang-ɣap
10 NW Chinese : źyañ$_{hab}$

No.	**Char.**	**Nishida**	**Sofronov**	**More Pis'men**
1		221-042 LĬu	0153 ldi̭u	3267

GLOSS : **T'E$_{HO}$** 特合

Middle Chinese : d'ək ɣap
10 NW Chinese : deg$_{hab}$

No.	**Char.**	**Nishida**	**Sofronov**	**More Pis'men**
1		001-161 th^{w}ɨ	1137 thI̭we	1111

GLOSS : **TI$_{HO}$** 底合

Middle Chinese : tiei ɣap
10 NW Chinese : tei$_{hab}$

No.	**Char.**	**Nishida**	**Sofronov**	**More Pis'men**
1		255-031 tĭụ	0555 tI̭u	1819

GLOSS : **TING$_{HO}$** 頂合

Middle Chinese : tieng ɣap
10 NW Chinese : tyeñ$_{hab}$

No.	**Char.**	**Nishida**	**Sofronov**	**More Pis'men**
1	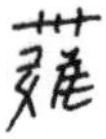	017-129 t^{w}eñ	0942 twIn	1306

GLOSS : HOTING 合頂

Middle Chinese : ɣaptieng
10 NW Chinese : habtyeń

No.	Char.	Nishida	Sofronov	More Pis'men
1		017-129 tʷeń	0942 twIn	1306

GLOSS : TSUHO 足合

Middle Chinese : tsi̯wokɣap
10 NW Chinese : tsughab

No.	Char.	Nishida	Sofronov	More Pis'men
1		181-085 ⁿdzǐu	4212 tsIwu	1787

GLOSS : TZ'UHO 束合

Middle Chinese : ts'i̯eɣap
10 NW Chinese : ts'ihab

No.	Char.	Nishida	Sofronov	More Pis'men
1		018-101 šʷǐo	0751 śi̯uo	1750
2		204-048 tshĭə̃	3647 tshI̭wen	0524

GLOSS : OHO 訛合

Middle Chinese : nguaɣap
10 NW Chinese : 'guahab

No.	Char.	Nishida	Sofronov	More Pis'men
1		139-041 ɣõ	1689 .on	1686

2	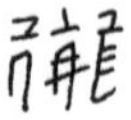	107-121 ɣõ	4477 wo	N.L.

<u>GLOSS</u> : **YUEH$_{\mathbf{HO}}$** 藥合

Middle Chinese : i̯ak ɣap
10 NW Chinese : yag hab

No.	**Char.**	**Nishida**	**Sofronov**	**More Pis'men**
1		259-052 ʔyiʷo	1633 .i̯uo	1753
2		196-041 ʔyʉɦ	1672 .i̯uo	4492

DIACRITIC K'OU 口

NOTE : This diacritic does not represent the sound k"ou 口 but a modification of either the initial or the final. As such it will be indicated by either **I** or **F**, preceding or following the character affected.

<u>GLOSS</u> : **CHI**$_F$ 即口

Middle Chinese : tsiet$_F$
10 NW Chinese : tsir$_F$

No	Char.	Nishida	Sofronov	More Pis'men
1	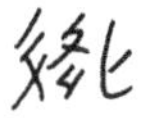	204-07j rɨr	3936 rI̭ə̣	2483

<u>GLOSS</u> : ^{I}**CH'ING** 口精

Middle Chinese : ^{I}tsi̯ãng
10 NW Chinese : ^{I}tsîṅ

No.	Char.	Nishida	Sofronov	More Pis'men
1		107-061 ⁿdzeɦ	4475 ndzI̭e	2648
2	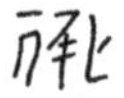	103-061 ⁿdziě̃	0303̂' ndzIe	2880
3	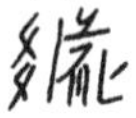	211-121 ⁿdzẽ	5676̂' ndzI̭e	2655
4	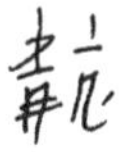	146-053 ⁿdzẽ̆	1666 ndzI̭e	2912

<u>GLOSS</u> : ^{I}**CHUAN** 口縳

Middle Chinese : ^{I}d̂'i̯wän
10 NW Chinese : ^{I}jwâṅ

No.	Char.	Nishida	Sofronov	More Pis'men
1		204-076 fa	3352 vi̭ạ	1966

GLOSS : ^{I}**FU** 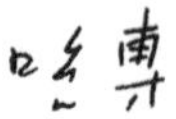

Middle Chinese : ^{I}b̑'i̯wak
10 NW Chinese : ^{I}b'âg

No.	Char.	Nishida	Sofronov	More Pis'men
1		204-077 naɦ	3352 via	1966
2	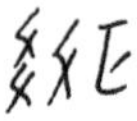	239-071 far	N.L.	N.L.

GLOSS : ^{I}**HEI** 

Middle Chinese : ^{I}χək
10 NW Chinese : ^{I}heg

No.	Char.	Nishida	Sofronov	More Pis'men
1	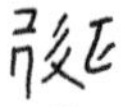	107-073 ŋhĭaɦ	4479 nIa	0770
2	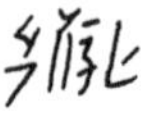	181-105 ŋhaw	4̂216 nIaw	3684

GLOSS : ^{I}**HUAI** 

Middle Chinese : ^{I}ɣwǎi
10 NW Chinese : ^{I}hwei

No.	Char.	Nishida	Sofronov	More Pis'men
1		007-098 ɣeɦ	2074 xIwêi	1263
2		041-069 ɣẽ	1̂417 xwai	1391

GLOSS : ^{I}**I** 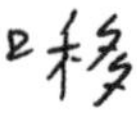

Middle Chinese : ^{I}ie
10 NW Chinese : ^{I}i

No.	Char.	Nishida	Sofronov	More Pis'men
1		004-082 ɓiɦ	0006 z̀i	3447
2		104-051 ɓir	0017 z̀i̭e	4894
3		108-072 ɓiɦ	4359 z̀i	0407
4	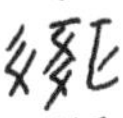	204-10g' ɓwIɦ	3496 z̀wẹi	2076
5		017-120 ʔyị	0827 .iei	2035
6		230-072 ɓi	4776 z̀Iei	2071
7	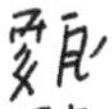	297-051 maɦ	4999 .iə	N.L.
8		N.L.	4333 z̀wẹi	2077

GLOSS : ^{I}I-CHIANG 口移將

Middle Chinese : ^{I}ie̯-tsi̯ang
10 NW Chinese : ^{I}i-tsyań

No.	Char.	Nishida	Sofronov	More Pis'men
1		118-041 ɓzɔɦ	4677 z̀I̭ọn	4751

GLOSS : ^{I}I-CHIN 口移金

Middle Chinese : ^{I}ie̯-ki̯əm
10 NW Chinese : ^{I}i-kim

No.	Char.	Nishida	Sofronov	More Pis'men
1		233-082 stshĭẽ	3050 sI̭wan	N.L.

GLOSS : ^{I}I-CH'ING 口移青

Middle Chinese : ^{I}ie - ts'ieng
10 NW Chinese : ^{I}i̍ - ts'eń

No.	Char.	Nishida	Sofronov	More Pis'men
1		039-112 zih	1566 zIe	1910

GLOSS : ^{I}KE 口隔

Middle Chinese : ^{I}kɛk
10 NW Chinese : ^{I}keg

No.	Char.	Nishida	Sofronov	More Pis'men
1	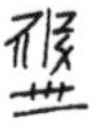	319-091 kew	N.L.	N.L.

GLOSS : $_{I}$K'E 口客

Middle Chinese : $_{I}$k'ɒk
10 NW Chinese :
$_{I}$kag

No.	Char.	Nishida	Sofronov	More Pis'men
1		315-031 khe	1328 khêi	N.L.
2	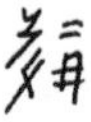	236-067 khe^{Y}	2642 khâi	N.L

GLOSS : $_{I}$K'E 刻

Middle Chinese : $_{I}$k'ɒk
10 NW Chinese : $_{I}$kag

No.	Char.	Nishida	Sofronov	More Pis'men
1		105-062 khɨ	2989 khi	1057

GLOSS : $_{I}$KO $_{2}$ 割

Middle Chinese : $_{I}$kât
10 NW Chinese : $_{I}$kar

No.	Char.	Nishida	Sofronov	More Pis'men
1		204-06f ka	3763 z̀iə	1147
2		0̇09-121 kaɦ	N.L.	N.L.

GLOSS : ^{I}K'O ^{2}磕

Middle Chinese : ^{I}k'âp
10 NW Chinese : ^{I}kab

No.	Char.	Nishida	Sofronov	More Pis'men
1	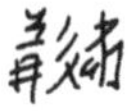	N.L.	N.L.	N.L.
2		017-09c khạ	0908 kha	N.L.

GLOSS : $_{I}$KOU $_{2}$ 苟

Middle Chinese : $_{I}$kə̣u
10 NW Chinese : $_{I}$Kaû

No.	Char.	Nishida	Sofronov	More Pis'men
1	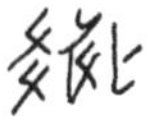	211-084 kǐʉr	N.L.	N.L.

GLOSS : LA$_{I}$ 辣$_{a}$

Middle Chinese : la:$_{F}$
10 NW Chinese : la$_{F}$

No.	Char.	Nishida	Sofronov	More Pis'men
1		N.L.	4374 lha	3054

GLOSS : ^{I}LA 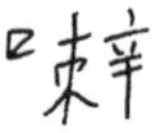

Middle Chinese : ^{I}la:
10 NW Chinese : ^{I}la

No.	Char.	Nishida	Sofronov	More Pis'men
1		188-031 raɦ	2843 lha	2809

GLOSS : ^{I}LA 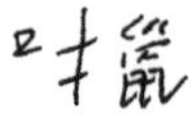

Middle Chinese : ^{I}li̯äp
10 NW Chinese : ^{I}lyab

No.	Char.	Nishida	Sofronov	More Pis'men
1	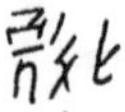	289-081 ɓzar	4860 ża	0603
2		157-065 ɓzar	1760 ża	2340
3		017-09L *	0686 ndza	2668
4		106-041 -ɓzar	1893 ża	3573
5		004-082 ɓiɦ	0006 żi	3447
6		026-105 ⁿdzaɦ	4847 ndẓi̭ə̂	2640
7		307-051 tsar	0408 tsạ	2354
8		139-111 tshõ	1685 tsə̣	2106
9		269-082 tshõ	N.L.	N.L.
10		N.L.	N.L.	N.L.
11		N.L.	N.L.	N.L.

GLOSS : $_{I}$LA 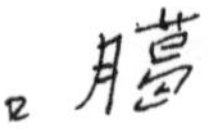

Middle Chinese : $_{I}$lât
10 NW Chinese : $_{I}$ɦa

No.	Char.	Nishida	Sofronov	More Pis'men
1		039-061 ɨạ	1545 ldạ	1957

GLOSS : ILAI 口來

Middle Chinese : Ilâi
10 NW Chinese : Ilai

No.	Char.	Nishida	Sofronov	More Pis'men
1	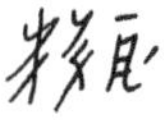	088-121 *	5477 lhei	3060

GLOSS : ILANG 口浪

Middle Chinese : Ilâng
10 NW Chinese : Ilaṅ

No.	Char.	Nishida	Sofronov	More Pis'men
1	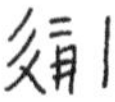	204-07d rĭɔɦ	3362 li̭o	3849

GLOSS : ILE 口勒

Middle Chinese : Ilək
10 NW Chinese : Ileg

No.	Char.	Nishida	Sofronov	More Pis'men
1	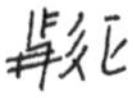	315-071 lɨɦ	1338 liə	0994
2		211-053 lɨɦ	5̂675 li̭ə	1001
3		017-153 lhɨɦ	0739 li̭ə	0995
4		276-052 -ɨI-	3̂365 lie	3370
5		N.L.	N̂.L.	N.L.

GLOSS : **LE$_F$** 勒$_a$

Middle Chinese : Lək$_F$
10 NW Chinese : leg$_F$

No.	**Char.**	**Nishida**	**Sofronov**	**More Pis'men**
1		204-066 lhɨ	3881 lhə	N.L.

GLOSS : **LENG$_F$** 冷$_a$

Middle Chinese : lieng:$_F$
10 NW Chinese : leṅ$_F$

No.	**Char.**	**Nishida**	**Sofronov**	**More Pis'men**
1		028-102 lhʷIĥ	2564 lhə	N.L.

GLOSS : **^{I}LI** 力

Middle Chinese : ^{I}liək
10 NW Chinese : ^{I}lîg

No.	**Char.**	**Nishida**	**Sofronov**	**More Pis'men**
1		287-061 rir	4911 rie	2324

GLOSS : **LI$_F$** 力$_a$

Middle Chinese : liɔk$_F$
10 NW Chinese : lîg$_F$

No.	**Char.**	**Nishida**	**Sofronov**	**More Pis'men**
1	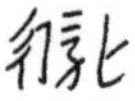	205-072 lhi	3313 lhiə	N.L.
2	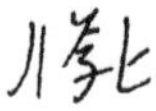	041-086 LẼ	1392 lỊ	1919

GLOSS : $_{I}$LI $_{a}$ 離

Middle Chinese : $_{I}$ljie
10 NW Chinese : $_{I}$lwi

No.	Char.	Nishida	Sofronov	More Pis'men
1		017-142 li	0700 lie	3373

GLOSS : $_{I}$LI $_{a}$ 里

Middle Chinese : $_{I}$Lji
10 NW Chinese : $_{I}$lwi

No.	Char.	Nishida	Sofronov	More Pis'men
1		017-142 li	0700 lie	3373

GLOSS : $_{I}$LIANG $_{a}$ 良

Middle Chinese : $_{I}$liang
10 NW Chinese : $_{I}$lian

No.	Char.	Nishida	Sofronov	More Pis'men
1		205-067 lhiɔɦ	3327 lio	1604

GLOSS : $LIANG_{F}$ 量$_{a}$

Middle Chinese : liang-$_{F}$
10 NW Chinese : $lian_{F}$

No.	Char.	Nishida	Sofronov	More Pis'men
1		017-068 la	0997 lho	3049

GLOSS : LIEH$_F$ 烈

Middle Chinese : li̯ät$_F$
10 NW Chinese : ly̑ar$_F$

No.	Char.	Nishida	Sofronov	More Pis'men
1		204-041 lhe	3420 ldi̭a	3657

GLOSS : ^{I}LING 領

Middle Chinese : ^{I}b'ieng
10 NW Chinese : ^{I}leń

No.	Char.	Nishida	Sofronov	More Pis'men
1		080-021 rǐẹ	5233 rịẹ	2225
2		208-082 rǐẽ	23̂87 rịẹ	4806
3		031-067 rǐẽ	39̂77 ldI̭e	N.L.

GLOSS : LING$_F$ 領

Middle Chinese : b'ieng$_F$
10 NW Chinese : leń$_F$

No.	Char.	Nishida	Sofronov	More Pis'men
1		039-111 lheñ	1594 lhịə	N.L.
2	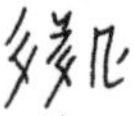	204-096 lhe	36̂90 lhịə	N.L.
3		265-001 lhi	06̂73 z̀ạ	1877

GLOSS : $_{I}$LING $_{2}$領

Middle Chinese : $_{I}$b'ieng
10 NW Chinese : $_{I}$leṅ

No.	Char.	Nishida	Sofronov	More Pis'men
1		N.L.	5275	N.L.
			.iwe	
2	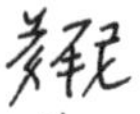	N.L.	N.L.	N.L.
3		007-088	2020	4876
		rir	rie̯	
4		080-021	5233	2225
		ríẹ	ri̭ẹ	

GLOSS : ^{I}LING ^{2}命

Middle Chinese : ^{I}li̭ăng
10 NW Chinese : ^{I}leṅ

No.	Char.	Nishida	Sofronov	More Pis'men
1		N.L.	0674	1877
			mbIẹ	
2	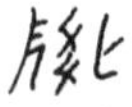	137-081	1317	4636
		mbẹ	mbIe	
3		N.L.	1234	3980
			mbIn	
4		204-o8k	3380	3977
		mbeñ	mbIn	
5		039-094	1232	1873
		mbẹ	mbI̭ẹ	

GLOSS : LING$_{F}$ ^{2}令$_{o}$

Middle Chinese : li̭ăng$_{F}$
10 NW Chinese : len$_{F}$

No.	Char.	Nishida	Sofronov	More Pis'men
1	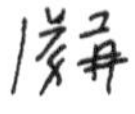	039-126	1562	2832
		lạ	lhi̭ə̣	

GLOSS : ^{I}LING 令

Middle Chinese : ^{I}liang
10 NW Chinese : ^{I}len

No.	Char.	Nishida	Sofronov	More Pis'men
1		203-061 rIr	5647 rę	N.L.
2	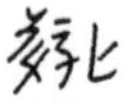	236-062 rIr	2692 rẹ	4857
3		017-076 rẹ	0994 rại	4769
4	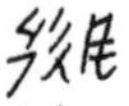	181-081 -rẹ	4247 rại	4770
5	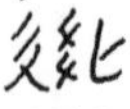	204-07j rɨr	3936 rI̭ə̣	2483
6	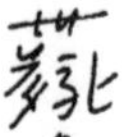	017-121 -rIr	0818 rę	4856
7		028-084 rI	2591 riə̆	4987
8	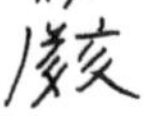	039-12b rʉr	1557 rẹ	2424
9	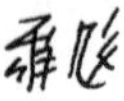	162-061 rIr	5114 re	N.L.
10		017-091 re	0711 rai	4768
11		085-063 rẹ	0618 rại	2212
12		104-061 rIr	0013 rə̣	4859

GLOSS : ^{I}LIU 留

Middle Chinese : ^{I}Li̭ə̂u
10 NW Chinese : ^{I}lu

No.	Char.	Nishida	Sofronov	More Pis'men
1		130-101 lǐər	1792 ri̭ẹɯ	3548

GLOSS : ^{I}LIU 六

Middle Chinese : ^{I}liuk
10 NW Chinese : ^{I}lug

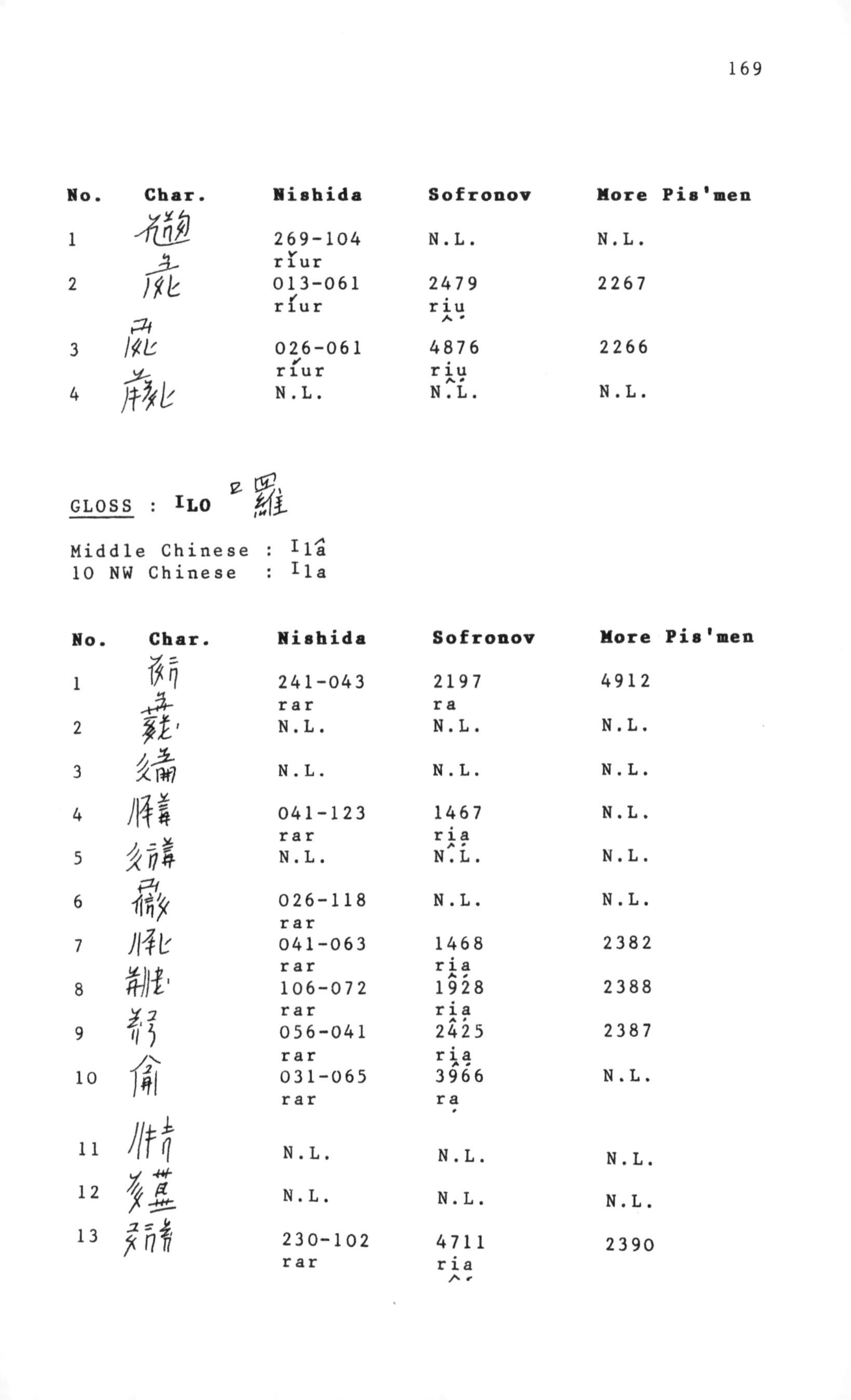

No.	Char.	Nishida	Sofronov	More Pis'men
1		269-104 rǐur	N.L.	N.L.
2		013-061 ríur	2479 ri̭ụ	2267
3		026-061 ríur	4876 ri̭ụ	2266
4		N.L.	N.L.	N.L.

GLOSS : ¹LO ² 羅

Middle Chinese : ¹lâ
10 NW Chinese : ¹la

No.	Char.	Nishida	Sofronov	More Pis'men
1		241-043 rar	2197 ra	4912
2		N.L.	N.L.	N.L.
3		N.L.	N.L.	N.L.
4		041-123 rar	1467 ri̭ạ	N.L.
5		N.L.	N.L.	N.L.
6		026-118 rar	N.L.	N.L.
7		041-063 rar	1468 ri̭ạ	2382
8		106-072 rar	1928 ri̭ạ	2388
9		056-041 rar	2425 ri̭ạ	2387
10		031-065 rar	3966 rạ	N.L.
11		N.L.	N.L.	N.L.
12		N.L.	N.L.	N.L.
13		230-102 rar	4711 ri̭ạ	2390

GLOSS : ^{I}LOU 婁

Middle Chinese : ^{I}liu
10 NW Chinese : ^{I}l

No.	Char.	Nishida	Sofronov	More Pis'men
1		170-051 ləw	5089 leɰ	4174

GLOSS : ^{I}LU 魯

Middle Chinese : ^{I}luo:
10 NW Chinese : ^{I}lu

No.	Char.	Nishida	Sofronov	More Pis'men
1		N.L.	N.L.	N.L.

GLOSS : LUI_F 縲

Middle Chinese : $ljwi_F$
10 NW Chinese : lwi_F

No.	Char.	Nishida	Sofronov	More Pis'men
1		112-063 lh^{w}ɪɦ	0312 lhwi	2814

GLOSS : LUI_F 淚

Middle Chinese : $ljwi_F$
10 NW Chinese : lwi_F

No.	Char.	Nishida	Sofronov	More Pis'men
1		N.L.	N.L.	N.L.

GLOSS : IMA ᴮ麻

Middle Chinese : Ima
10 NW Chinese : Ima

No.	Char.	Nishida	Sofronov	More Pis'men
1		230-066 maɦ-	4745 ma	0729

GLOSS : IMEI ᴮ每

Middle Chinese : Imuai
10 NW Chinese : Imai

No.	Char.	Nishida	Sofronov	More Pis'men
1		007-087 mɛ	1850 mei	1207

GLOSS : IMING ᴮ命

Middle Chinese : Imjwɒng
10 NW Chinese : Imen

No.	Char.	Nishida	Sofronov	More Pis'men
1		026-101 mbɛ	4884 mbIe	1875
2		310-081 mieɦ	2971 mbIe	4149
3		135-001 mbeɦ	1309 mbIn	3982
4		039-094 mbɛ	1232 mbIe	1873
5		085-063 re	0618 rai	2212
6		204-08k mbeɦ	3380 mbIn	3977
7	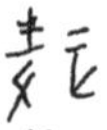	N.L.	1729 mbIe	1339
8	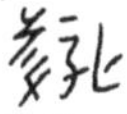	236-062 rIr	2691 mbIn	3983
9		N.L.	N.L.	N.L.
10	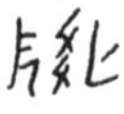	137-081 mbɛ	1317 mbIe	4636

GLOSS : IMO 没

Middle Chinese : Imuət
10 NW Chinese : Ibor

No.	Char.	Nishida	Sofronov	More Pis'men
1		075-082 mʉɦ	1273 mə	0884
2		017-111 mʉ	0991 mə	1128
3		124-051 mɨr	0029 miə	2455
4		259-051 mʉɦ	1649 mI	1020
5		204-074 mu	3421 mə	1129
6		238-072 mʉɦ	2530 mI	1022
7		N.L.	0893 mə	N.L.
8	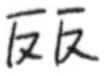	255-041 mʉr	0484 mə	2419

GLOSS : IMU 暮

Middle Chinese : Imuo:
10 NW Chinese : Imu

No.	Char.	Nishida	Sofronov	More Pis'men
1	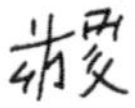	N.L.	N.L.	N.L.

GLOSS : INENG 能

Middle Chinese : Inəng
10 NW Chinese : Iniń

No.	Char.	Nishida	Sofronov	More Pis'men
1	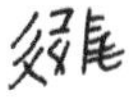	204-116 ndʉ	3847 nə	1130
2		192-071 -ndɨ	2901 ndI	3841
3		026-134 ndɨ	4927 ndI	3833
4		183-071 ndIr	5807 ndI̭ə	4977
5		007-093 mdɨ	1819 ndI	3840
6		026-062 ndɨ	4925 ndI	3834

GLOSS : **NENG$_F$** 能

Middle Chinese : nəəng$_I$
10 NW Chinese : niń$_I$

No.	Char.	Nishida	Sofronov	More Pis'men
1		218-061 nɨ	5351 ndə	0540
2	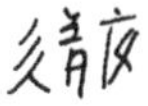	204-133 nɨ	3671 nI	3831
3	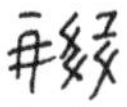	N.L.	0360 nIə	3889
4		236-052 nɨ̣	2750 nI̭wə̣	N.L.

GLOSS : **$_I$NI**$_2$ 你

Middle Chinese : $_I$ngie̯-
10 NW Chinese : $_I$ni

No.	Char.	Nishida	Sofronov	More Pis'men
1	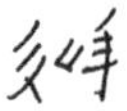	N.L.	3769 nI̭e	1346
2		110-053 neɦ	2875 nIn	4011

GLOSS : ꜀NI-TSU ꜀尼卒

Middle Chinese : ꜀ńi-tsuət
10 NW Chinese : ꜀'di-tsur

No.	Char.	Nishida	Sofronov	More Pis'men
1		205-046 ⁿdzoɦ	3335 ndzI̭ə̣	2631

GLOSS : ꜀NIANG ꜀娘

Middle Chinese : ꜀niäng
10 NW Chinese : ꜀nyań

No.	Char.	Nishida	Sofronov	More Pis'men
1		182-067 nhe	4612 nIwo	4356
2		123B-062 nur	0431 nụ	2251

GLOSS : ꜀NU ꜀奴

Middle Chinese : ꜀nuo
10 NW Chinese : ꜀nu

No.	Char.	Nishida	Sofronov	More Pis'men
1		N.L.	N.L.	N.L.

GLOSS : ꜀PO ꜀百

Middle Chinese : ꜀pɒk
10 NW Chinese : ꜀peg

No.	Char.	Nishida	Sofronov	More Pis'men
1		107-074 pỊ	4473 pê̤i	2015

GLOSS : IP'IAO 嘌

Middle Chinese : Ip'i̯aŭ
10 NW Chinese : Ip'ŷau

No.	Char.	Nishida	Sofronov	More Pis'men
1		017-109 rI-	0933 ri̯ə	N.L.
2	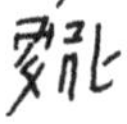	297-066 ri	5042 ri̭ə	4982

GLOSS : IPU 吥

Middle Chinese : Ipi̯ə̂u=
10 NW Chinese : Ipû

No.	Char.	Nishida	Sofronov	More Pis'men
1		269-092 pǏu	2318 pI̭e	N.L.

GLOSS : IPU 哺

Middle Chinese : Ipiu=
10 NW Chinese : Ipu

No.	Char.	Nishida	Sofronov	More Pis'men
1		199-001 -puɦ	5553 pu	3173
2		159-041 xar	3072 .ạ	2335
3		182-103 pǏụ	4645 pI̭ụ	0129

GLOSS : ISANG 嗓

Middle Chinese : Isâng
10 NW Chinese : Isań

No.	Char.	Nishida	Sofronov	More Pis'men
1		139-072 sɔɦ	1688 so	4298

GLOSS : ɪSUI 碎

Middle Chinese : ɪsuại
10 NW Chinese : ɪsai

No.	Char.	Nishida	Sofronov	More Pis'men
1		047-051 sǝw	2245 sweɰ	1469

GLOSS : ɪTE 嘚

Middle Chinese : ɪd'ậi
10 NW Chinese : ɪtig

No.	Char.	Nishida	Sofronov	More Pis'men
1		236-021 tɨ	2704 tI	1032

GLOSS : ɪTO 哆

Middle Chinese : ɪtâ
10 NW Chinese : ɪta

No.	Char.	Nishida	Sofronov	More Pis'men
1		N.L.	N.L.	N.L.
2		124-041 tɪ̃õ̤	0030 tÎon	4742

GLOSS : ɪTO 多

Middle Chinese : ɪtâ
10 NW Chinese : ɪta

No.	Char.	Nishida	Sofronov	More Pis'men
1	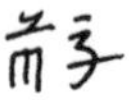	N.L.	N.L.	N.L.

GLOSS : IT'O ꜀托

Middle Chinese : It'âk
10 NW Chinese : It'ag

No.	Char.	Nishida	Sofronov	More Pis'men
1		194-041 thU	2834 *	0207

GLOSS : ITS'A ꜀擦

Middle Chinese : Itṣ'ât
10 NW Chinese : Iç'ar

No.	Char.	Nishida	Sofronov	More Pis'men
1		017-12h tẹ̃	0693 tha	3624

GLOSS : ITS'ANG ꜀藏

Middle Chinese : Its'ang
10 NW Chinese : Its'aṅ

No.	Char.	Nishida	Sofronov	More Pis'men
1		102-082 tshã	0116 ndzwon	2613

GLOSS : ITS'ANG ꜀蒼

Middle Chinese : Its'âng
10 NW Chinese : Its'aṅ

No.	Char.	Nishida	Sofronov	More Pis'men
1		007-081 tshõ	2067 tshon	1675

GLOSS : ITSE 責

Middle Chinese : Itṣɐk
10 NW Chinese : Içėg

No.	Char.	Nishida	Sofronov	More Pis'men
1		005-105 tṣIě	N.L.	N.L.

GLOSS : ITSE 賊

Middle Chinese : Idz'ək
10 NW Chinese : Idzeg

No.	Char.	Nishida	Sofronov	More Pis'men
1		157-064 ndzɨ	1741 tse	3288
2		028-112 tsI	2595 tse	3289

GLOSS : ITSO 左

Middle Chinese : Itsa=
10 NW Chinese : Idza

No.	Char.	Nishida	Sofronov	More Pis'men
1	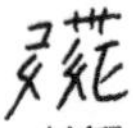	230-111 tsɔr	4720 tsṳo	2532
2		017-11g tsɔr	0845 tsṳo	2533

GLOSS : ITSU 祖

Middle Chinese : Itsuo=
10 NW Chinese : Itsu

No.	Char.	Nishida	Sofronov	More Pis'men
1		009-131 cə̃	4689 tsen	0482

GLOSS : ITSU $_{2}$足

Middle Chinese : Itsi̭wok
10 NW Chinese : Itsǔg

No.	Char.	Nishida	Sofronov	More Pis'men
1		028-141 tsĭuɦ	2555 tswu	0155
2		155-041 tsĭu	4516 tsI̭wu	1827

GLOSS : IT'UI ^{2}推

Middle Chinese : It'uậi
10 NW Chinese : It'ai

No.	Char.	Nishida	Sofronov	More Pis'men
1		017-107 th^{w}I̩-	1042 śi̭e	N.L.

GLOSS : IWANG $_{2}$亡

Middle Chinese : Imi̯wang
10 NW Chinese : I'b̊waṅ

No.	Char.	Nishida	Sofronov	More Pis'men
1	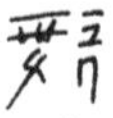	297-055 car	0247 vio	2193
2		017-097 -wior	0732 viuo	2584

GLOSS : IWEI ^{2}未

Middle Chinese : Imjwe̯i-
10 NW Chinese : I'bwî

No.	Char.	Nishida	Sofronov	More Pis'men
1		202-061 maɦ	5588 mba	3617

2	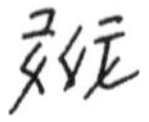	230-051 mbạ	4763 mbIạ	1977

GLOSS : IWEN 2 昷

Middle Chinese : I.uən
10 NW Chinese : Iyun

No.	Char.	Nishida	Sofronov	More Pis'men
1		154-041 ŋhiɦ	0451 ngwu	0210

GLOSS : IWO 2 我

Middle Chinese : Inga=
10 NW Chinese : I'ga

No.	Char.	Nishida	Sofronov	More Pis'men
1		026-113 ŋaɦ	4943 nga	0572

GLOSS : IWU 2 悟

Middle Chinese : Inguo-
10 NW Chinese : I'go

No.	Char.	Nishida	Sofronov	More Pis'men
1	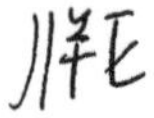	041-088 ŋur	1389 ngụ	2240

DUAL DIACRITICS

<u>GLOSS</u> : ApLAshe 合辣舌

Middle Chinese : ɣạp la: dz'i̯ät

10 NW Chinese : hablaçar

No.	Char.	Nishida	Sofronov	More Pis'men
1		184-051 lhʷạ	5501 lhi̯wạ	2822
2		236-08c lhʷạ	N.L.	N.L.

DIACRITIC CHUNG 重

GLOSS : **LANG$_{\text{CHUNG}}$** 浪重

Middle Chinese : lâng$_{\text{d̂'i̯wang=}}$

10 NW Chinese : laṅ$_{\text{juṅ}}$

No.	Char.	Nishida	Sofronov	More Pis'men
1		107-041 rõ	4478 ldi̯ọn	4749

GLOSS : **CHUNG^{LING}** 重領

Middle Chinese : d̂'i̯wang=b'ieng

10 NW Chinese : juṅleṅ

No.	Char.	Nishida	Sofronov	More Pis'men
1		057-041 lĭẽ	0668 ldI̯en	4140

GLOSS : **MA$_{\text{CHUNG}}$** 馬重

Middle Chinese : ma=d̂'iwang

10 NW Chinese : ma$_{\text{juṅ}}$

No.	Char.	Nishida	Sofronov	More Pis'men
1		221-041 ma-	0157 mbâ	N.L.
2		221-091 ma	N.L.	N.L.

<u>GLOSS</u> : **NENG CHUNG** 能重

Middle Chinese : nəeng d͡'iwang

10 NW Chinese : niṅ juṅ

No.	Char.	Nishida	Sofronov	More Pis'men
1	[illegible]	N.L.	N.L.	N.L.

DIACRITIC CH'ING 輕

GLOSS : LECH'ING 勒輕

Middle Chinese : lək k'i̯äng

10 NW Chinese : leg kyeṅ

No.	Char.	Nishida	Sofronov	More Pis'men
1	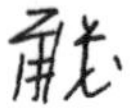	170-061 lɔw	5087 leɰ	4178

GLOSS : CH'INGMO 輕末

Middle Chinese : k'i̯äng muât

10 NW Chinese : kyeṅ'bor

No.	Char.	Nishida	Sofronov	More Pis'men
1		008-091 mạ	N.L.	N.L.

GLOSS : MOCH'ING 麼輕

Middle Chinese : muâ k'i̯äng

10 NW Chinese : ma kyeṅ

No.	Char.	Nishida	Sofronov	More Pis'men
1		180-093 mɪ̌or	4135 *	4970

GLOSS : **MO CH'ING** 麼輕

Middle Chinese : mua= k'i̯ăng

10 NW Chinese : ma kyeṅ

No.	**Char.**	**Nishida**	**Sofronov**	**More Pis'men**
1		018-081 ma	0183 mIn	3257

GLOSS : **MO CH'ING** 沒輕

Middle Chinese : muet k'i̯ăng

10 NW Chinese : 'bor kyeṅ

No.	**Char.**	**Nishida**	**Sofronov**	**More Pis'men**
1		018-081 ma	0183 mIn	3257
2		239-051 mʉ	5135 mu	0102
3	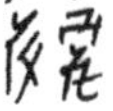	241-071 mi̯ɔɦ	2223 mI̯o	4349

GLOSS : **MU CH'ING** 暮輕

Middle Chinese : muo= k'i̯ăng

10 NW Chinese : mu kyeṅ

No.	**Char.**	**Nishida**	**Sofronov**	**More Pis'men**
1		N.L.	N.L.	N.L.

GLOSS : OCH'ING 遏輕

Middle Chinese : ·ât k'i̯äng

10 NW Chinese : ʔar kyeṅ

No.	Char.	Nishida	Sofronov	More Pis'men
1		204-08n nhah	3818 nga	3549

GLOSS : P'UCH'ING 普輕

Middle Chinese : p'uo k'i̯äng

10 NW Chinese : po kyeṅ

No.	Char.	Nishida	Sofronov	More Pis'men
1	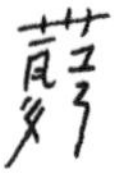	017-134 phuĥ	0696 phI̯o	4383

PART III

FACSIMILE

Manuscript A

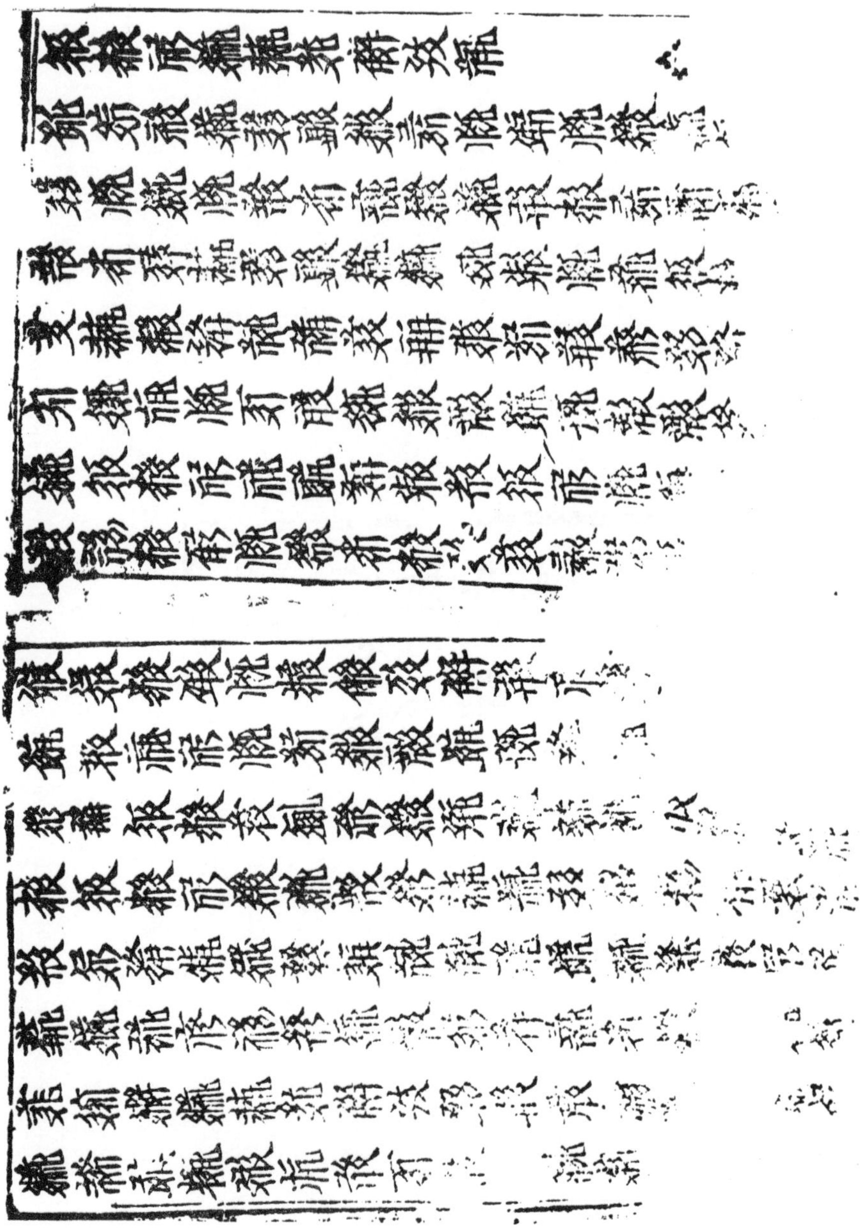

番漢合時掌中珠序

凡君子者為物豈可忘己故未嘗不學為
己亦不絕物故未嘗不教學則以智成己
欲襲古迹教則以仁利物以救今時兼番
漢文字者論末則殊考本則同何則先聖
後聖其揆未嘗不一故也然則今時人者
番漢語言可以俱備不學番言則豈和番
人之衆不會漢語則豈入漢人之數

智者漢人不敬漢有賢士番人不崇若此
者由語言不通故也如此則有逆前言故
茂才稍學番漢文字曷敢默而弗言不避
慚怍准三才集成番漢語節略一本言音
分辨語句昭然言音未切教者能整語句
雖俗學人易會號為合時掌中珠賢哲覩
斯幸莫哂焉時乾祐庚戌二十一年　月
日骨勒茂才謹序

精謀巳悟溺□
□□□□茲
合時掌中珠
□□□□□

没□天□

没□天□
各□形□
普□上□

没□天□
盈□相□
悟□中□

没没
勿

勒□地□

勒□地□
各□形□
普□上□

勒□地□
盈□相□
悟□中□

勒□地□
渫谷□用□
名□下□

辛尼□人□

人體上

人相中

人事下

天乾

皇天

旻天

昊天

上天

四

九霄

一清

虛空

日月

金烏

玉兔

桂技

星宿

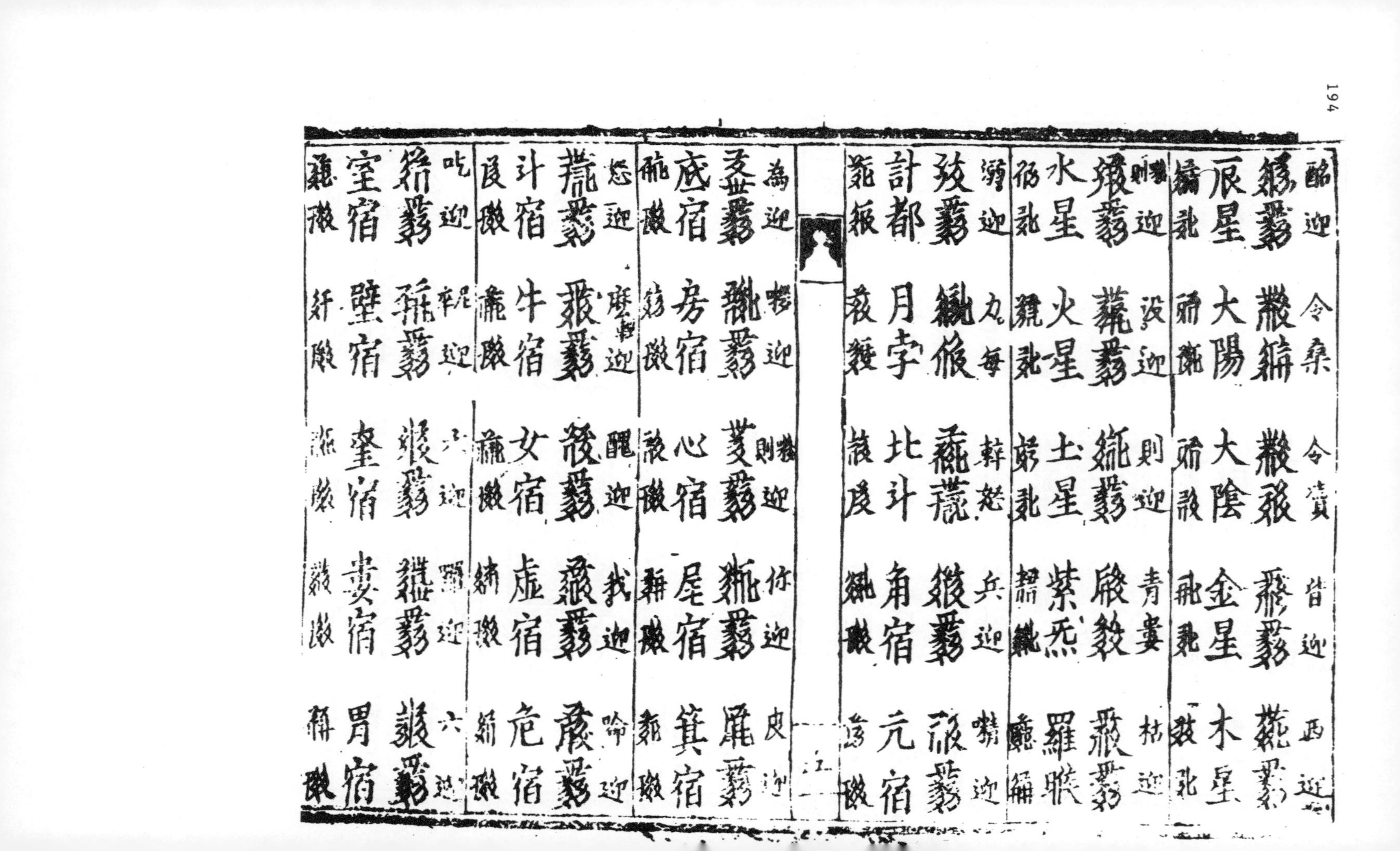

[illegible]	辰星	[illegible]	酩迎
[illegible]	大陽	[illegible]	令桑
[illegible]	大陰	[illegible]	令讚
[illegible]	金星	[illegible]	皆迎
[illegible]	木星	[illegible]	西迎
[illegible]	水星	[illegible]	[illegible]迎
[illegible]	火星	[illegible]	設迎
[illegible]	土星	[illegible]	則迎
[illegible]	紫炁	[illegible]	青婁
[illegible]	羅睺	[illegible]	枯迎
[illegible]	計都	[illegible]	[illegible]迎
[illegible]	月孛	[illegible]	丸每
[illegible]	北斗	[illegible]	韓怒
[illegible]	角宿	[illegible]	兵迎
[illegible]	亢宿	[illegible]	[illegible]迎
[illegible]	底宿	[illegible]	為迎
[illegible]	房宿	[illegible]	[illegible]迎
[illegible]	心宿	[illegible]	[illegible]迎
[illegible]	尾宿	[illegible]	你迎
[illegible]	箕宿	[illegible]	皮迎
[illegible]	斗宿	[illegible]	悠迎
[illegible]	牛宿	[illegible]	[illegible]迎
[illegible]	女宿	[illegible]	醍迎
[illegible]	虛宿	[illegible]	我迎
[illegible]	危宿	[illegible]	嗆迎
[illegible]	室宿	[illegible]	吃迎
[illegible]	壁宿	[illegible]	卒尼迎
[illegible]	奎宿	[illegible]	六迎
[illegible]	婁宿	[illegible]	[illegible]迎
[illegible]	胃宿	[illegible]	六迎

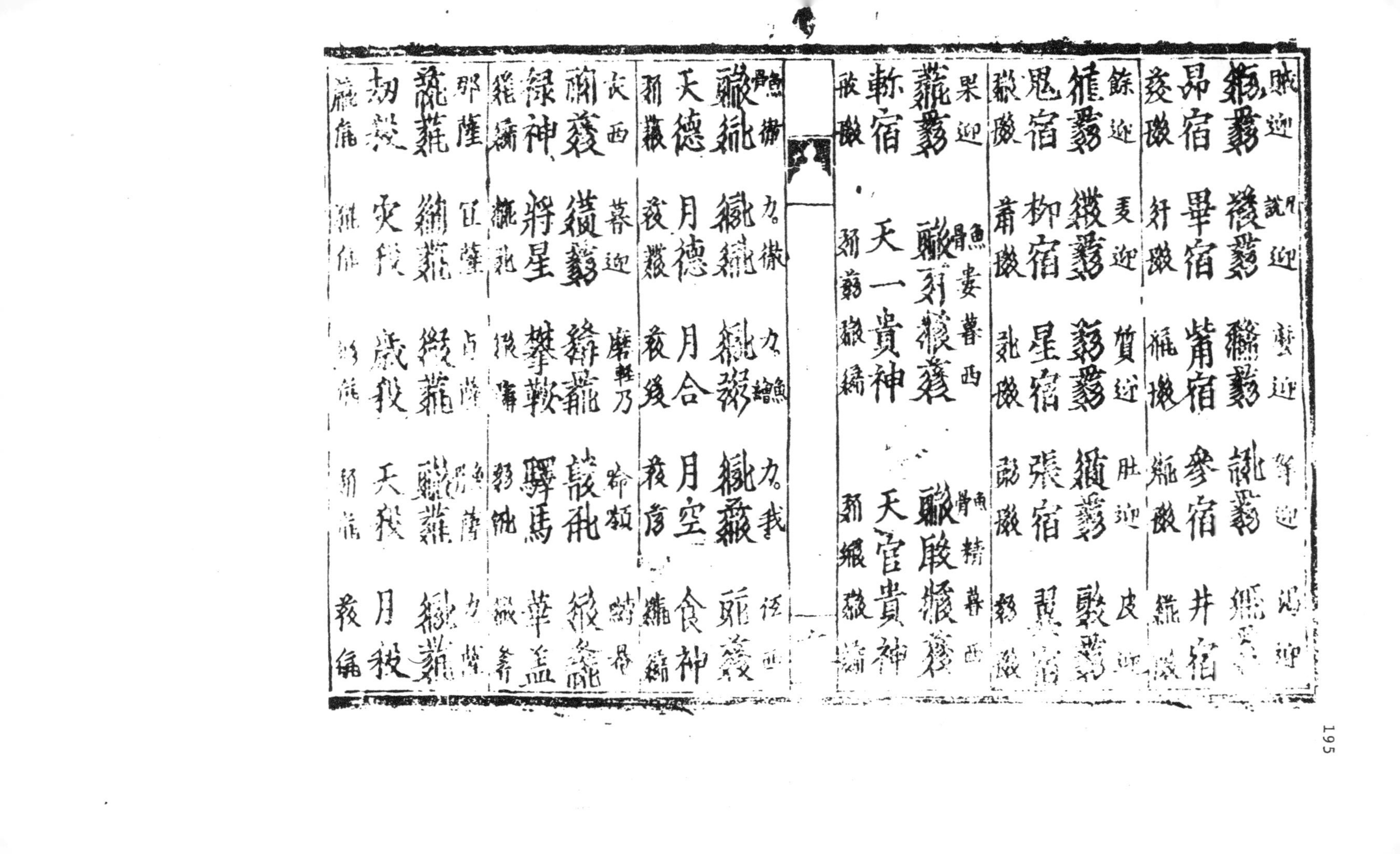

昴宿
畢宿
觜宿
參宿
井宿

鬼宿
柳宿
星宿
張宿
翼宿

軫宿
天一貴神
天官貴神

天德
月德
月合
月空
食神

祿神
將星
攀鞍
驛馬
華蓋

切殺
災殺
歲殺
天殺
月殺

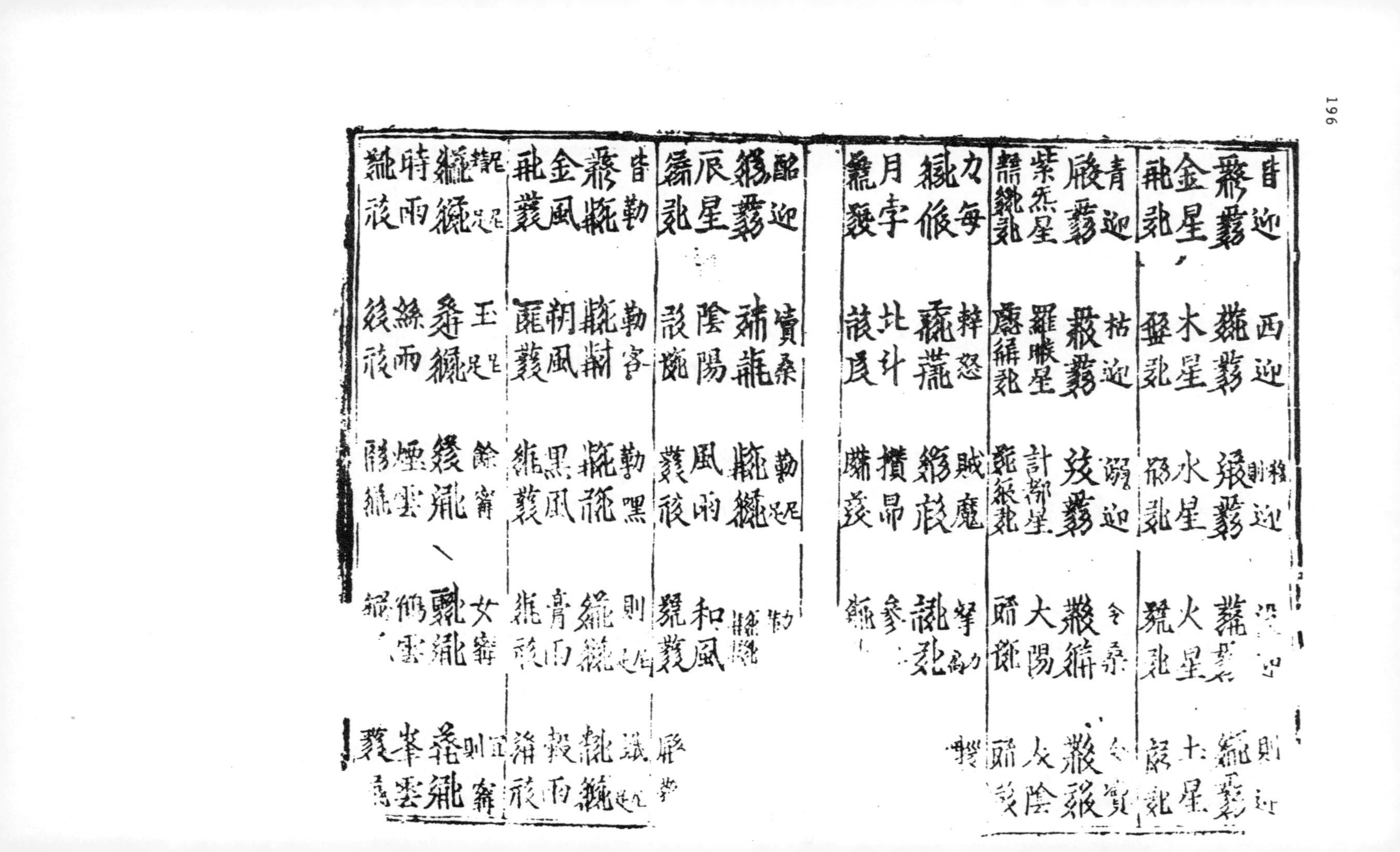

金星	紫炁星	月孛	辰星	金風	時雨
木星	羅睺星	北斗	陰陽	朔風	絲雨
水星	計都星	攙槍	風雨	黑風	煙雲
火星	太陽	參	和風	膏雨	鶴雲
土星	太陰			穀雨	峯雲

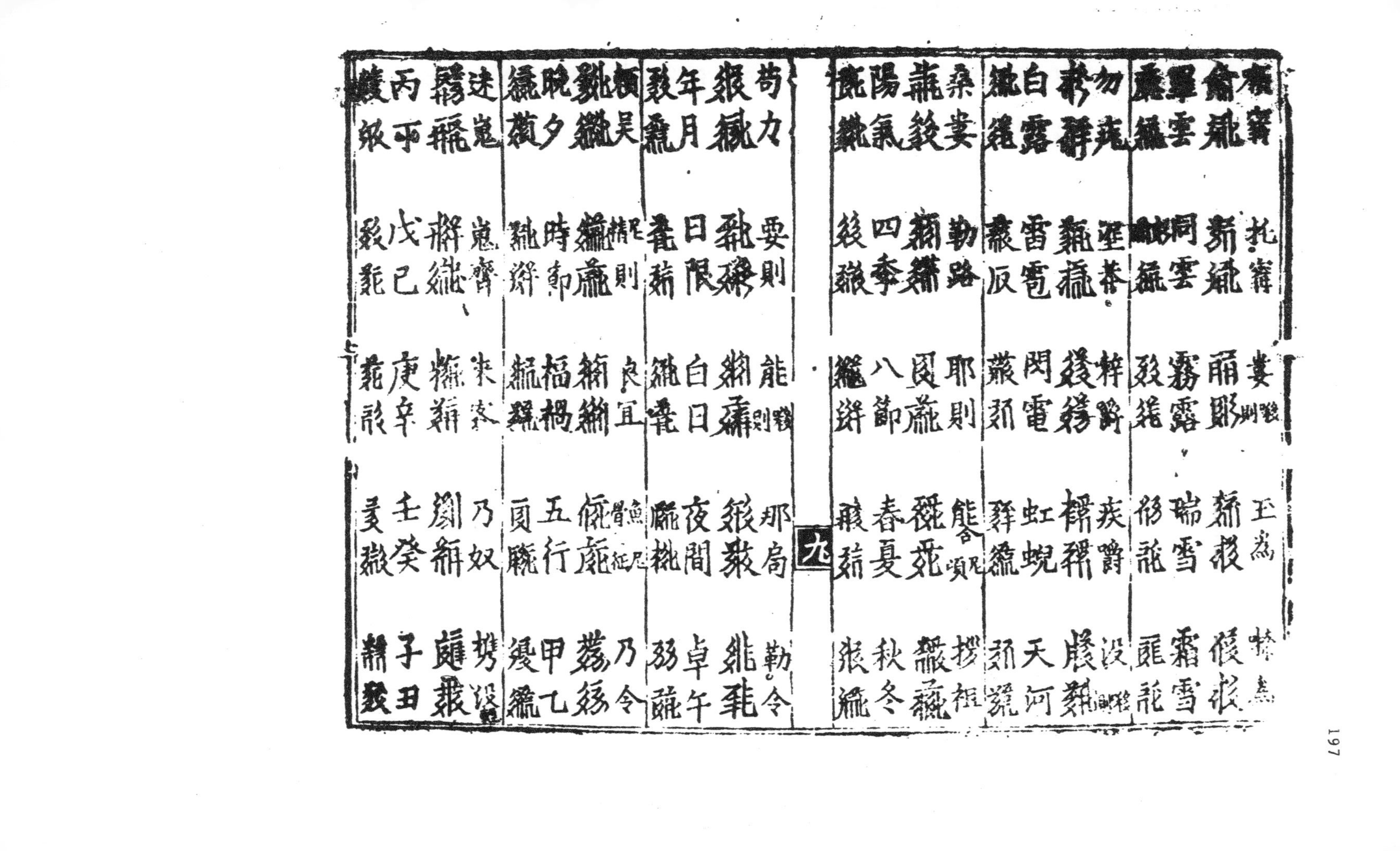

[illegible] 雲 ([illegible] 寶)	白露 (物羌)	陽氣 (桑婁)	九	年月 (苟力)	晚夕 ([illegible] 昊)	丙丁 (迷嵬)
同雲 (扎寧)	雷雹 (埿恭)	四季 (勒路)		日限 (要則)	時節 ([illegible] 則)	戊己 (嵬齊)
霧露 (婁郎)	閃電 ([illegible])	八節 (耶則)		白日 (能 [illegible])	福禍 (良宜)	庚辛 (來[illegible])
瑞雪 (王爲)	虹蜺 (疾[illegible])	春夏 (能頂)		夜間 (那局)	五行 ([illegible])	壬癸 (乃奴)
霜雪 ([illegible])	天河 (設 [illegible])	秋冬 (捞祖)		卓午 (勒令)	甲乙 (乃令)	子丑 (携[illegible])

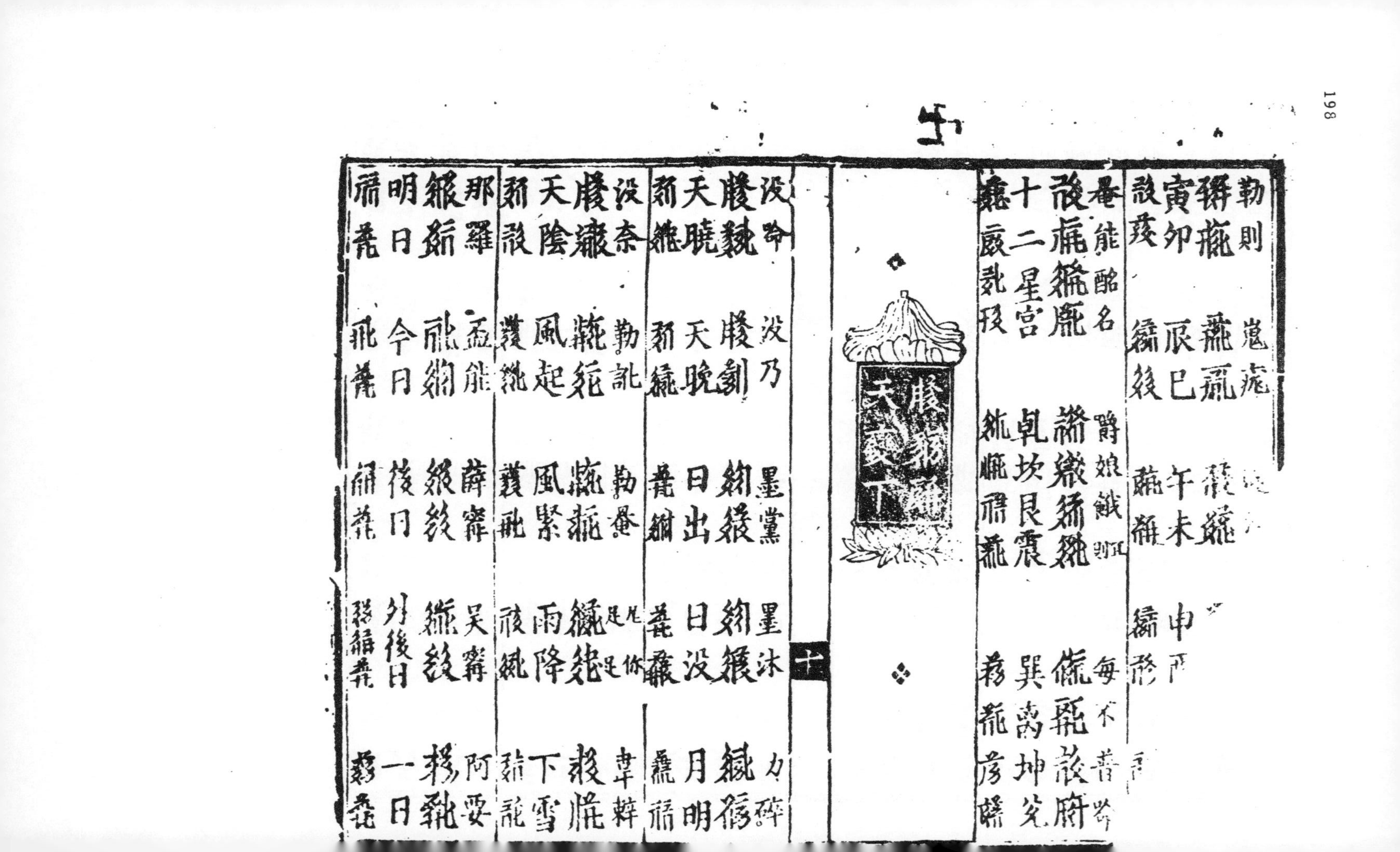

勒則 寅卯
嵬瘥 辰巳
午未
申酉

菴能 酩名 十二星宮
爵娘 鐵 乾坎艮震
每不 普 巽离坤兌

十

没吟 天曉
没乃 天晚
墨黨 日出
墨沐 日没
力碎 月明

没奈 天陰
勒訛 風起
勒疊 風緊
尼足 你足 雨降
韋粹 下雪

那羅 明日
孟能 今日
薛寗 後日
吴寗 外後日
阿要 一日

能要 [Tangut] 二日 [Tangut]
孟能 背能 [Tangut] 今日 一日 [Tangut]
阿 苟能苟 [Tangut] 一年 二年 [Tangut]
孟 [illegible] [Tangut] 今年 [Tangut]

斜韋 [Tangut] 來年 [Tangut]
易韋 [Tangut] 去歲 [Tangut]
能韋 [Tangut] 前年 [Tangut]
阿力傍 [Tangut] 一个月 [Tangut]
浪 [illegible] [Tangut] 正月 [Tangut]

吟力 [Tangut] 月 [Tangut]
嚕力 [Tangut] 閏月 [Tangut]
勿 則嵬 嶺 粹 [Tangut] 東南西北 [Tangut]
勒 領 勒 [illegible] [Tangut] 四方四隅 [Tangut]

十二

地體上

勒 [Tangut] 地 [Tangut]
部 [Tangut] 坤 [Tangut]
奧 [illegible] [Tangut] 一獨 [Tangut]
令勒 [Tangut] 大地 [Tangut]
疊勒 [Tangut] 十地 [Tangut]

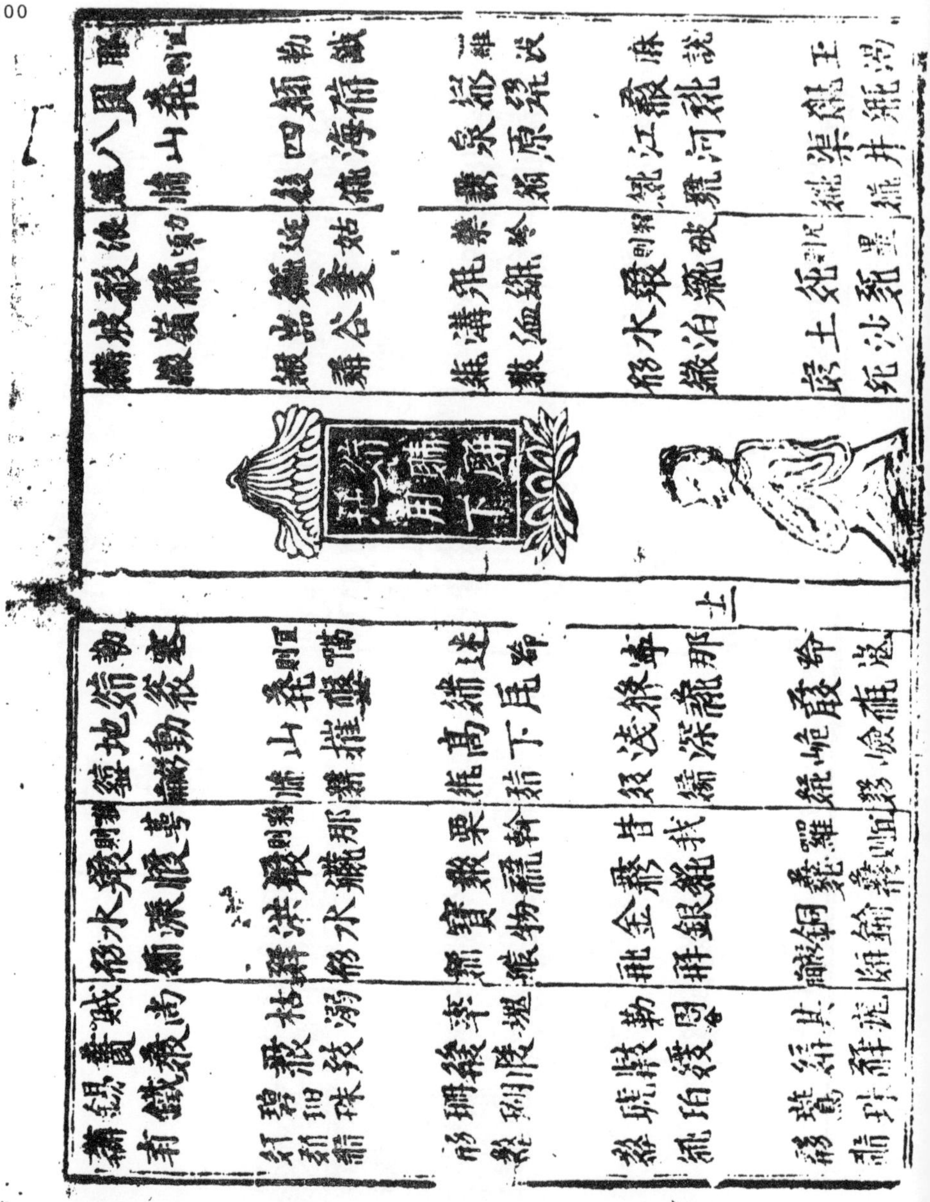
地用下
八山
四海
泉原
江河
渠井
谷
溝洫
水治
土沙
地動
山
高下
淺深
寶物
金銀
洪水
珊瑚
琥珀
珠
鐵

黑乙 [illegible] [illegible]
[illegible] 瑠璃 [illegible]
迎那 [illegible] [illegible]
[illegible] 瑪瑙 [illegible]
王拍 [illegible] [illegible]
[illegible] 開渠 [illegible]
渦盧 [illegible] [illegible]
[illegible] 鑿井 [illegible]
勒每 [illegible] 依
[illegible] 塵土 [illegible]

勒 [illegible] [illegible]
[illegible] 天 [illegible]
勒 [illegible] [illegible]
[illegible] 地程 [illegible]
勒羅 [illegible] [illegible]
[illegible] 田疇 [illegible]
勒乙 [illegible] [illegible]
[illegible] 松炭 [illegible]
盧乙 [illegible] [illegible]
[illegible] 石炭 [illegible]

訛麁 [illegible] [illegible]
[illegible] 園林 [illegible]
麻 [illegible] [illegible]
[illegible] 花菓 [illegible]
托緑 [illegible] [illegible]
[illegible] 牡丹花 [illegible]
則赤 [illegible] [illegible]
[illegible] 芍藥花 [illegible]
則尚 [illegible] [illegible]
[illegible] 山丹花 [illegible]

十三

餓里 [illegible] [illegible]
[illegible] 海棠花 [illegible]
梁栢 [illegible] [illegible]
[illegible] 龍栢花 [illegible]
出令 [illegible] [illegible]
[illegible] 梅花 [illegible]
勿尼 [illegible] [illegible]
[illegible] 葵花 [illegible]

勿能 [illegible] [illegible]
[illegible] 芍葵花 [illegible]
要哺 [illegible] [illegible]
[illegible] 雞冠花 [illegible]
皆精 [illegible] [illegible]
[illegible] 金錢花 [illegible]
則 [illegible] [illegible]
[illegible] 水紅花 [illegible]

盧吹 [illegible] [illegible]
[illegible] 石竹花 [illegible]
王石 [illegible] [illegible]
[illegible] 萱草花 [illegible]
乙 [illegible] [illegible]
[illegible] 玉井花 [illegible]
膃 [illegible] [illegible]
[illegible] 蓮花 [illegible]
西麻 [illegible] [illegible]
[illegible] 菜本 [illegible]

注音	漢義
麻	菜子
没杏	栗杏
辛麻	梨
余麻	檎
能[illegible]	櫻桃
諾	胡桃
麦諾	蒲桃
嵬梅	龍眼
則麻	協枝
能麻	李子
水麻	揥子
吒麻	橘子
則麻	甘蔗
卒則尼	棗
盧嵬	石榴

十四

注音	漢義
諾麻	桃
麦吴	柳榆
勒柔	松栢
悉那	菜蔬
里那	香菜
悉那	芥菜
抽那	薄荷
末那	菠薐
由那	茵蔯
流那	百菜
羅赤	蔓菁
李羅	蘿蔔
路長凡	瓠子
全耶	茄子
羅那	蔓菁菜

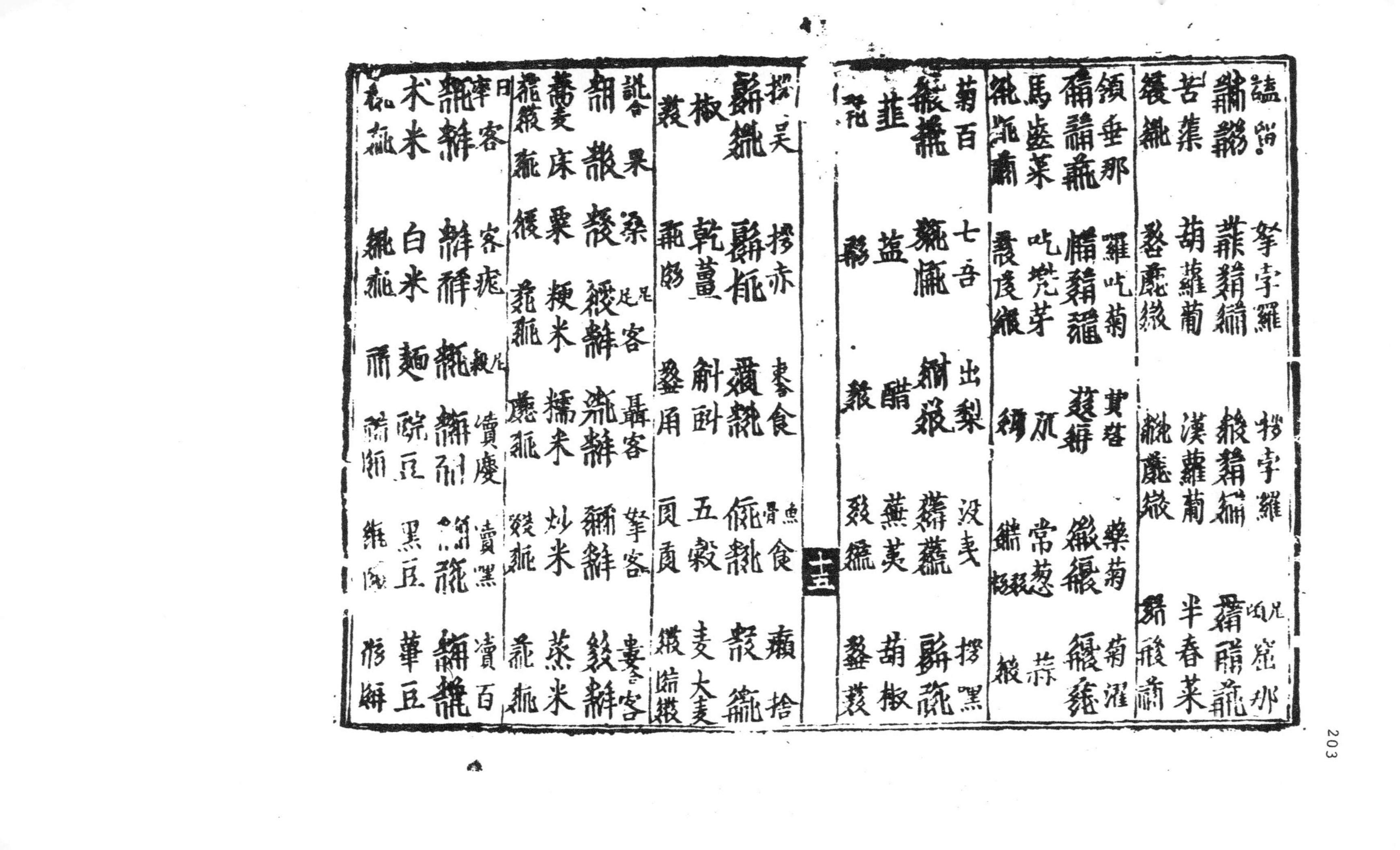

謳㖷　苦蕖
箏字羅　葫蘿蔔
撈字羅　漢蘿蔔
崖那　半春菜

領垂那　馬齒菜
羅吃菊　吃芥芽
貫喈　瓜
藥菊　常葱
菊澀　蒜

菊百　韮
七吾　盐
出梨　醋
没夷　蕪荑
撈嘿　葫椒

十五

撈吴　椒
撈赤　乾薑
東嗇食　斛㪷
骨食　五穀
癩捨　麦　大麦

訛合　蕎麦
果　床
桑　粟
足尼客　粳米
聶客　糯米
箏客　炒米
妻客　蒸米

日寧客　术米
客疪　白米
尼穀　麵
讀慶　豌豆
讀嘿　黑豆
讀百　華豆

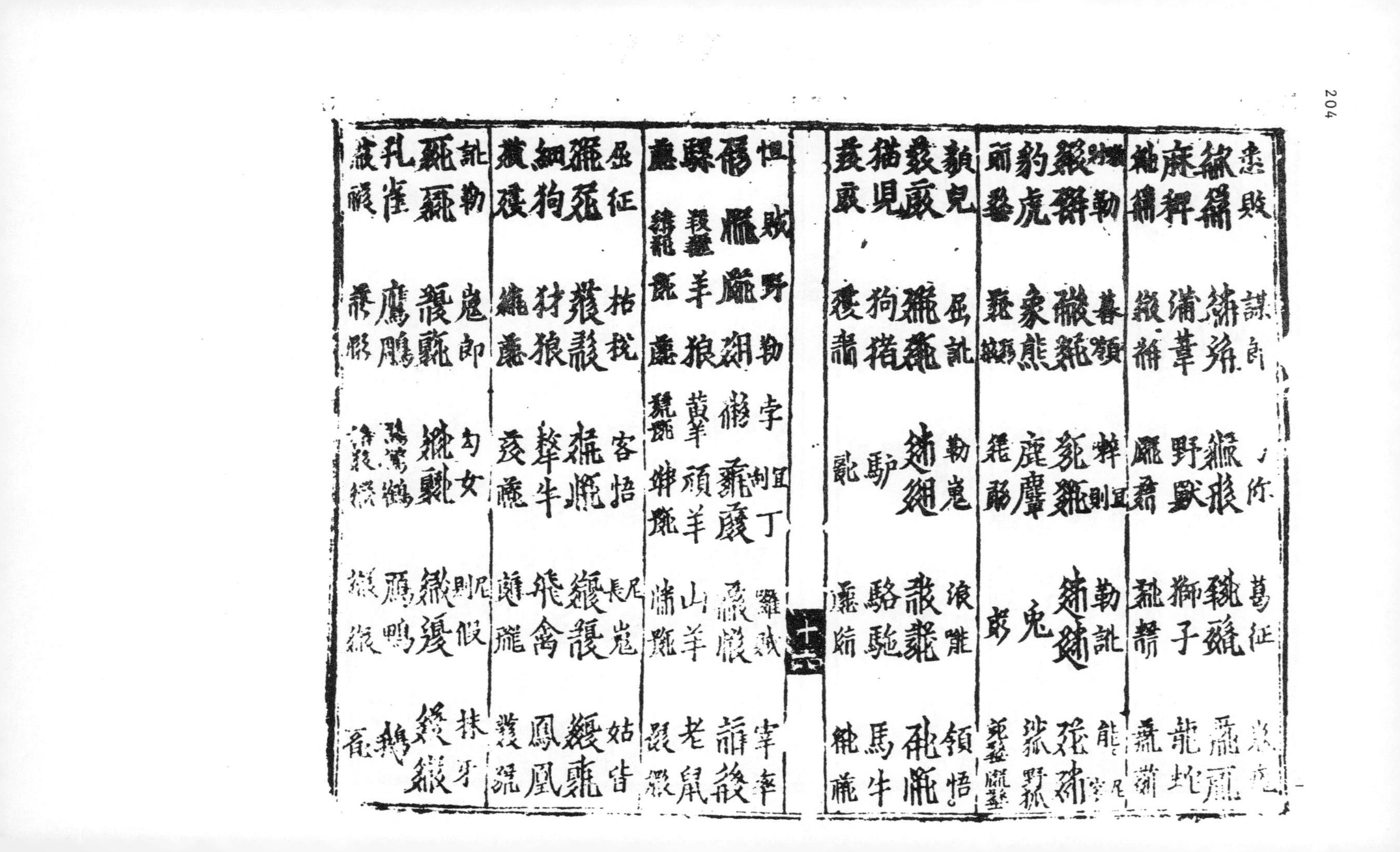

麻稗　蒲葦　野獸　獅子　龍蛇

豹虎　象熊　鹿麞　兔　狐　野狐

貓兒　狗猪　駒　駱駝　馬牛

十六

羊　狼　黃羊　頑羊　山羊　老鼠

細狗　豺狼　犛牛　飛禽　鳳凰

孔雀　鷹鷂　鴈鴨

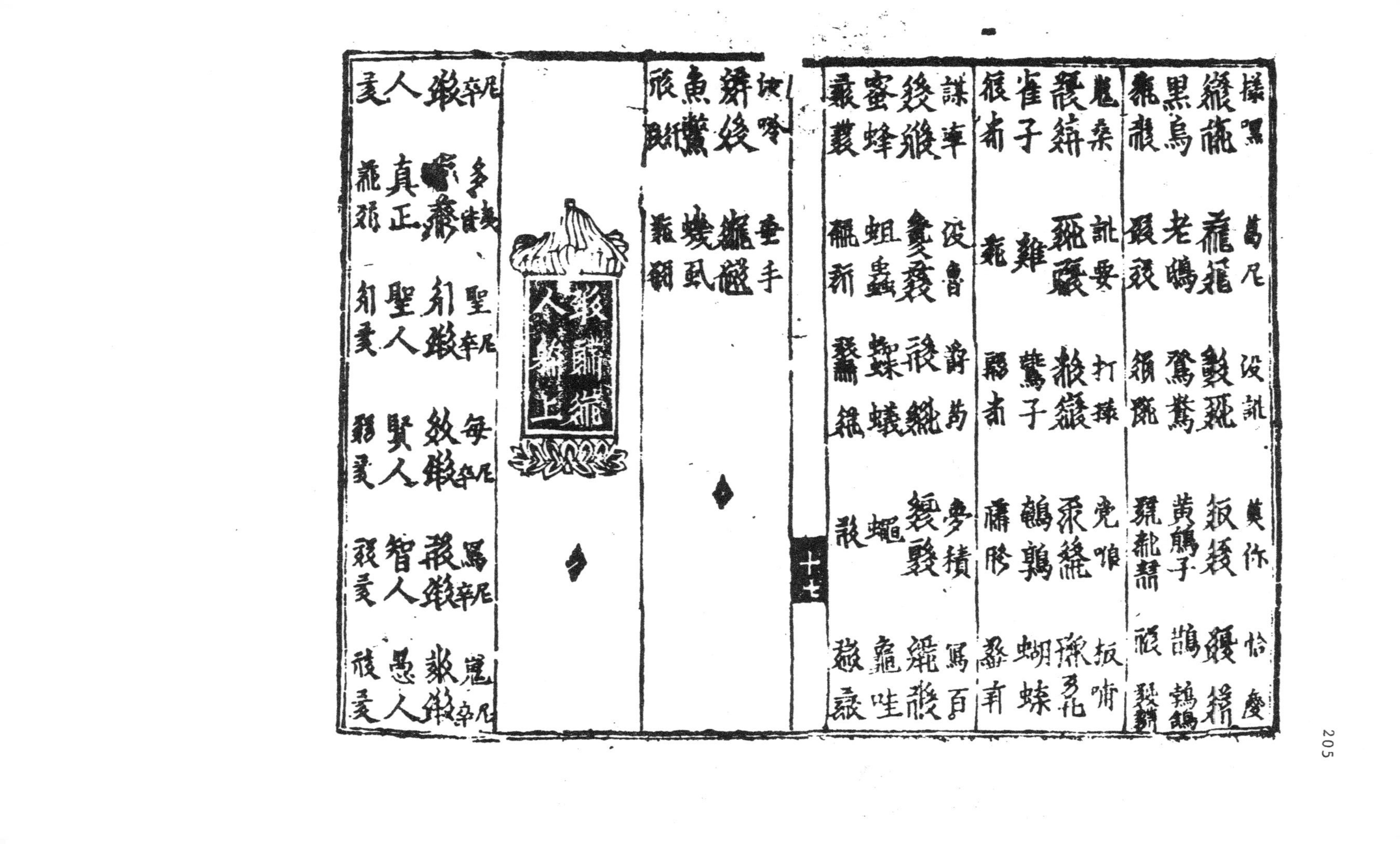

揉嘿 黑鳥
葛尼 老鴟
没訛 鴛鴦
莫作 黄鶯子
恰慶 鵲 鵓鴿

嵬桑 雀子
訛要 雞
打揉 鷹子
党唯 鵪鶉
扳哺 蝴蝶

謀華 蜜蜂
没魯 蛆蟲
蔚葛 蛛蟻
夢積 蠅
寫百 龜蛙

十七

泥吟 魚
垂手 蟣虱

人 上

尼卒 人
多 真正
聖 尼卒 聖人
每 尼卒 賢人
寫 尼卒 智人
嵬 尼卒 愚人

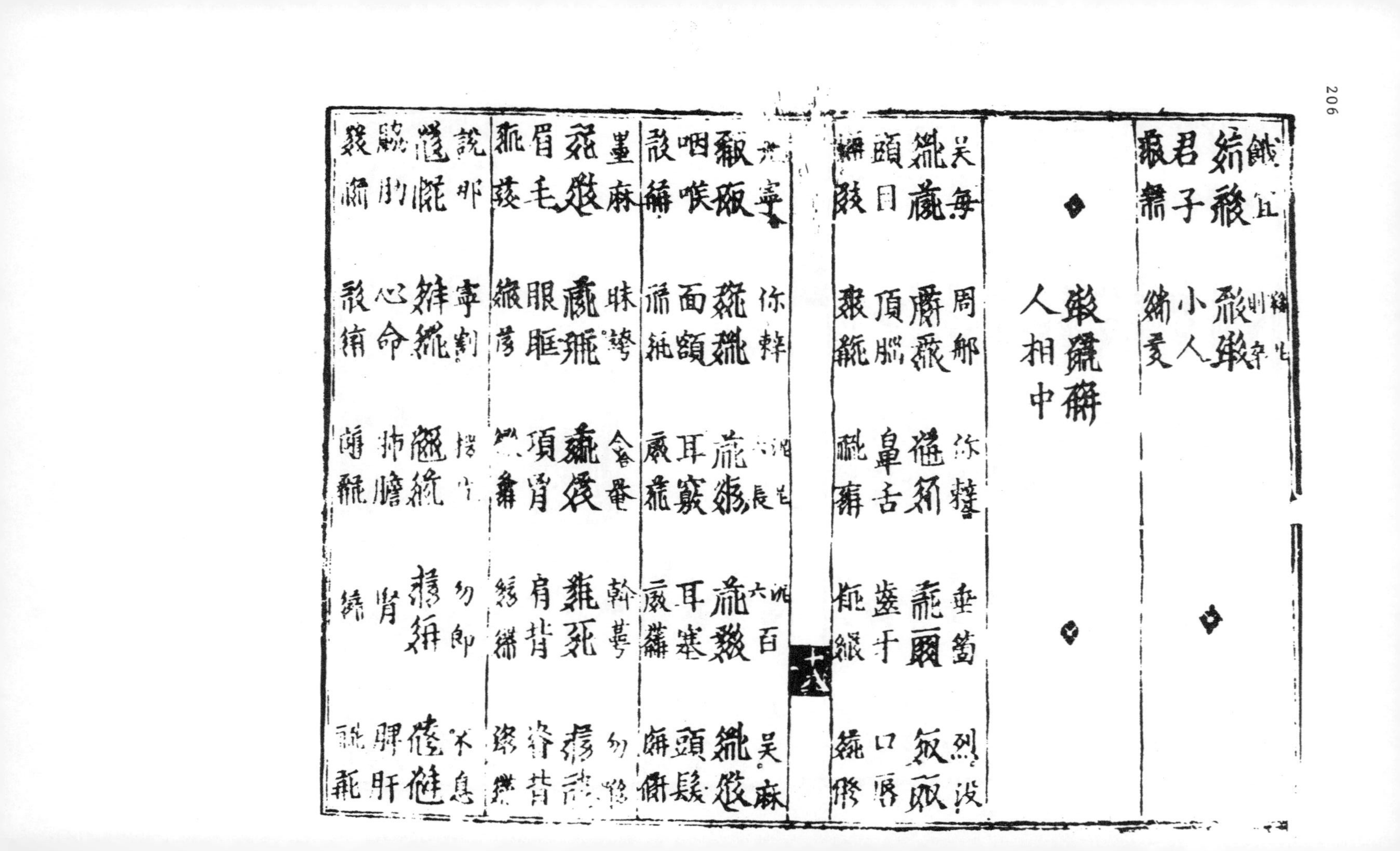

君子 餓丘
小人

人相中

Chinese	Chinese gloss
頭目	吴每
頂腦	周郁
鼻舌	你犨
齒牙	垂萄
口唇	烈沒
咽喉	[illegible]
面頰	你斡
耳竅	[illegible]
耳塞	六百
頭髮	吴麻
眉毛	墨麻
眼眶	昧彎
項胃	令畨
肩背	斡萼
脊背	勿悠
脇肋	說那
心命	寧劃
肺膽	措[illegible]
腎	勿郎
脾肝	不息

十六

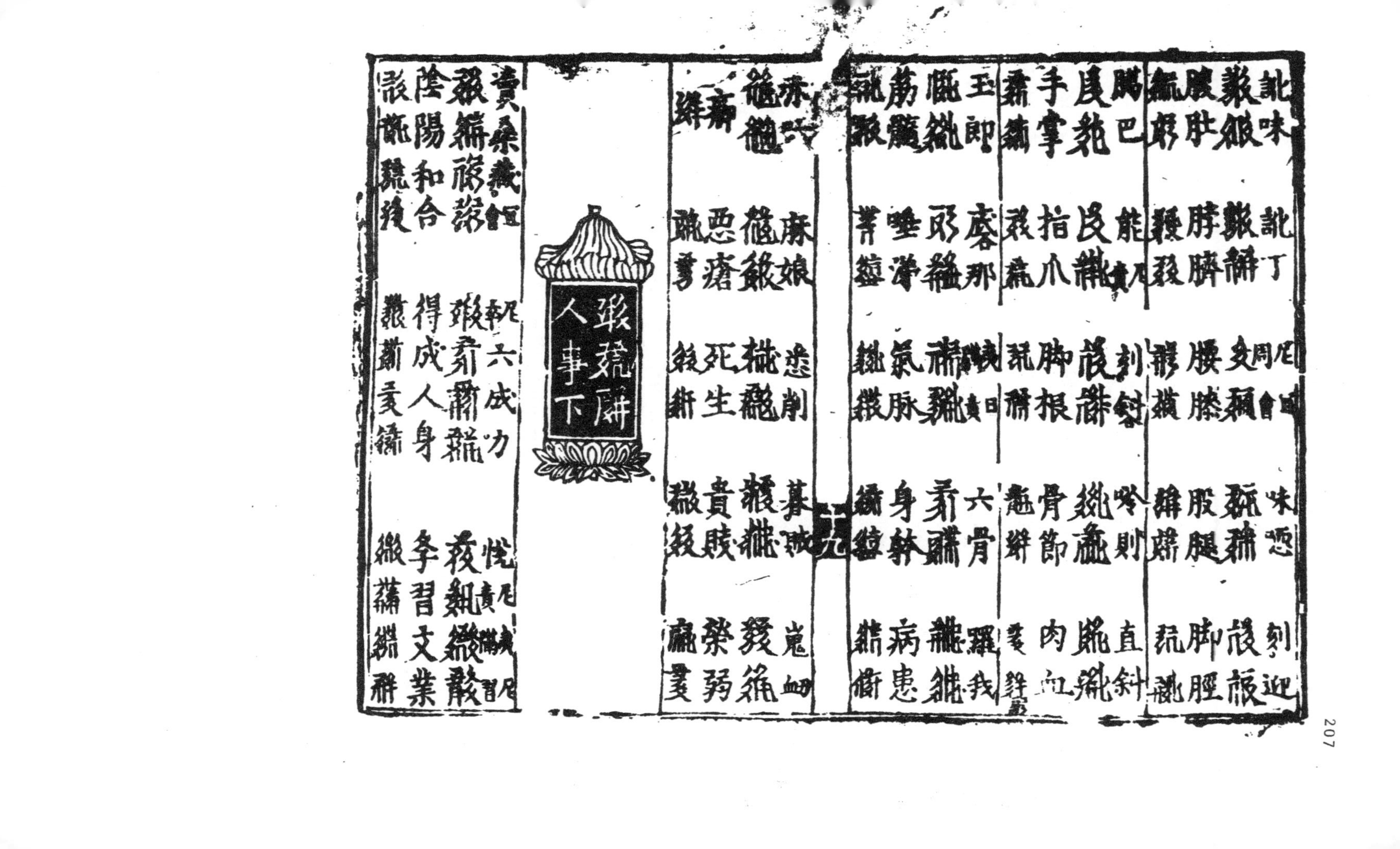

訛味 腹肚　　賜巴 手掌　　王郎 筋

訛丁 脖臍　　能尼責 指爪　　麼那 唾滓

尼周交會 腰膝　　刹 脚根　　訖日責 氣脈

味恧 股腿　　吟則 骨節　　六骨 身軀

刻迎 脚脛　　直斜 肉血　　羅我 病患

麻娘 惡瘡

悉削 死生

慕 貴賤

嵬皿 榮弱

人事下

責桑 陰陽和合

尼六成力 得成人身

悦尼責 斈習文業

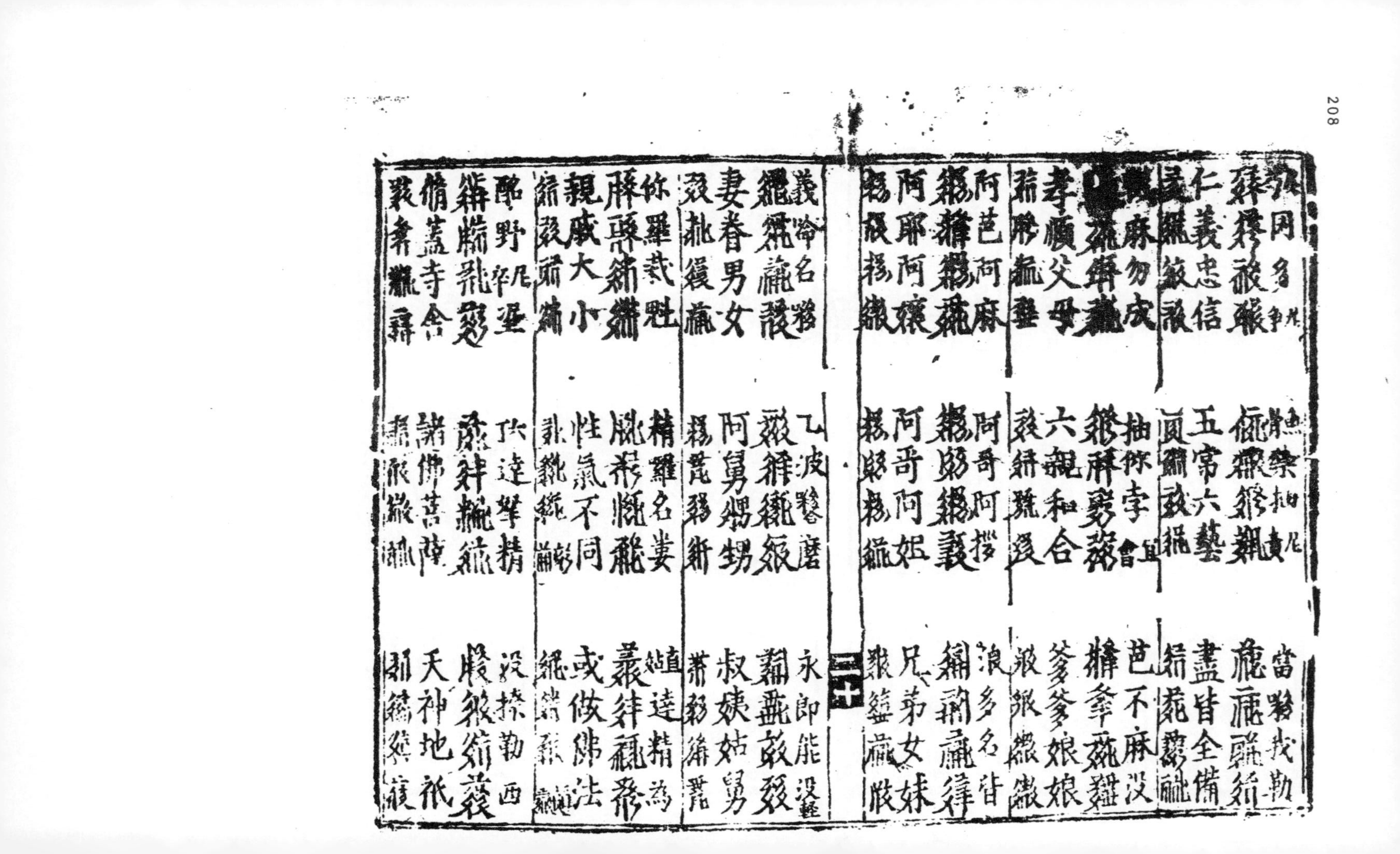

同多 尹尤
仁義忠信

麻勿戊
孝順父母

阿芭阿麻
阿耶阿孃

義泠名務
妻眷男女

你羅栽甡
親戚大小

酩野 卒尼 埿
倩蓋寺舍

觸禁 抽 貴尼
五常六藝

抽你 孛 會 罝
六親和合

阿哥阿 撥
阿哥阿姐

乙波 磬 磨
阿舅甥甥

精羅名 婁
性氣不同

伙達 挈 精
諸佛菩薩

當 黠 找 勒
盡皆全備

芭不麻 没
爹爹娘娘

浪多名 皆
兄弟女妹

二十

永郎能 没輕
叔姨姑舅

直姑 達精 爲
或做佛法

没 捺勒 西
天神地祇

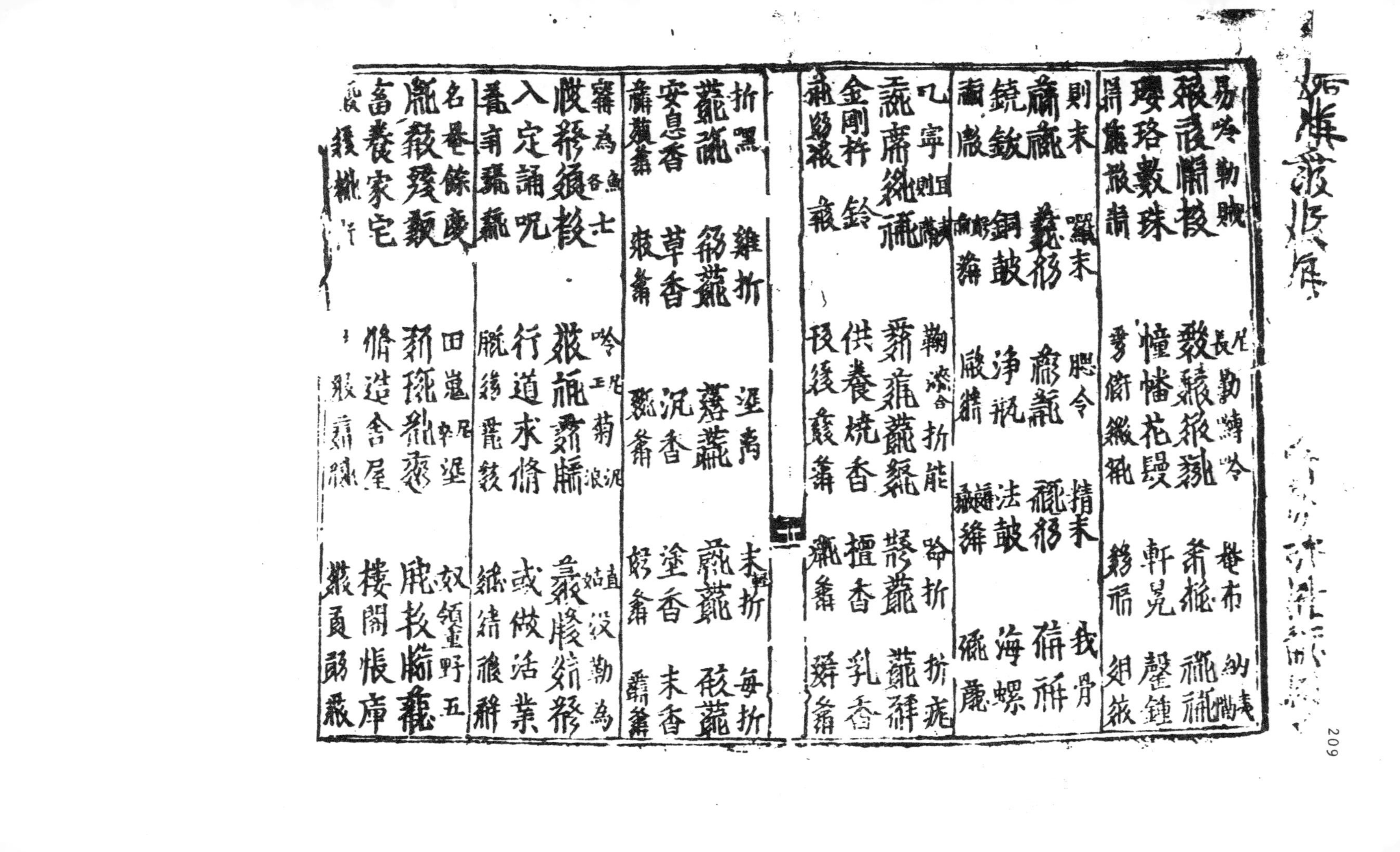

十一

易吟勒賊	瓔珞數珠
尼長勤嚩吟令	幢幡花鬘
檐布	軒冕
納衣	磬鍾
則末	鐃鈸
囉末	銅鼓
腮令	淨瓶
精末	法鼓
我骨	海螺
乞寧則且	金剛杵
	鈴
勒涂合折能	供養燒香
吟折	檀香
折㢋	乳香
折罵	安息香
雜折	草香
逕禹	沉香
末折	塗香
每折	末香
為魚士	入定誦呪
吟王尼葡浪泥	行道求脩
直姑没勤為	或做活業
名疊餘慶	畜養家宅
田嵬卒尼逕	修造舍屋
奴領重野五	樓閣帳庫

堂　廚　庖　廂　廊　重　楸　平　五　楸

六　椎　枕　樂　枇　杖　椽　棟　欄　杆

桂　御　提　木　石　頂　抖　拱　墻　圈

田　合　和　坐　運　土　木　植　木　匠

匠　体　工　斤　斧　鑿　鋸　鑷　鈴

三十二

刀　桶　鑽　木　檻　碟　赤　沙

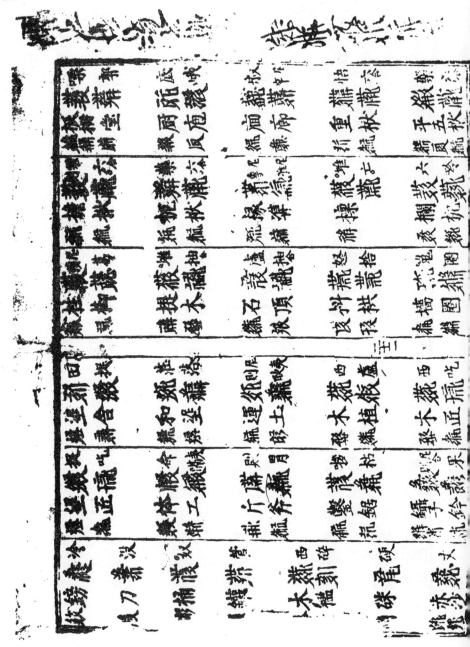

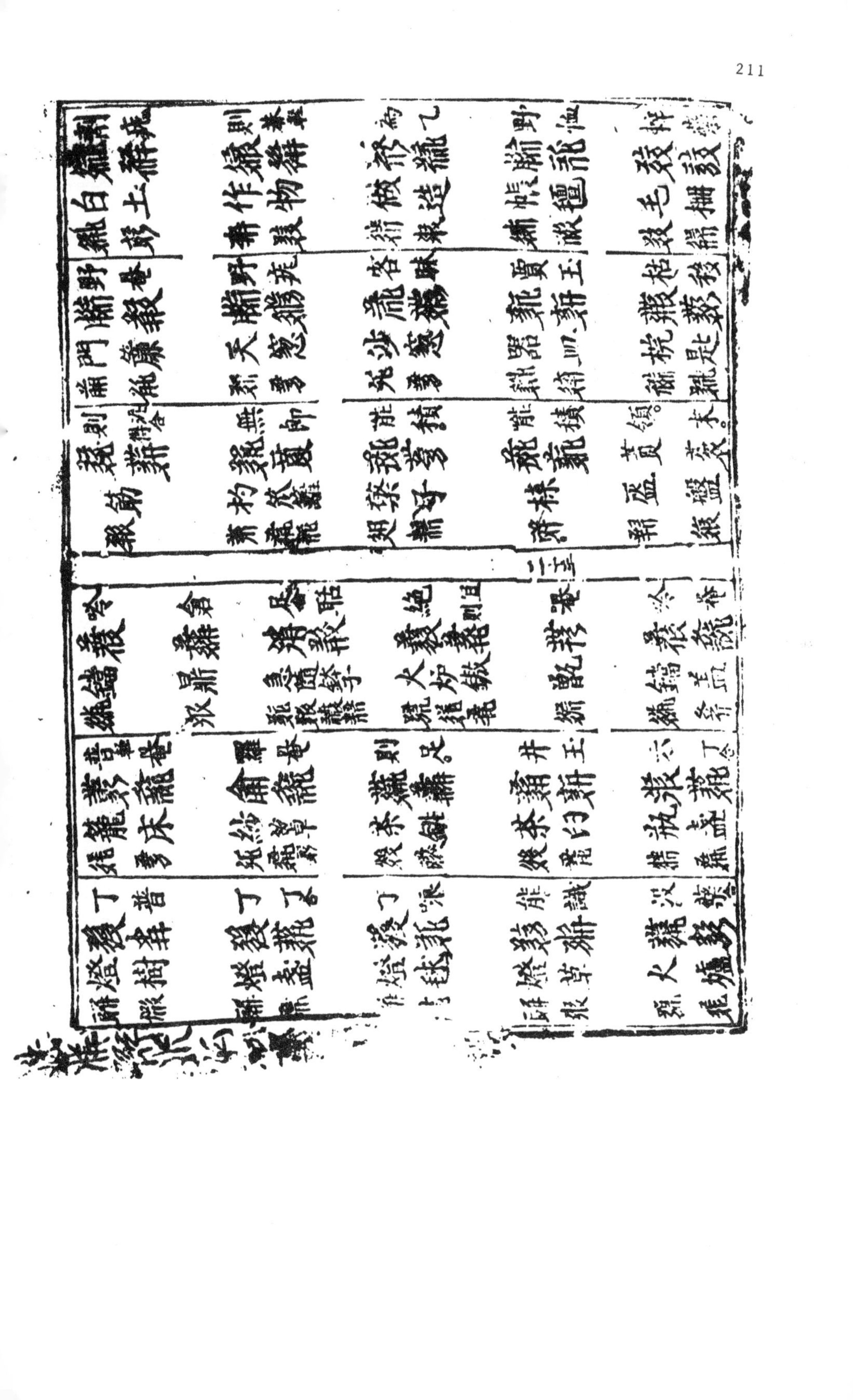

[illegible]

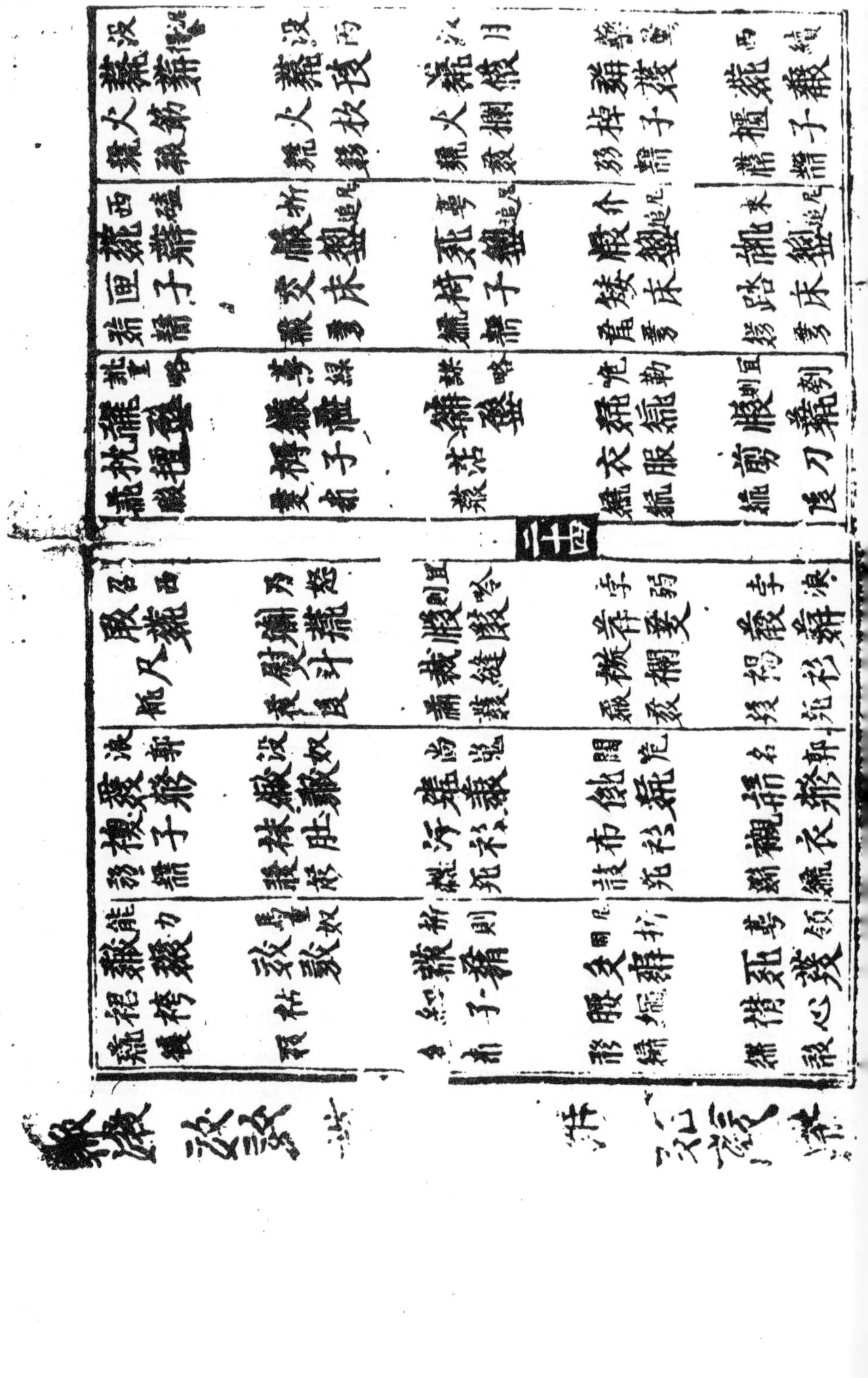

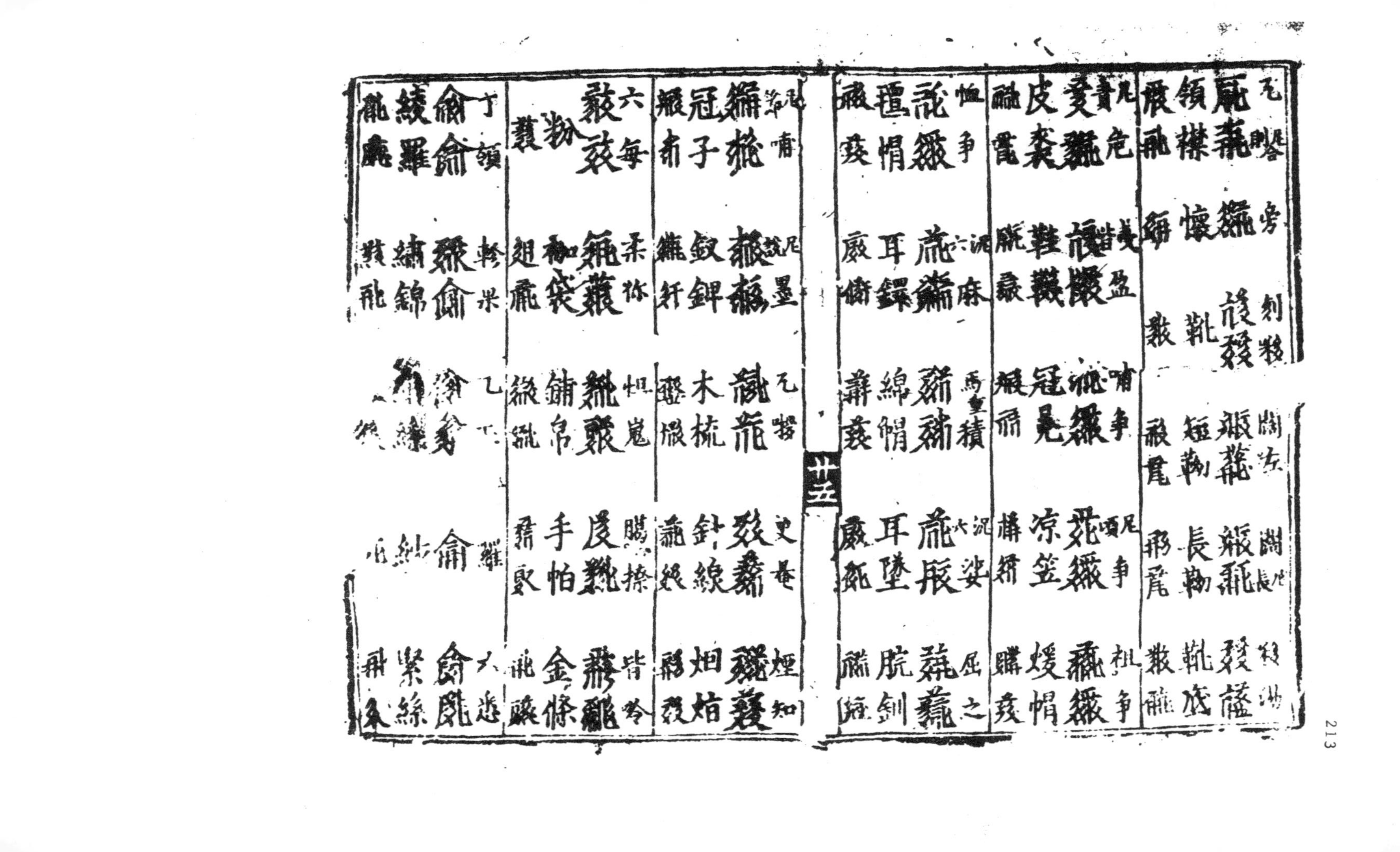

領襟 [illegible] [illegible] 短靿 長靿 [illegible]

皮裘 [illegible] 冠冕 涼笠 煖帽

[illegible]帽 耳鐶 綿帽 耳墜 腕釧

廿五

冠子 釵鉀 木梳 針線 烟焰

[illegible] 袈裟 [illegible]帛 手帕 金條

[illegible] 錦 [illegible] [illegible] 緊絲

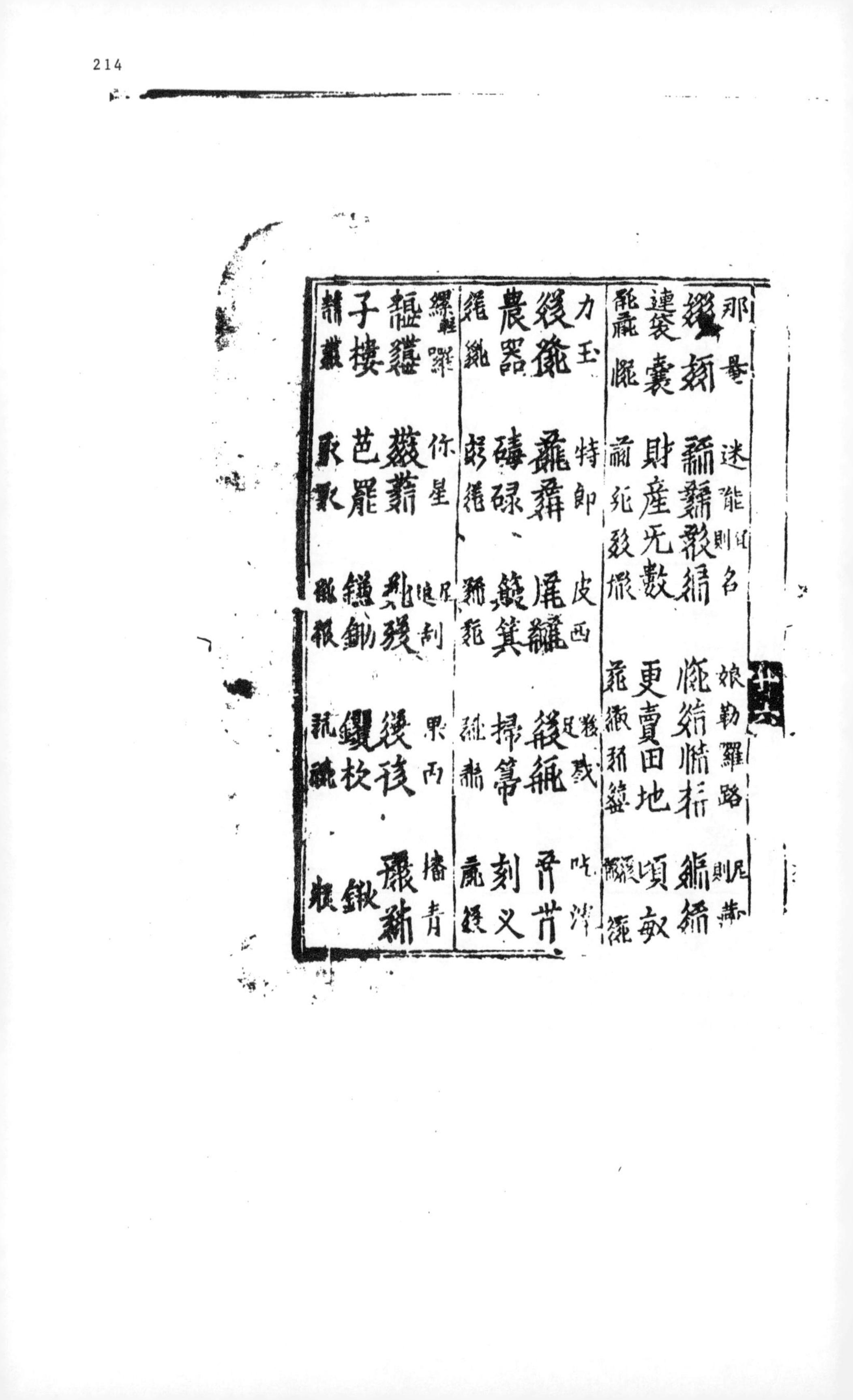

那皆　迷能則囗名　娘勒羅路　尼則蒂

[illegible]

連袋囊　財產无數　更賣田地　頃畝

[illegible]

力玉　特郎　皮西　幾足戴　吃澤

[illegible]

農器　磚碌　簸箕　掃箒　刻义

[illegible]

繰囉　你星　尼浪剖　果丙　播青

[illegible]

子樓　芭籬　鑱劁　钁枚　鍬

[illegible]

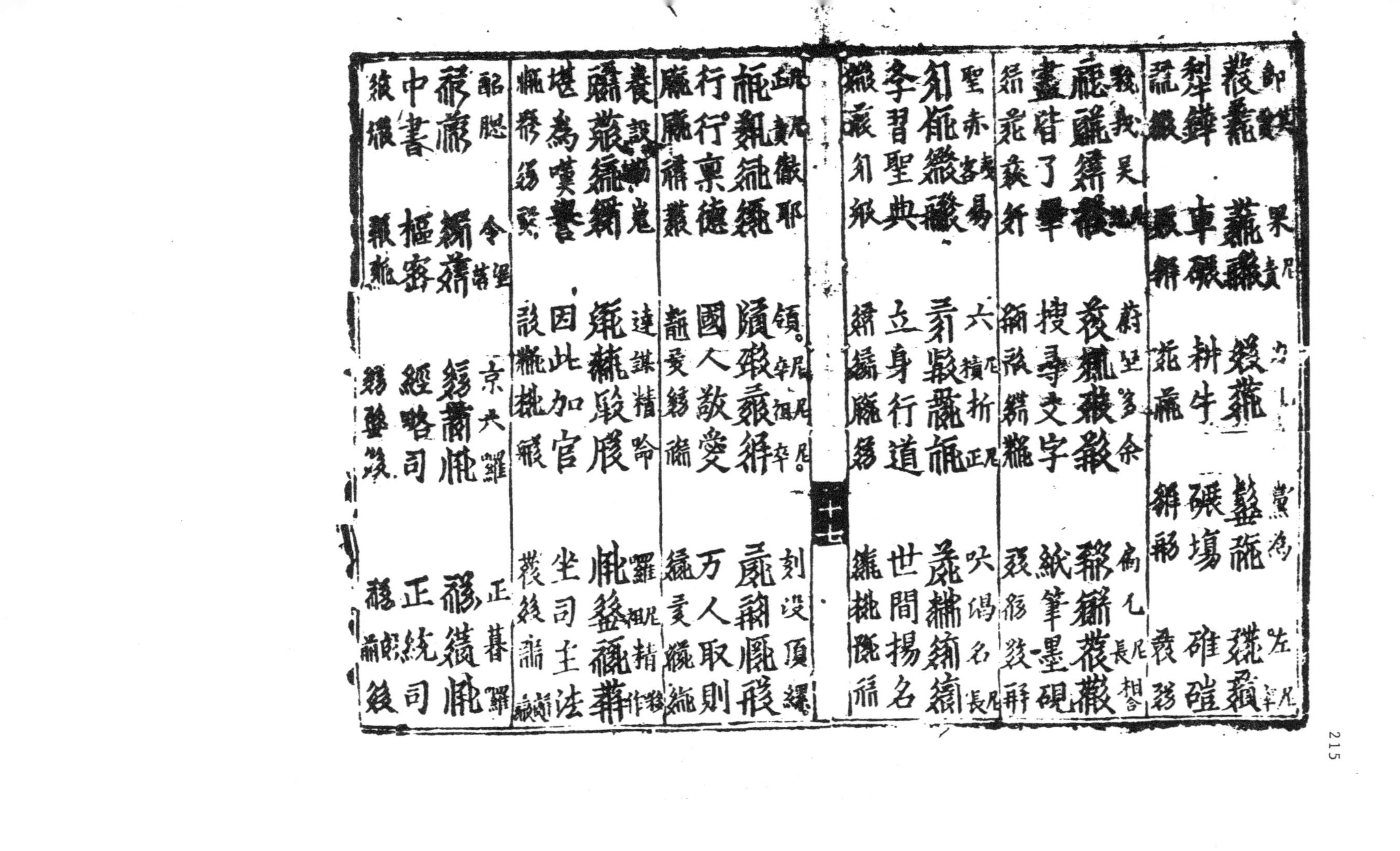

犁鏵　車　耕牛　碾場　碓磑

盡皆了畢　搜尋文字　紙筆墨硯

李習聖典　立身行道　世間揚名

行行禀德　國人敬愛　万人取則

堪為嘆譽　因此加官　坐司主法

中書　樞密　經略司　正統司

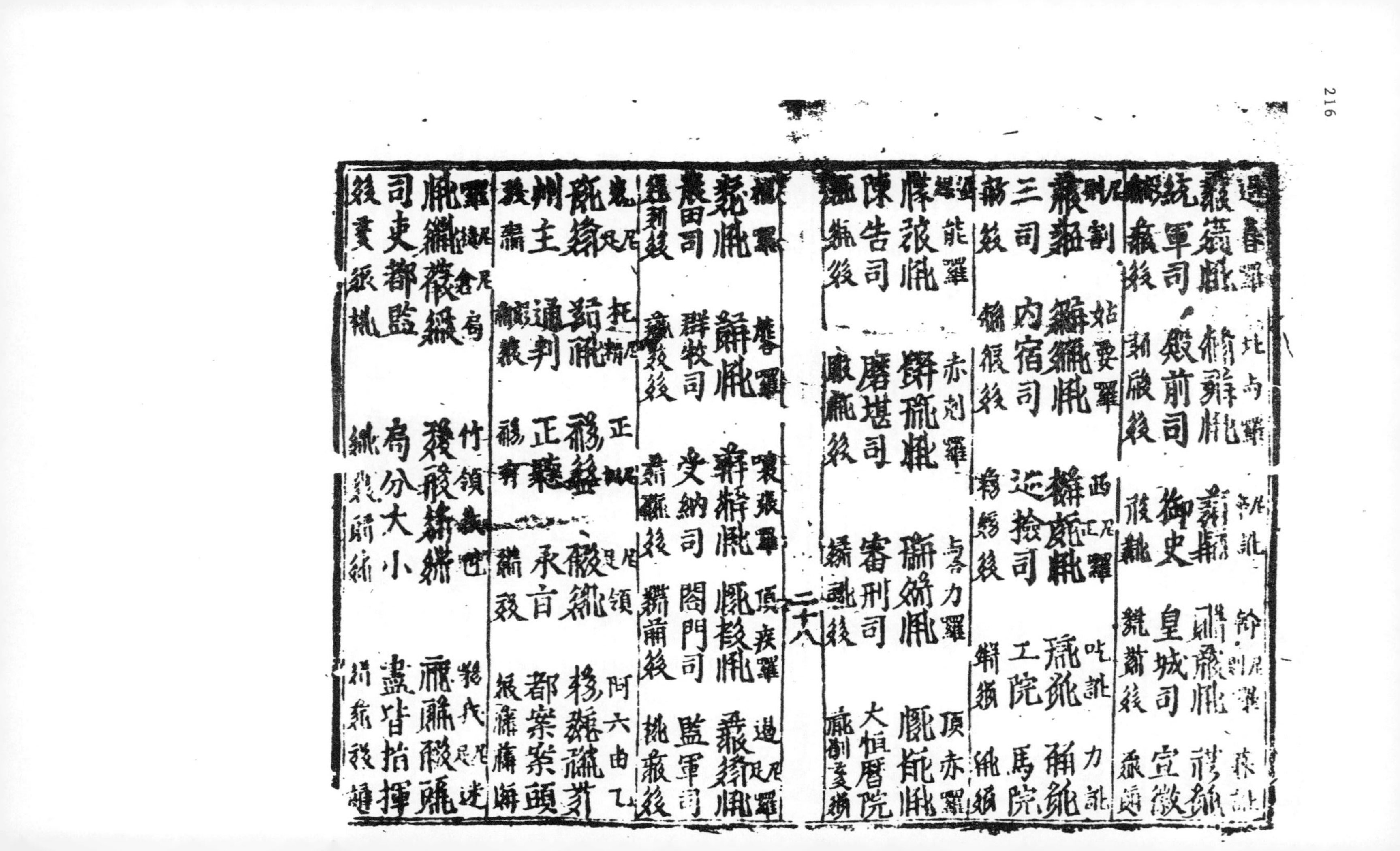

統軍司　殿前司　御史　皇城司　宣徽

三司　內宿司　巡撿司　工院　馬院

陳告司　磨堪司　審刑司　大恒曆院

二十八

農田司　群牧司　受納司　閤門司　監軍司

州主　通判　正聽　承旨　都案

司吏　都監　烏分大小　盡皆指揮

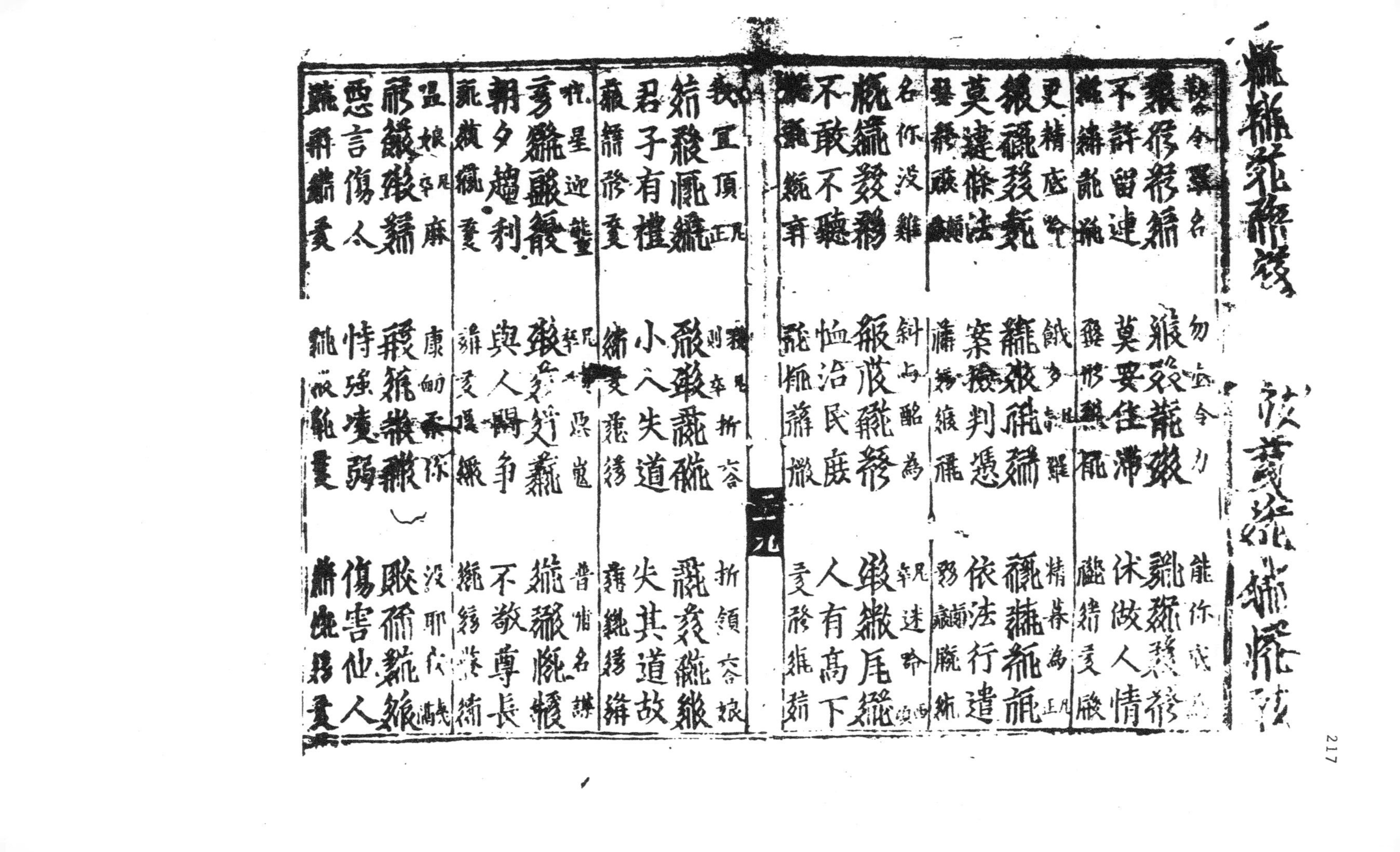

不許留連
莫違條法
不敢不聽
莫要住滯
案檢判憑
恤治民庶
休做人情
依法行遣
人有高下
君子有禮
朝夕趨利
惡言傷人
小人失道
與人鬪爭
恃强凌弱
失其道故
不敬尊長
傷害他人

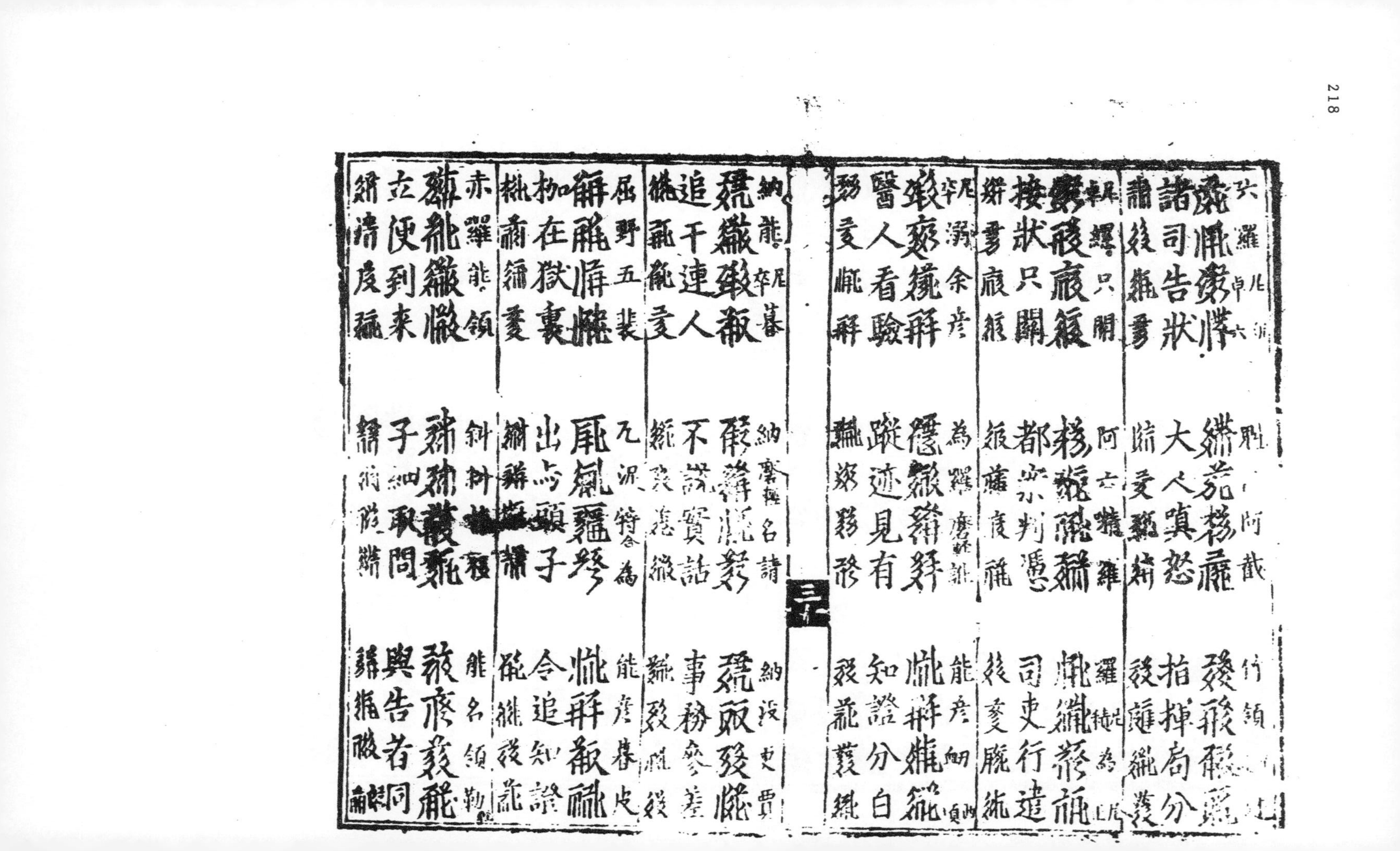

諸司告狀
接狀只關
醫人看驗
追干連人
枷在獄裏
立便到來

大人嗔怒
都案判憑
蹤迹見有
不說實話
出與頭子
子細取問

指揮局分
司吏行遣
知證分白
事務參差
令追知證
與告若同

三十

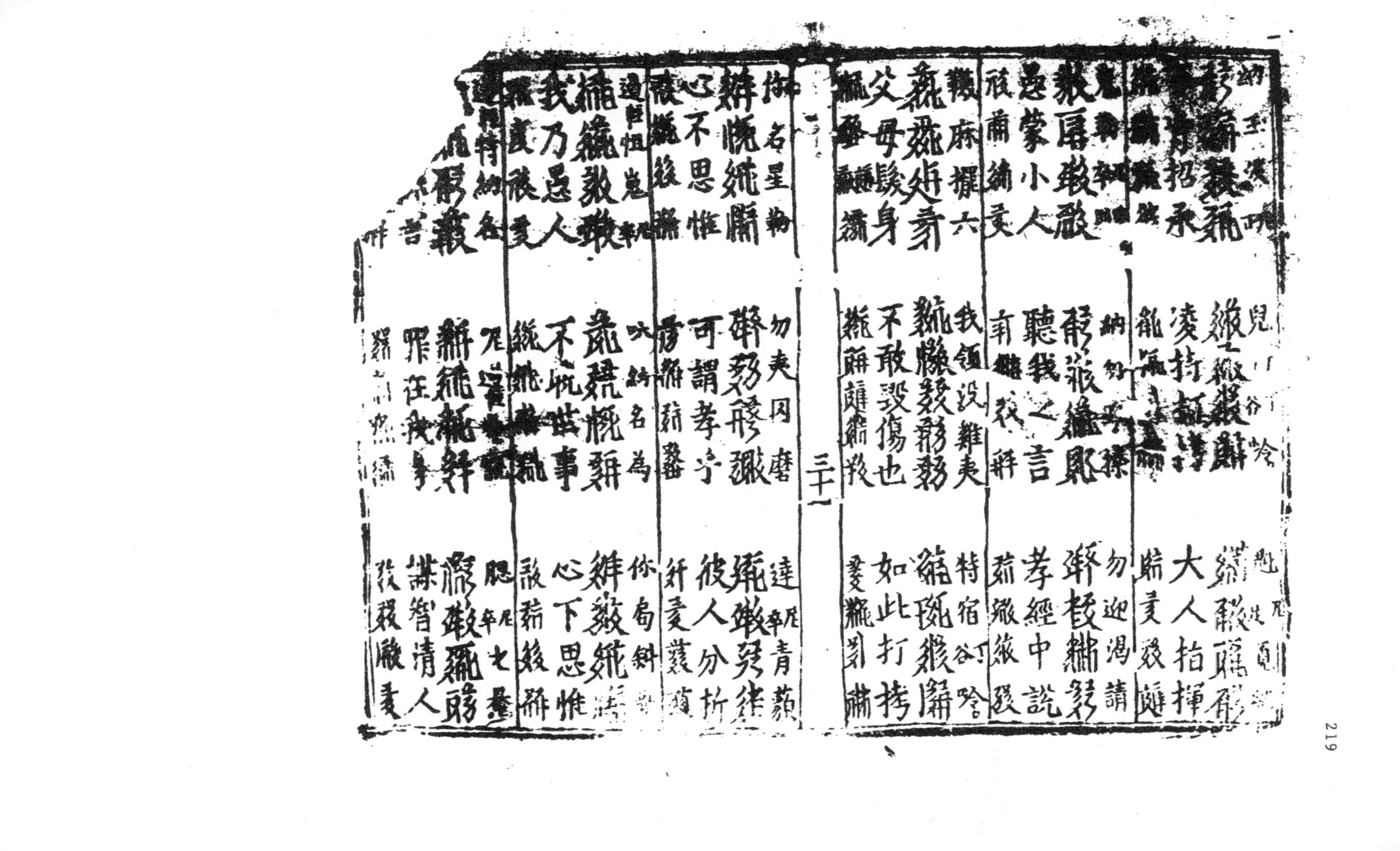

招承

聽我之言

不敢毀傷也

大人指揮

孝經中說

如此打拷

三十一

心不思惟

我乃愚人

可謂孝子

不忺世事

罪在我身

彼人分析

心下思惟

謀智清人

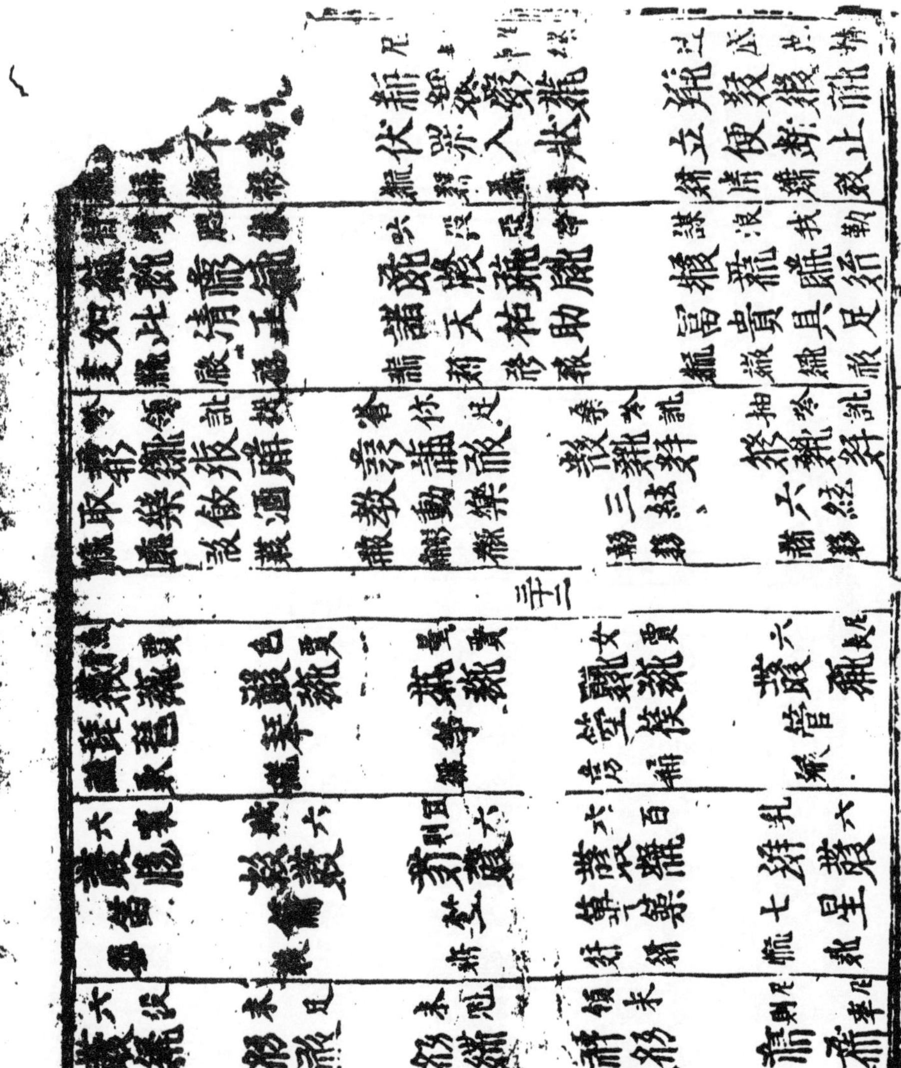

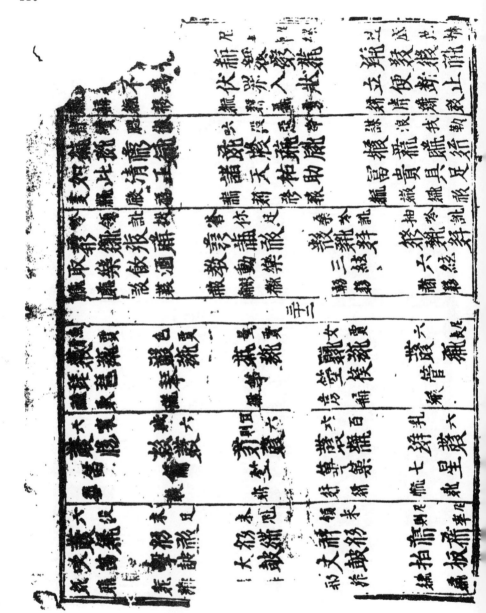

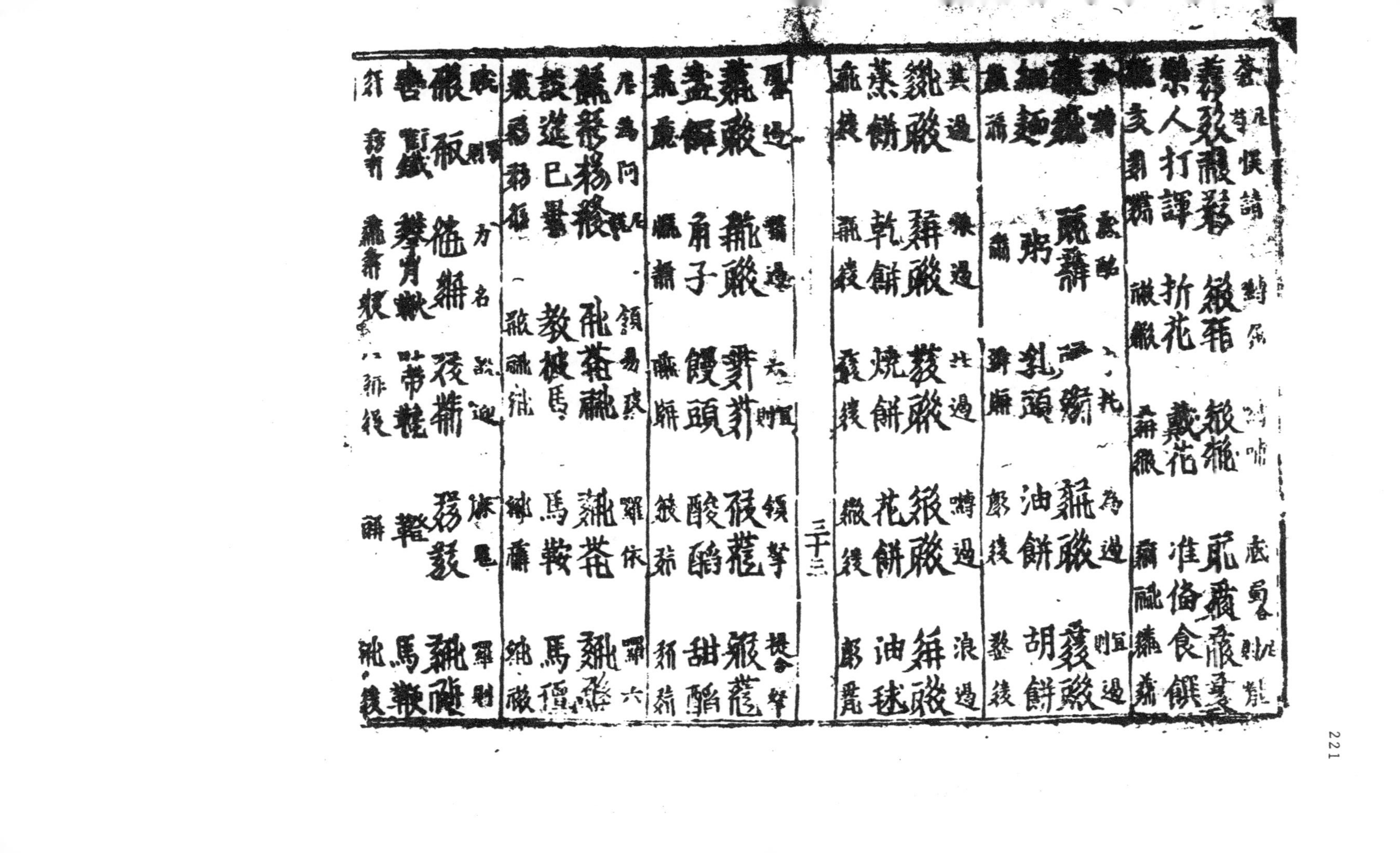

人　打諢　折花　戴花　准備　食饌

麵　粥　亂頭　油餅　胡餅

乾餅　燒餅　花餅　油毬

三十三

扇子　饅頭　酸餡　甜餡

已　教　馬　馬

鐵　掌　背　帶　馬鞍

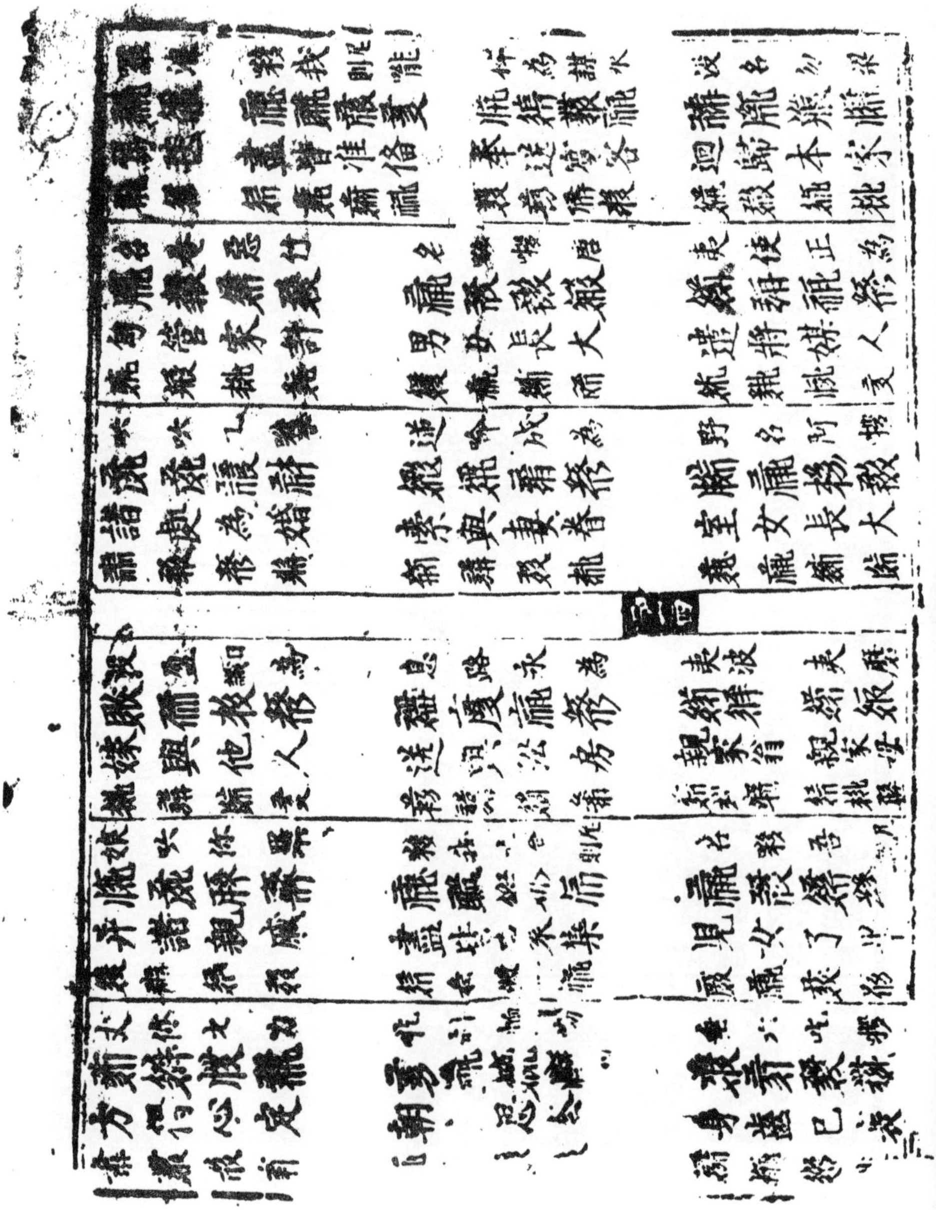

人壽百歲　七十者稀　凡君子者

不失於物　不累於己　能

豈滯一邊　雖然如此　世人

煩惱纏縛　爭名趨利　忘

逐物心動　起貪嗔癡　以

以貧為醜　由此業力　三界流轉

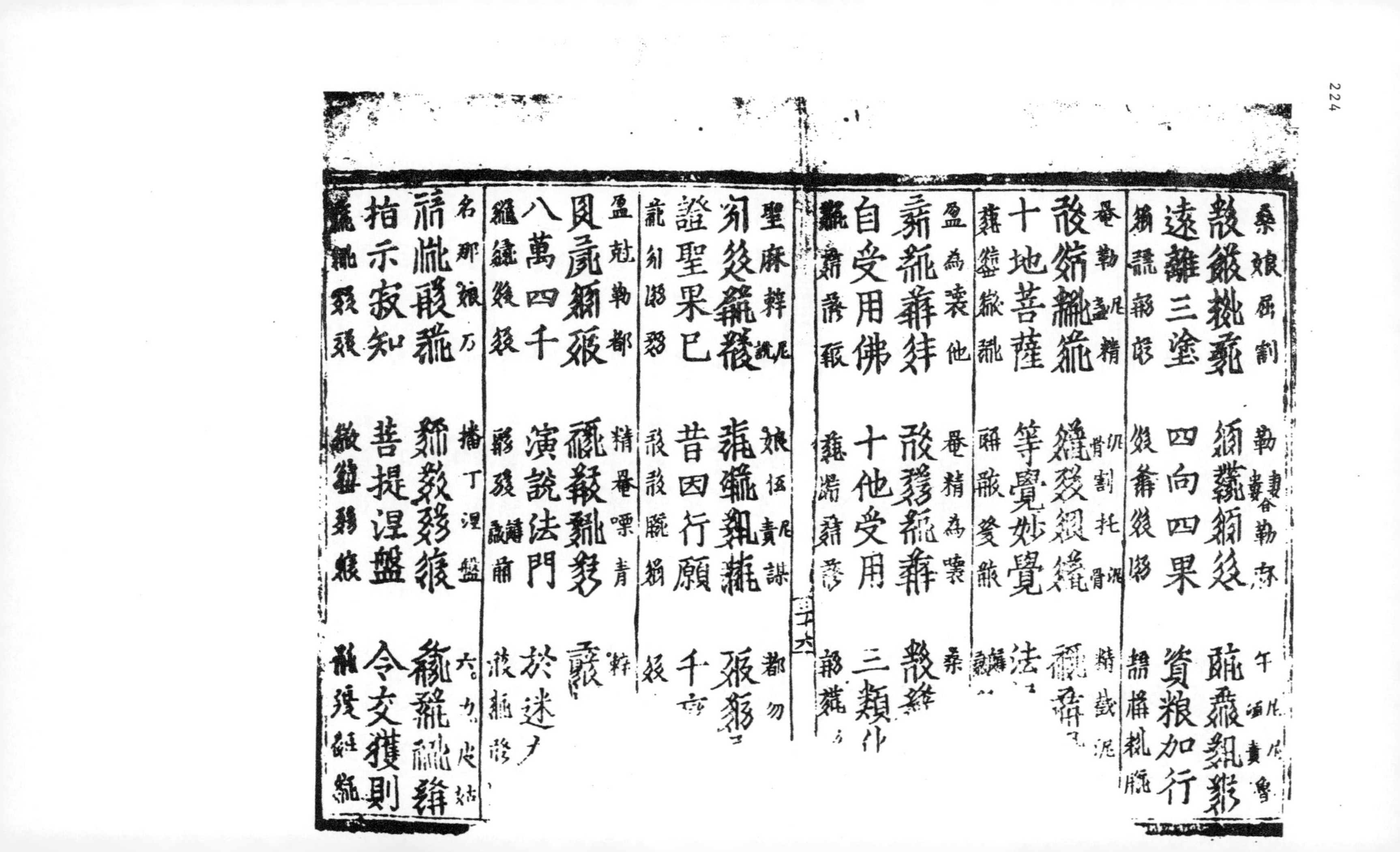

Chinese phonetic	Chinese
桑娘屈割	遠離三塗
勒妻合勒㮕	四向四果
午涌尼責尼魯	資粮加行
疊勒盡尼精	十地菩薩
㑧骨割托骨泥	等覺妙覺
精[illegible]泥	法[illegible]
盈為褱他	自受用佛
疊精為囊	十他受用
桑	三類化
聖麻粹訛尼	證聖果已
娘伍責尼謀	昔因行願
都勿	千[illegible]
盈尅勒都	八萬四千
精疊嘌青	演說法門
粹	於迷
名那娘乃	指示寂知
播丁涅盤	菩提涅盤
六力尼姑	令交獲則

六趣輪迴　苦報無量

修行觀心　得達聖道

合時掌中珠　竟

Manuscript B

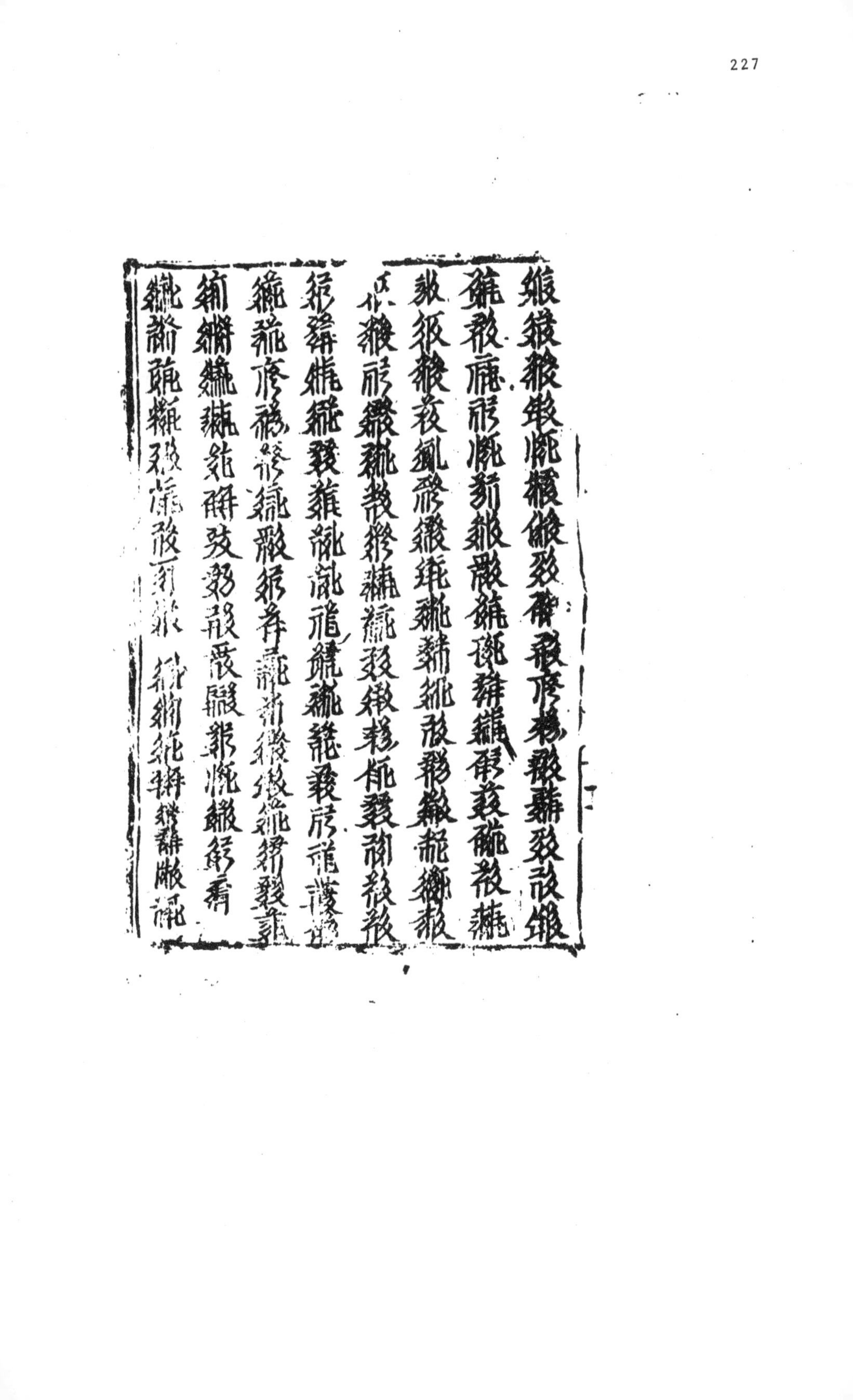

番漢合時掌中珠序

凡君子者為物豈可忘己故未嘗不學為己亦不絕物故未嘗不教學則以智成己欲襲古迹教則以仁利物以救今時兼番漢文字者論末則殊考本則同何則先聖後聖其揆未嘗不一故也然則今時人者番漢語言可以俱備不學番言則豈和番人之衆不會漢語則豈入漢人之數番有智者漢人不敬漢有賢士番人不崇若此者由語言不通故也如此則有逆前言故茂才稍學番漢文字曷敢默而弗言不避慚怍準三才集成番漢語節略一本言音分辨語句照然言音未切教者能整語句雖俗學人易會號為合時掌中珠賢哲覩斯幸莫哂焉時乾祐庚戌二十一年　月

日骨勒茂才謹序

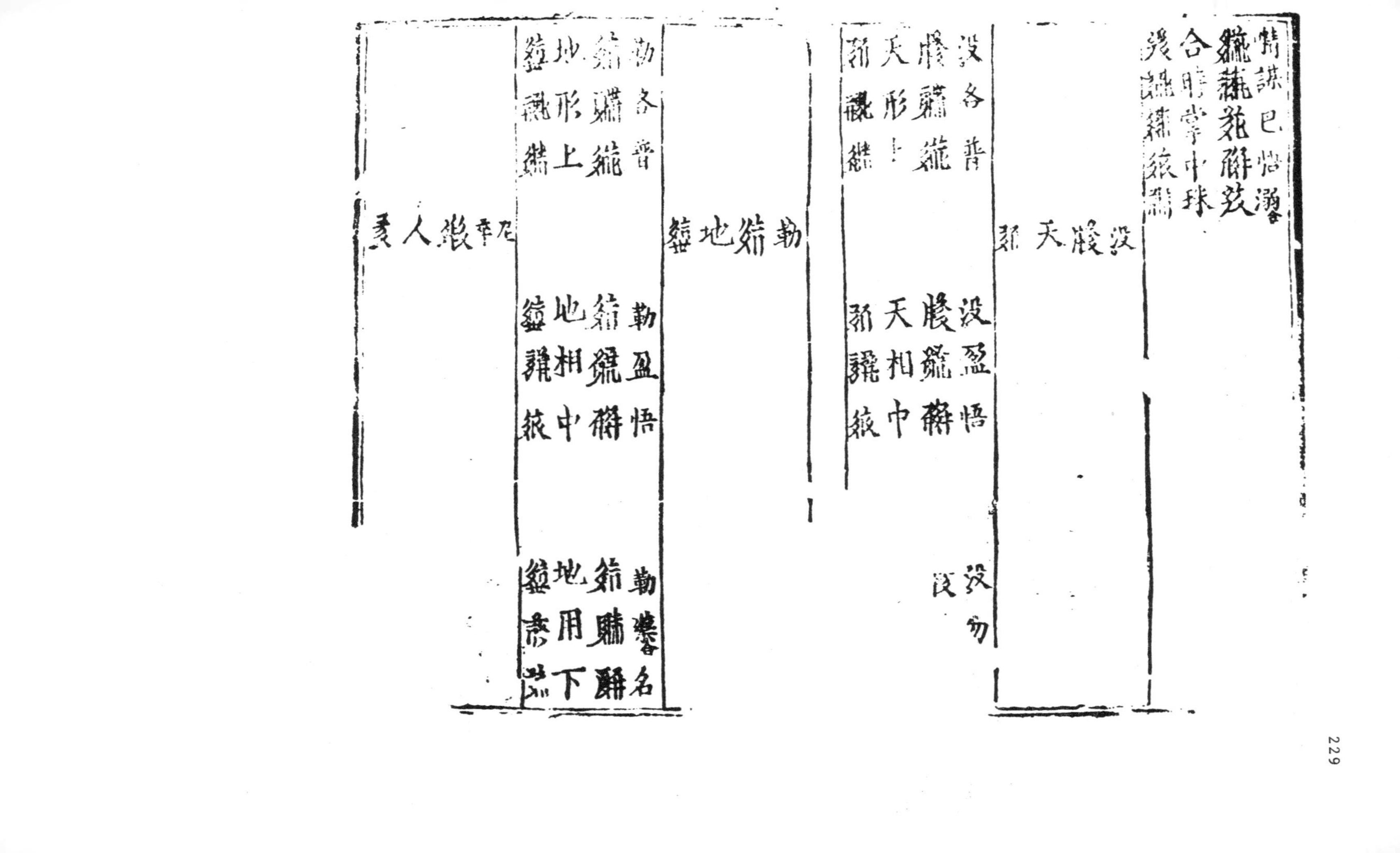

合時掌中珠

没 天

没各普
天形上

没盈悟
天相中

没勿

勒 地

勒各普
地形上

勒盈悟
地相中

勒名
地用下

人 卒尼

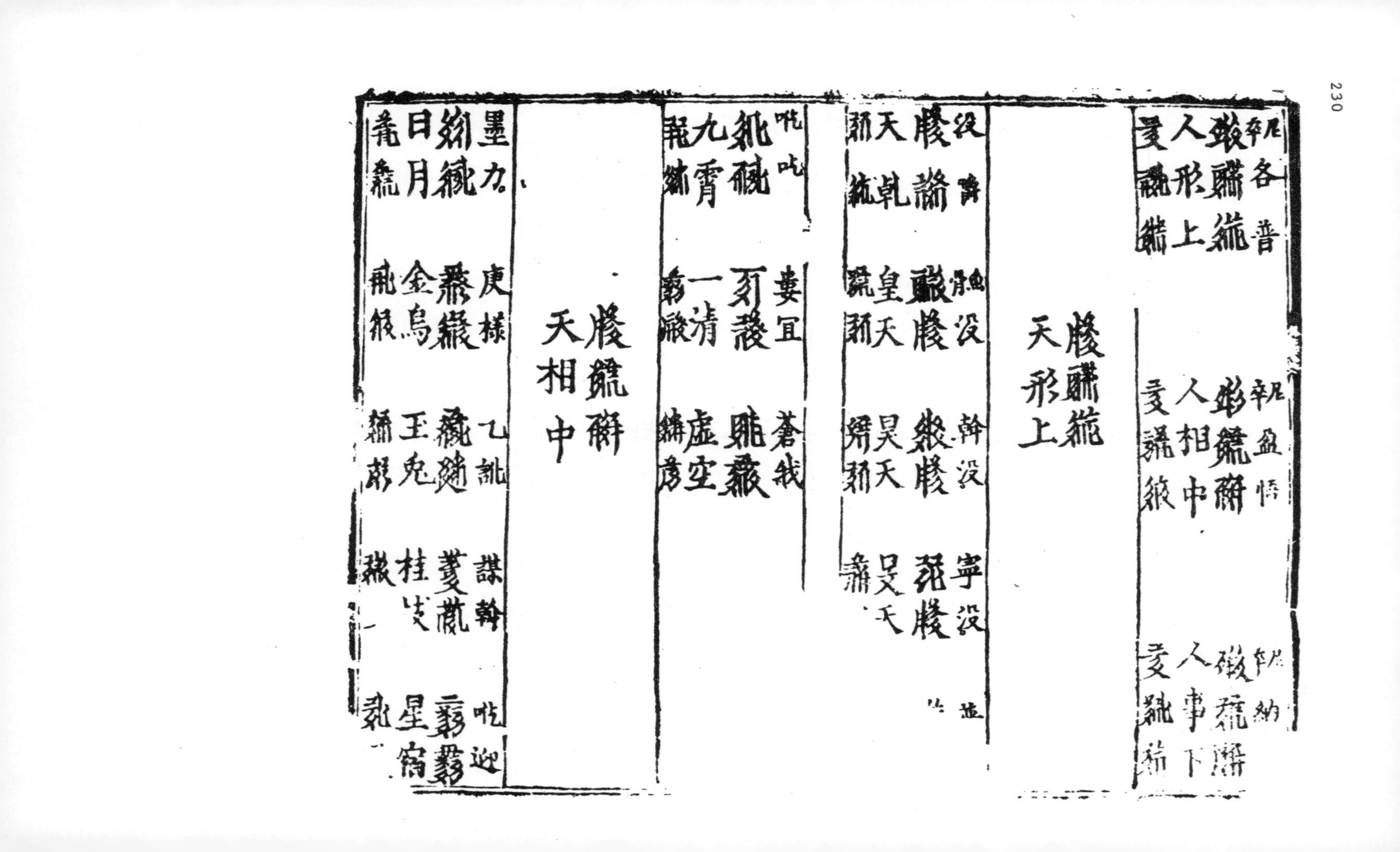

卒尼各普 人形上

卒尼盈悟 人相中

卒尼納 人事下

天形上

没 天乾

没 皇天

斡没 昊天

寧没 旻天

吪吪 九霄

妻宜 一清

蒼我 虚空

天相中

墨力 日月

庚様 金烏

乙訛 玉兎

謀斡 桂

吪迎 星宿

為迎	[illegible]	底宿	[illegible]
[illegible]	[illegible]	房宿	[illegible]
[illegible]	[illegible]	心宿	[illegible]
怒迎	[illegible]	斗宿	良皴
虔迎	[illegible]	牛宿	[illegible]
配迎	[illegible]	女宿	[illegible]
[illegible]	[illegible]	虚宿	[illegible]
		危宿	[illegible]
吒迎	[illegible]	室宿	[illegible]
犯迎	[illegible]	壁宿	[illegible]
六迎	[illegible]	奎宿	[illegible]
羅迎	[illegible]	婁宿	[illegible]
六迎	[illegible]	胃宿	[illegible]

五

賊迎	[illegible]	昂宿	[illegible]
詋迎	[illegible]	畢宿	[illegible]
麼迎	[illegible]	觜宿	[illegible]
箏迎	[illegible]	參宿	[illegible]
渴迎	[illegible]	井宿	[illegible]
餘迎	[illegible]	鬼宿	[illegible]
叐迎	[illegible]	柳宿	[illegible]
兵迎	[illegible]	角宿	[illegible]
肚迎	[illegible]		
皮迎	[illegible]		
果迎	[illegible]	軫宿	[illegible]
猜迎	[illegible]	亢宿	[illegible]
[illegible]	[illegible]	天	[illegible]

天德 劫殺 地殺 寡宿 地

月德 災殺 亡神 三丘 青龍

六害 歲殺 五墓

驛馬 天殺 三刑 歲星

華蓋 月殺 孤神 天羅

六二

白虎　玄武　寶瓶　磨蝎　巨蟹

人馬　天蝎　天秤　雙女　獅子

金牛　白羊　雙魚

七

逐星　掃星　天鼓　天火　天河

霹靂　陽燄　雨澤　封露　旋風

此掌中珠者三十[illegible]句內更新添十句

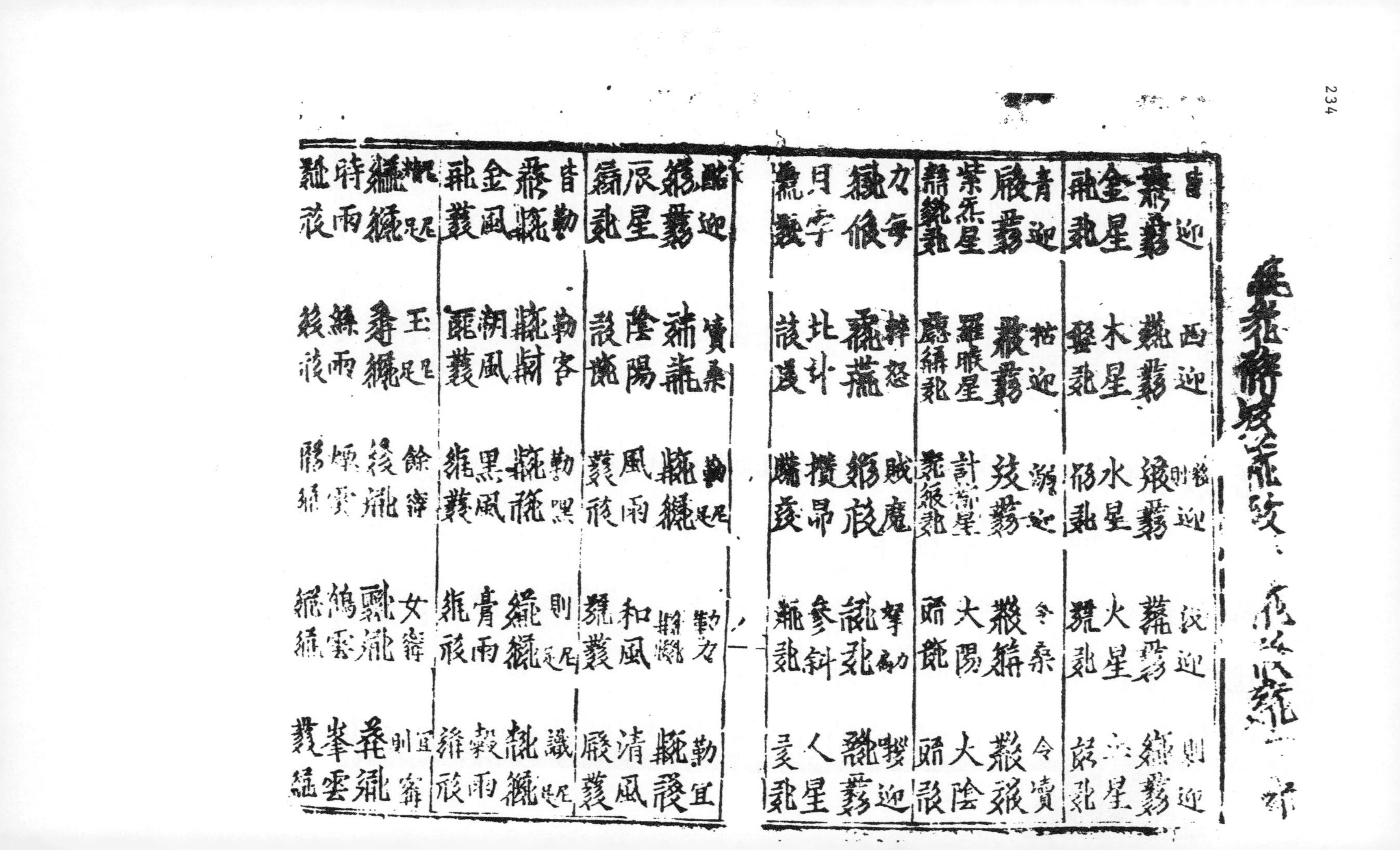

[illegible]致 [illegible]

旨迎 [illegible] 金星 [illegible]	青迎 [illegible] 紫炁星 [illegible]	力每 [illegible] 月孛 [illegible]	[illegible]迎 [illegible] 辰星 [illegible]	旨勤 [illegible] 金風 [illegible]	[illegible]尼 [illegible] 時雨 [illegible]
西迎 [illegible] 木星 [illegible]	枯迎 [illegible] 羅睺星 [illegible]	辞怒 [illegible] 北斗 [illegible]	賓桑 [illegible] 陰陽 [illegible]	勤客 [illegible] 湖風 [illegible]	王尼 [illegible] 綠雨 [illegible]
[illegible]迎 [illegible] 水星 [illegible]	游迎 [illegible] 計都星 [illegible]	賊魔 [illegible] 攢昴 [illegible]	[illegible]尼 [illegible] 風雨 [illegible]	勤嘿 [illegible] 黑風 [illegible]	餘寧 [illegible] 煙雲 [illegible]
設迎 [illegible] 火星 [illegible]	令桑 [illegible] 太陽 [illegible]	挐劢 [illegible] 參斜 [illegible]	勤力 [illegible] 和風 [illegible]	則尼 [illegible] 青雨 [illegible]	女寧 [illegible] 鳩雲 [illegible]
則迎 [illegible] 土星 [illegible]	令賓 [illegible] 太陰 [illegible]	[illegible]迎 [illegible] 人星 [illegible]	勤宜 [illegible] 清風 [illegible]	識尼 [illegible] 穀雨 [illegible]	則宜寧 [illegible] 峯雲 [illegible]

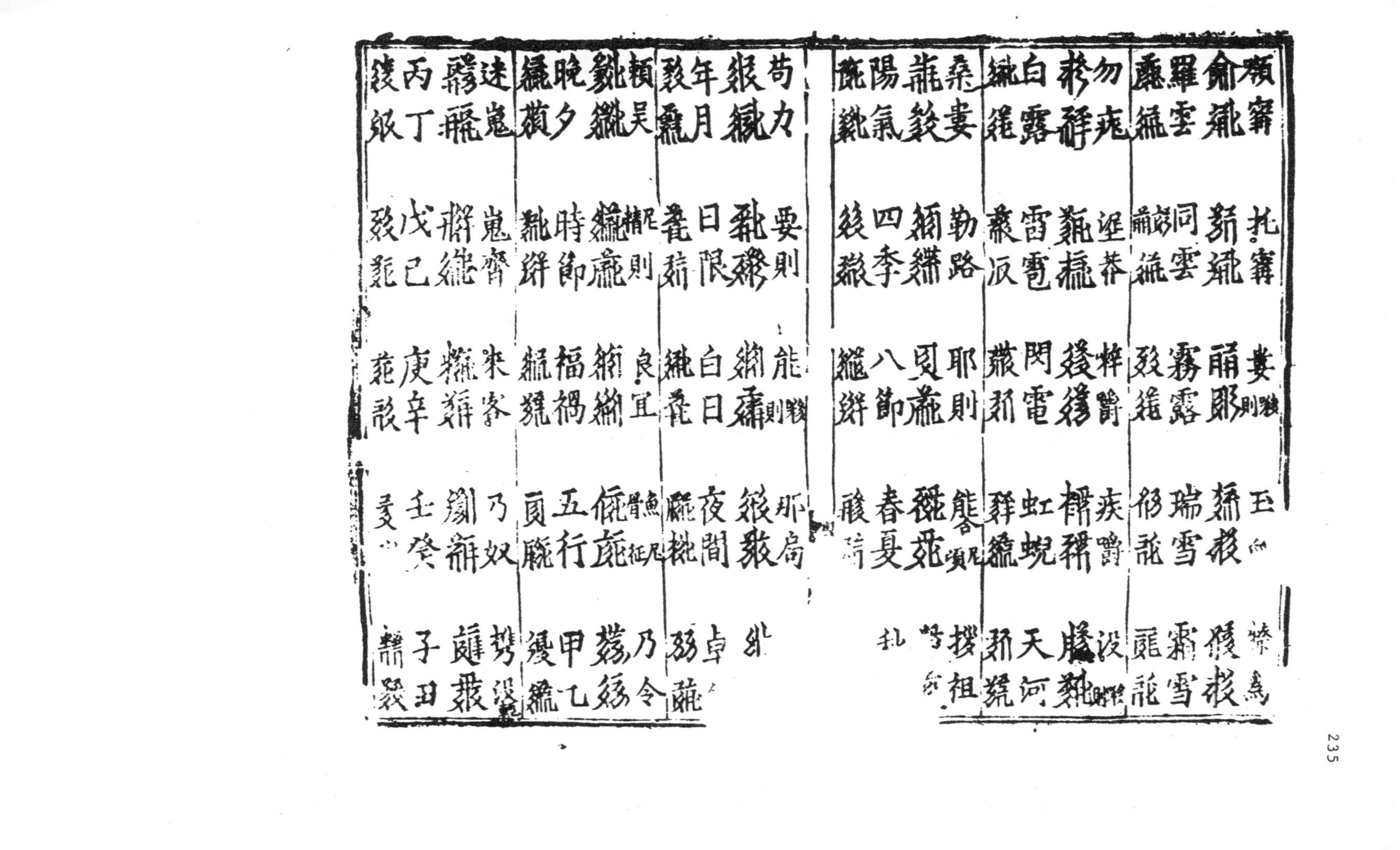

Chinese transcription	Tangut	Chinese	Tangut transcription
頻寧	[Tangut]	羅雲	[Tangut]
勿疾	[Tangut]	白露	[Tangut]
桑妻	[Tangut]	陽氣	[Tangut]
扎寧	[Tangut]	同雲	[Tangut]
逕恭	[Tangut]	霄雹	[Tangut]
勒路	[Tangut]	四季	[Tangut]
婁則	[Tangut]	霧露	[Tangut]
粹爵	[Tangut]	閃電	[Tangut]
耶則	[Tangut]	八節	[Tangut]
玉	[Tangut]	瑞雪	[Tangut]
疾爵	[Tangut]	虹蜺	[Tangut]
能昝	[Tangut]	春夏	[Tangut]
襟爲	[Tangut]	霜雪	[Tangut]
設	[Tangut]	天河	[Tangut]
撈	[Tangut]	祖	扎
苟力	[Tangut]	年月	[Tangut]
頼吳	[Tangut]	晚夕	[Tangut]
迷嵬	[Tangut]	丙丁	[Tangut]
要則	[Tangut]	日限	[Tangut]
尼精則	[Tangut]	時節	[Tangut]
嵬齊	[Tangut]	戊己	[Tangut]
能則	[Tangut]	白日	[Tangut]
良宜	[Tangut]	福禍	[Tangut]
來客	[Tangut]	庚辛	[Tangut]
那局	[Tangut]	夜間	[Tangut]
魚骨尼征	[Tangut]	五行	[Tangut]
乃奴	[Tangut]	壬癸	[Tangut]
北	[Tangut]	卓	[Tangut]
乃令	[Tangut]	甲乙	[Tangut]
勢没	[Tangut]	子丑	[Tangut]

Chinese reading	Chinese meaning
勒則	寅卯
嵬瘧	辰巳
迎没	午未
韋長	申酉
亦	戌亥

Chinese reading	Chinese meaning
叠能	十二
酩名	星宮
嚀娘 鐵則	乾坎艮震
每下 普吟	巽离坤兌

天變下

Chinese reading	Chinese meaning
没鈴	天曉
没乃	天晚
墨黨	日出
墨汶	日没
卜	[illegible]

Chinese reading	Chinese meaning
没奈	天陰
勒訛	風起
勒叠	風緊
足尼 足你	雨降
舟卒	下雪

Chinese reading	Chinese meaning
那羅	明日
孟能	今日
薛寧	後日
吳寧	外後日
阿要	一日

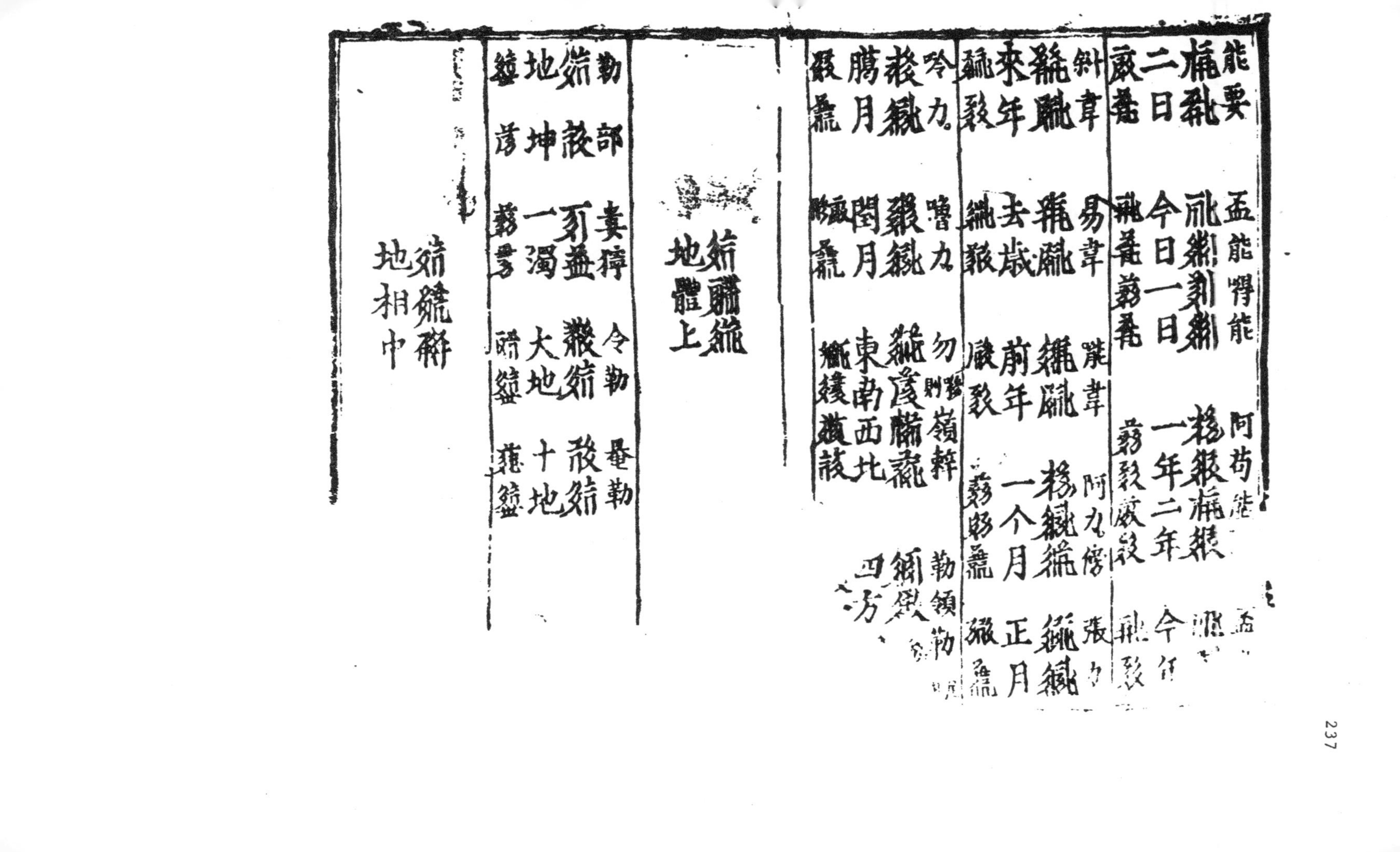

能要	[illegible]	二日	[illegible]
盃能 嘚能	[illegible]	今日 一日	[illegible]
阿苟能	[illegible]	一年 二年	[illegible]
[illegible]	[illegible]	今	[illegible]
斜韋	[illegible]	來年	[illegible]
易韋	[illegible]	去歲	[illegible]
罷韋	[illegible]	前年	[illegible]
阿尼嗒	[illegible]	一个月	[illegible]
張力	[illegible]	正月	[illegible]
吟力	[illegible]	腊月	[illegible]
嚕力	[illegible]	閏月	[illegible]
勿則 嶺粹	[illegible]	東南西北	[illegible]
勒領勒	[illegible]	四方	

[illegible] 地體上

勒	[illegible]	地	[illegible]
部	[illegible]	坤	[illegible]
婁嬣	[illegible]	一濁	[illegible]
令勒	[illegible]	大地	[illegible]
疊勒	[illegible]	十地	[illegible]

[illegible] 地相中

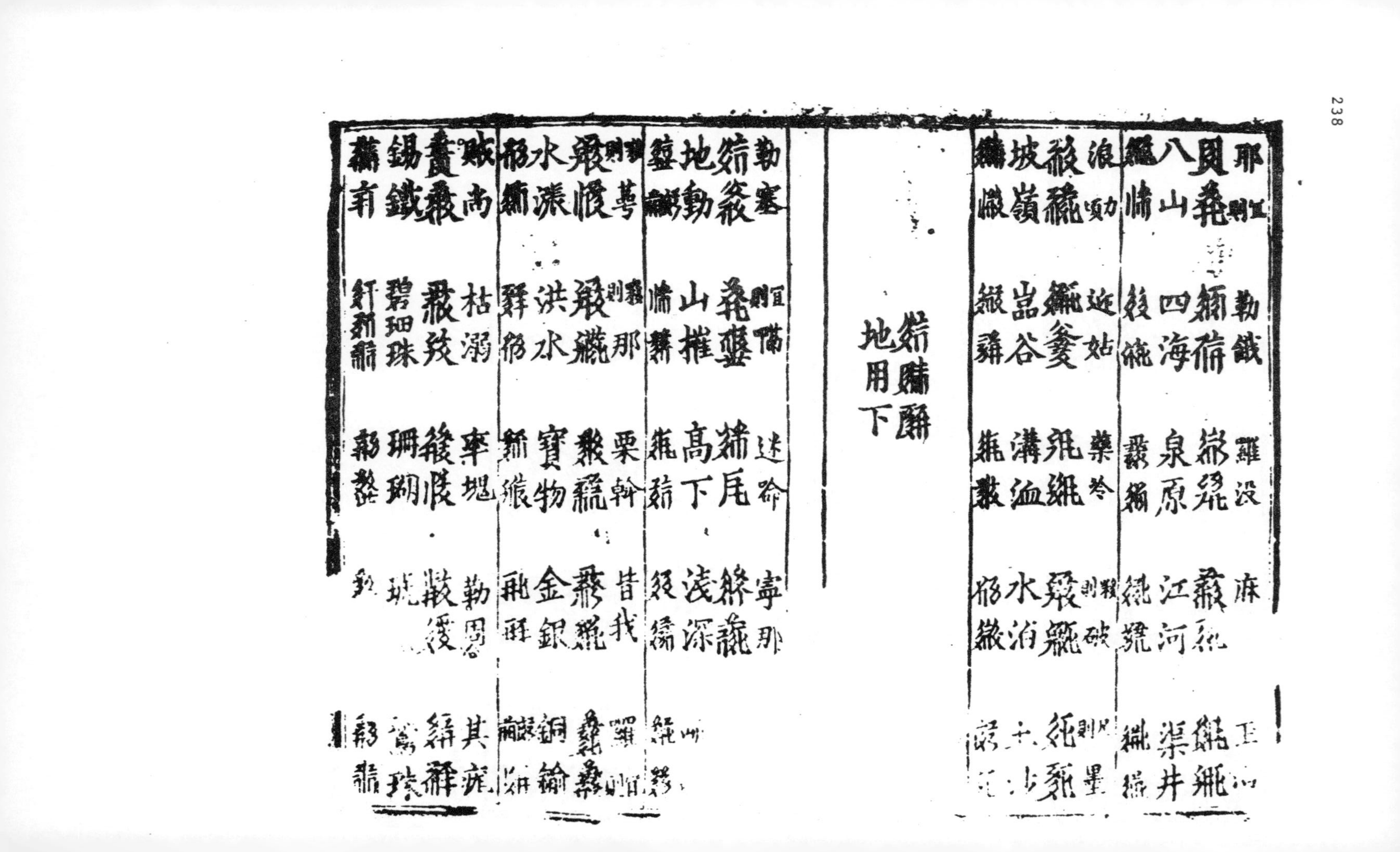

耶 [Tangut]	八山	[Tangut]
勒鐵 [Tangut]	四海	[Tangut]
羅没 [Tangut]	泉原	[Tangut]
麻 [Tangut]	江河	[Tangut]
王 [Tangut]	渠井	[Tangut]
浪 [Tangut]	坡嶺	[Tangut]
近姑 [Tangut]	嵓谷	[Tangut]
藥令 [Tangut]	溝洫	[Tangut]
破 [Tangut]	水泊	[Tangut]
墨 [Tangut]	十步	[Tangut]

[Tangut] 地用下

勒塞 [Tangut]	地動	[Tangut]
[Tangut]	山摧	[Tangut]
迷吟 [Tangut]	高下	[Tangut]
寧那 [Tangut]	淺深	[Tangut]
州 [Tangut]		
[Tangut]	水漲	[Tangut]
那 [Tangut]	洪水	[Tangut]
栗斡 [Tangut]	寶物	[Tangut]
昔我 [Tangut]	金銀	[Tangut]
[Tangut]	銅鍮	[Tangut]
賊尚 [Tangut]	錫鐵	[Tangut]
枯溺 [Tangut]	碧[illegible]珠	[Tangut]
率堰 [Tangut]	珊瑚	[Tangut]
勒罔合 [Tangut]	琥[illegible]	[Tangut]
其[illegible] [Tangut]	[illegible]珠	[Tangut]

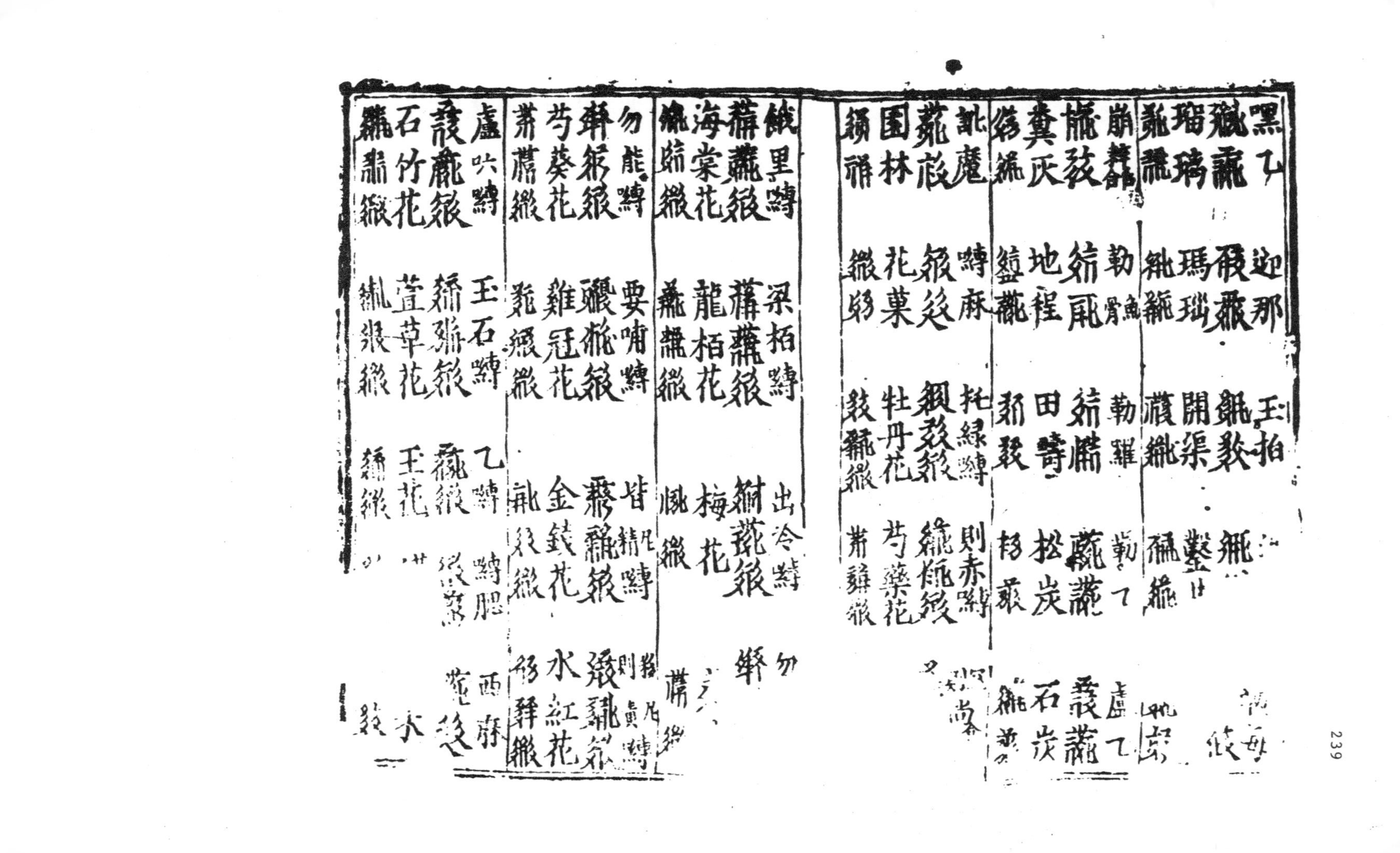

Chinese transcription	Tangut	Chinese	Tangut transcription
黑乙	[illegible]	瑠璃	[illegible]
迎那	[illegible]	瑪瑙	[illegible]
王拍	[illegible]	開渠	[illegible]
[illegible]	[illegible]	鑿	[illegible]
崩	[illegible]	糞灰	[illegible]
勒	[illegible]	地程	[illegible]
勒羅	[illegible]	田疇	[illegible]
勒7	[illegible]	松炭	[illegible]
訛魔	[illegible]	園林	[illegible]
嚩麻	[illegible]	花菓	[illegible]
托綠嚩	[illegible]	牡丹花	[illegible]
則赤嚩	[illegible]	芍藥花	[illegible]
餓里嚩	[illegible]	海棠花	[illegible]
梁拍嚩	[illegible]	龍栢花	[illegible]
出冷嚩	[illegible]	梅花	[illegible]
勿	[illegible]		
勿能嚩	[illegible]	芍葵花	[illegible]
要哺嚩	[illegible]	雞冠花	[illegible]
皆精凡嚩	[illegible]	金錢花	[illegible]
則	[illegible]	水紅花	[illegible]
盧吠嚩	[illegible]	石竹花	[illegible]
玉石嚩	[illegible]	萱草花	[illegible]
乙嚩	[illegible]	玉花	[illegible]
嚩胆	[illegible]		
西蘇	[illegible]		
盧乙	[illegible]	石炭	[illegible]
尚	[illegible]		

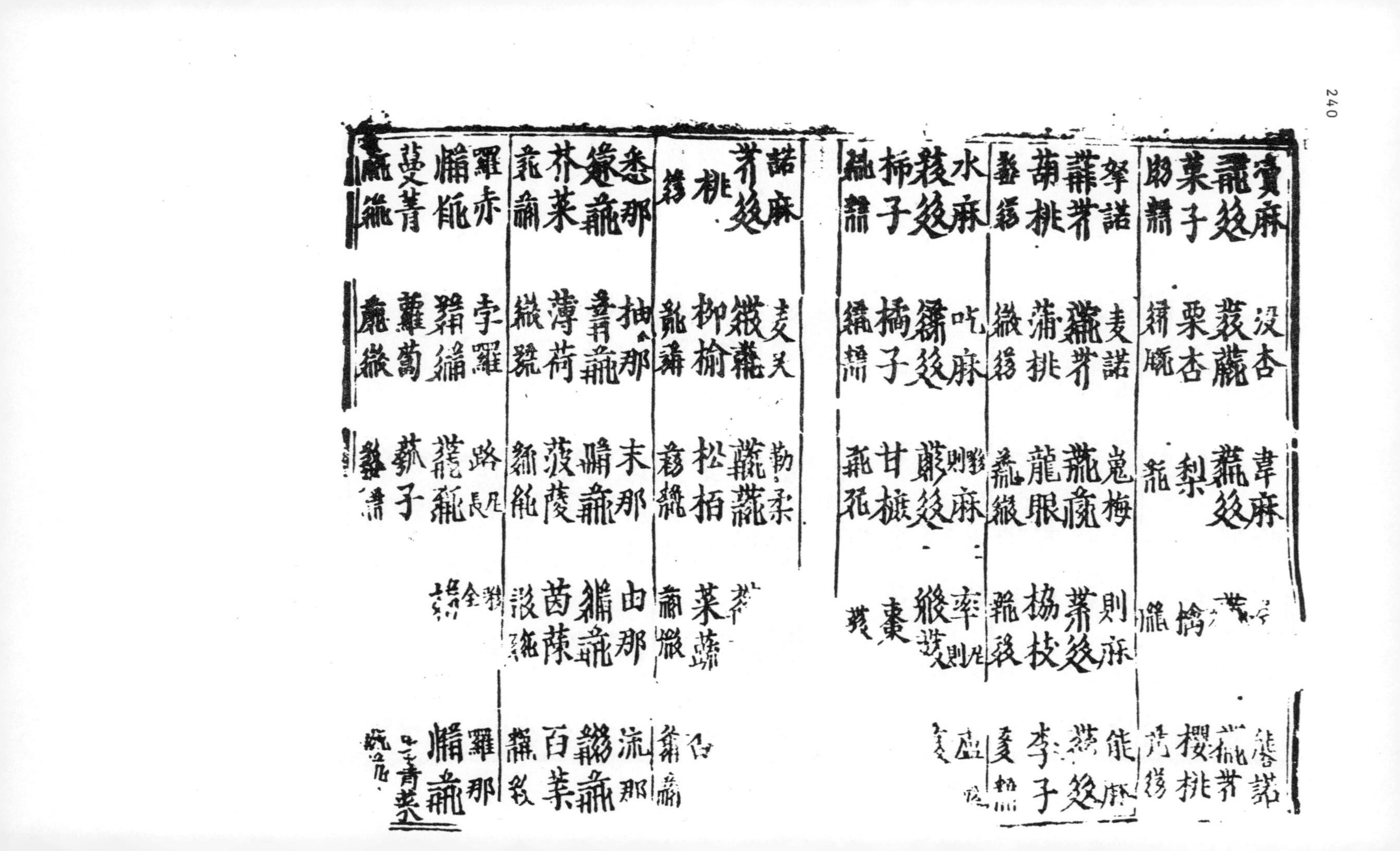

賣麻 菓子
拏諾 葫桃
水麻 柿子
諾麻 桃
悉那 芥菜
羅赤 蔓菁

没杏 栗杏
麦諾 蒲桃
吃麻 橘子
麦叉 柳榆
抽那 薄荷
孛羅 蘿蔔

韋麻 梨
嵬梅 龍眼
則麻 甘樜
勒柔 松栢
末那 菠薐
路 蘇子

檎
則麻 荔枝
率 棗
莱菔
由那 茵蔯
全

能麻 櫻桃
李子
盃
白
流那 百葉
羅那 青菜

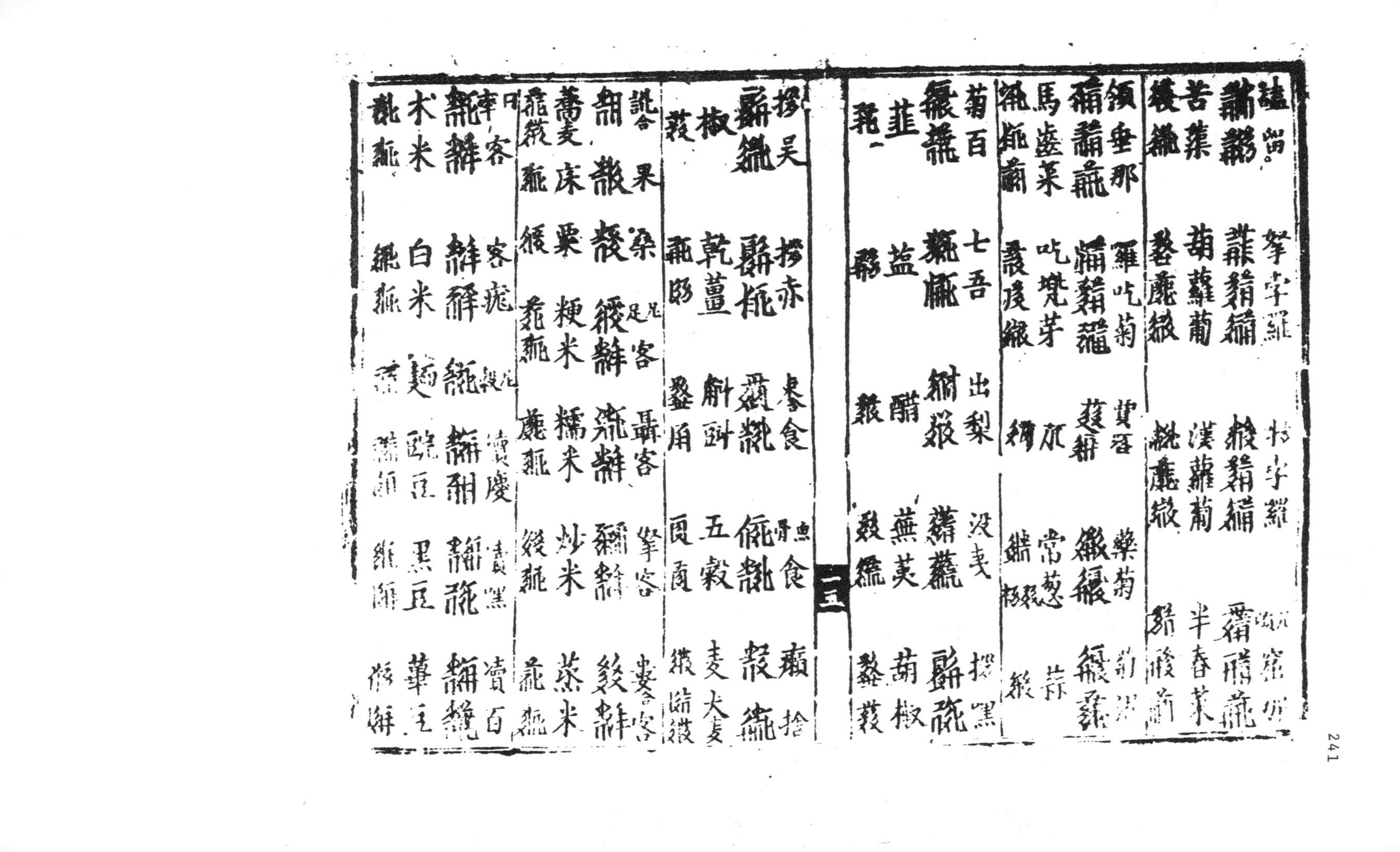

囉	[illegible]	苦菜	[illegible]
箏宰羅	[illegible]	葫蘿蔔	[illegible]
特宰羅	[illegible]	漢蘿蔔	[illegible]
窟	[illegible]	半春菜	[illegible]
領垂那	[illegible]	馬齒菜	[illegible]
羅吃菊	[illegible]	吃莧芽	[illegible]
貨苔	[illegible]	瓜	[illegible]
藥菊	[illegible]	常葱	[illegible]
菊	[illegible]	蒜	[illegible]
菊百	[illegible]	韭	[illegible]
七吾	[illegible]	藍	[illegible]
出梨	[illegible]	醋	[illegible]
沒夷	[illegible]	蕪荑	[illegible]
揬黑	[illegible]	葫椒	[illegible]

一五

揬吳	[illegible]	椒	[illegible]
揬赤	[illegible]	乾薑	[illegible]
參食	[illegible]	斛斗	[illegible]
骨魚食	[illegible]	五穀	[illegible]
癩捨	[illegible]	麥 大麥	[illegible]
訛合	[illegible]	蕎麥	[illegible]
果	[illegible]	床	[illegible]
桑	[illegible]	粟	[illegible]
足客	[illegible]	粳米	[illegible]
聶客	[illegible]	糯米	[illegible]
箏客	[illegible]	炒米	[illegible]
婁合客	[illegible]	蒸米	[illegible]
宰客	[illegible]	术米	[illegible]
客疵	[illegible]	白米	[illegible]
殺	[illegible]	麯	[illegible]
讀慶	[illegible]	豌豆	[illegible]
嘖黑	[illegible]	黑豆	[illegible]
噴百	[illegible]	華豆	[illegible]

Phonetic gloss	Meaning
恋敗	麻
謀郎	蒲葦
勿你	野獸
甚[illegible]	獅子
忠[illegible]	龍蛇
嘬則勒	豹虎
暮領	象熊
蚌則且	鹿麞
勒訛	兎
能[illegible]	野狐
顡兒	猫兒
屈訛	狗猪
勒嵬	駒
浪能	駱駝
領悟	馬
怛賊	騾
野勒	羊狼
孛則且丁	羣羊
[illegible]	山羊
屈征	細狗
枯我	犲狼
客捂	犛牛
長尼嵬	飛禽
姑白	鳳凰
訛物	孔雀
嵬郎	鷹鵰
勾女	鴛鴦
則尼假	鴈
林[illegible]	[illegible]

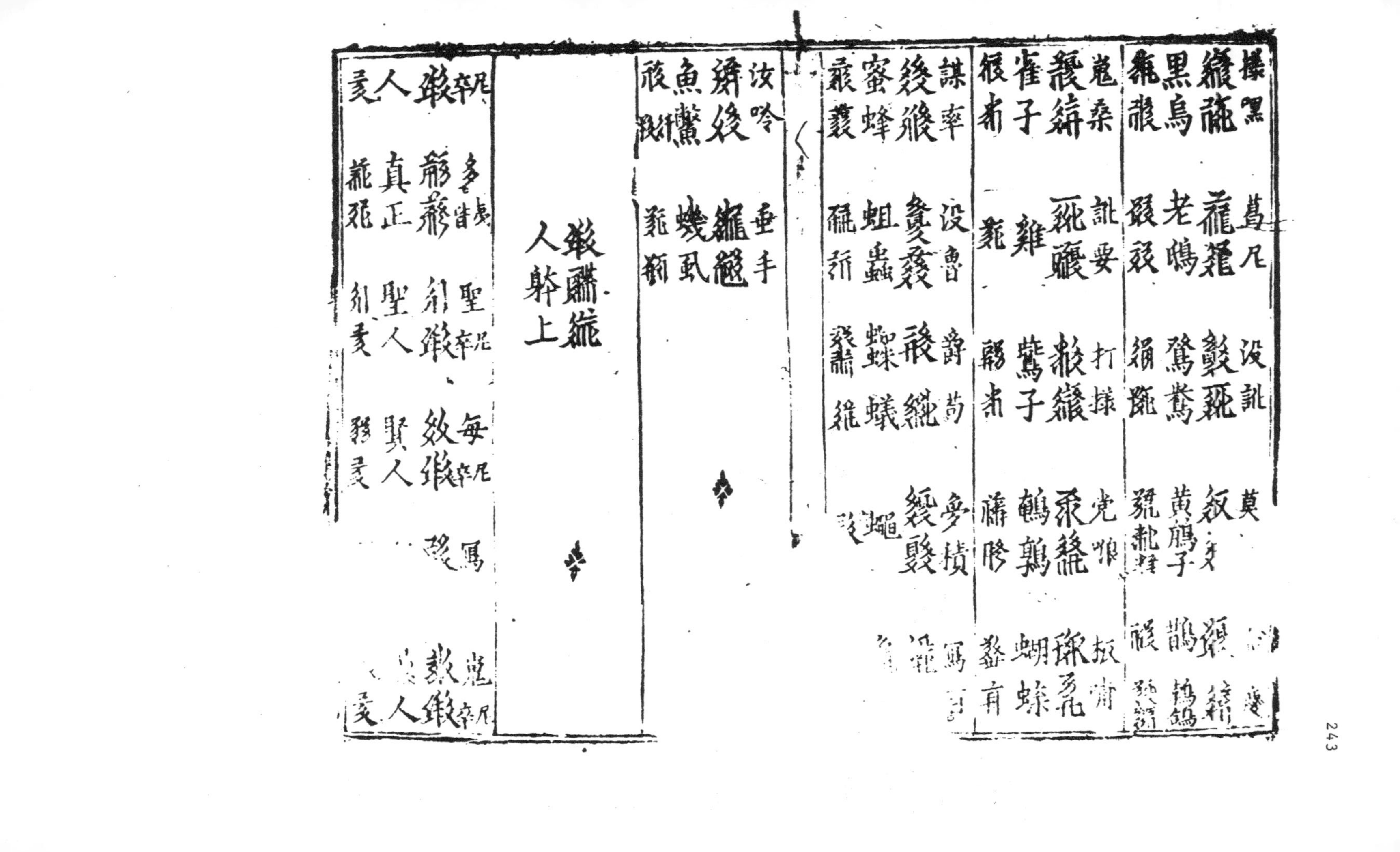

㮛罵 [illegible] 黑烏 [illegible]	葛尼 [illegible] 老鴟 [illegible]	設訛 [illegible] 鴛鴦 [illegible]	莫 [illegible] 黃鸝子 [illegible]
[illegible] 鵲 [illegible]	[illegible] 鵓鴿 [illegible]		
嵬桑 [illegible] 雀子 [illegible]	訛要 [illegible] 雞 [illegible]	打揲 [illegible] 鷂子 [illegible]	光 [illegible] 鵪鶉 [illegible]
扳 [illegible] 蝴蝶 [illegible]			
謀率 [illegible] 蜜蜂 [illegible]	没魯 [illegible] 蛆蟲 [illegible]	爵苟 [illegible] 蜘蟻 [illegible]	多 [illegible] 蜻蜓 [illegible]
寫 [illegible]			
汝吟 [illegible] 魚 [illegible]	垂手 [illegible] 蝦 [illegible]		

[illegible] 人 [illegible] 上

卒尼 [illegible] 人 [illegible]	多皆 [illegible] 真正 [illegible]	聖卒尼 [illegible] 聖人 [illegible]	每卒尼 [illegible] 賢人 [illegible]
寫 [illegible]			
嵬卒尼 [illegible] 人 [illegible]			

君子 宜
小人 則 兒

人相中

頭 吴　目 每
頂 周　腦 郁
鼻 你　舌 韓
齒 垂　牙 菌
口 烈　唇 没

十

咽 光　喉 寧
面 你　頷 粹
耳 六泥　竅 長尼
耳 六泥　塞 百
頭 吴　髮 麻

眉 墨　毛 麻
眼 昧　眶 誇
項 會　肩 疊
肩 幹　背 萼
脊 勿　背 勝

腸 説　肋 那
心 寧　命 割
肺 撈　膽 吃
腎 勿　郎
脾 不　肝 息

訛味 肚
訛丁 膀
膝
味 腿
刻迎 脚 脛

長巴 手掌
能 指爪
刻斜 脚根
吟則 骨節
直斜 肉血

玉郎 筋
麼那 唾涕
氣脈
六骨 身軀
羅我 病患

赤吹
麻娘 惡瘡
速劇 死生
貴賤
嵬 血 榮弱

黃桑
陰陽 和合
六成方 得成人身
悅 争習文業

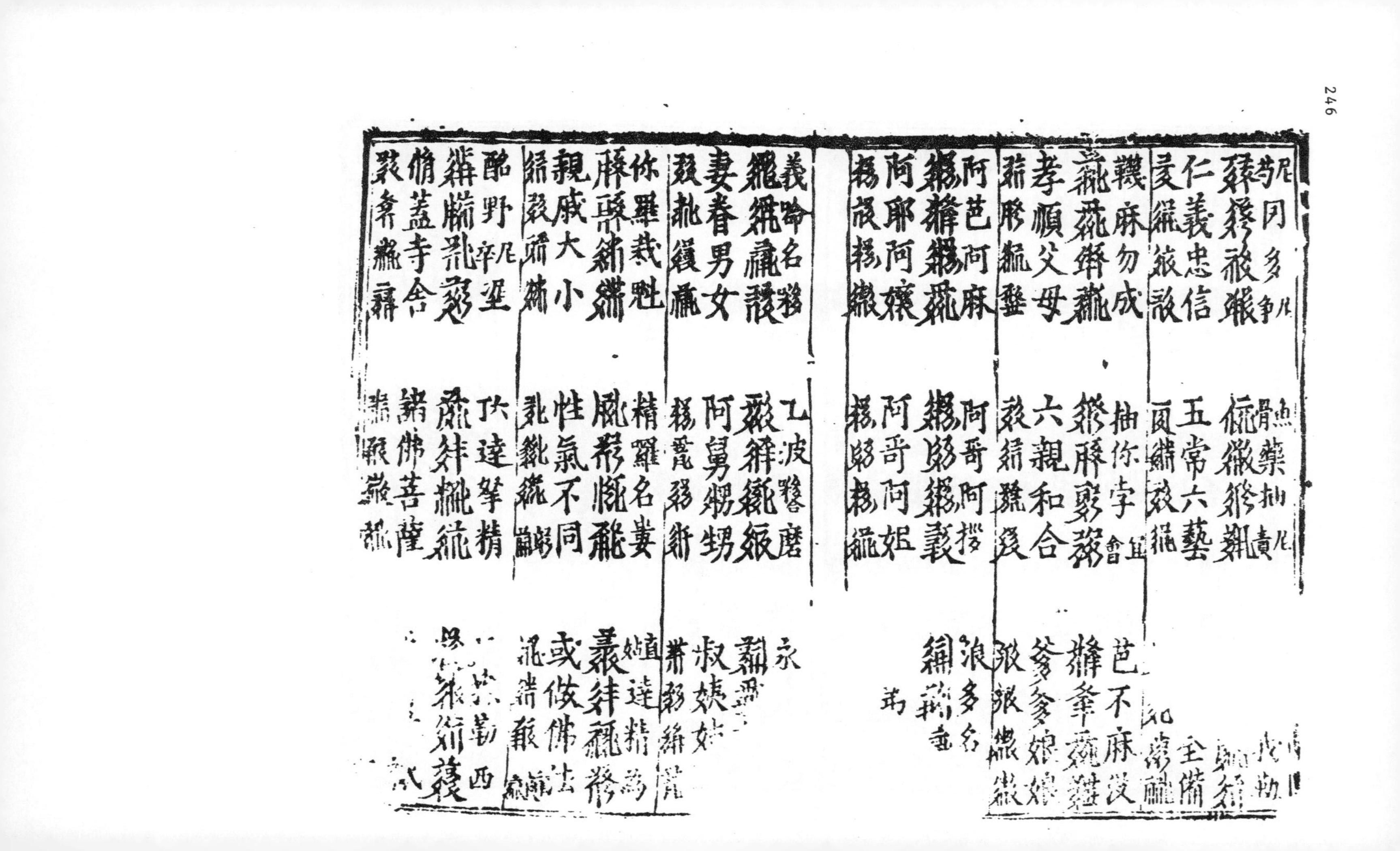

仁義忠信

孝順父母

阿耶阿孃

妻眷男女

親戚大小

僧蓋寺舍

五常六藝

六親和合

阿哥阿姐

阿舅甥甥

性氣不同

佛菩薩

全備

芭不麻沒

叔姨姑

或做佛法

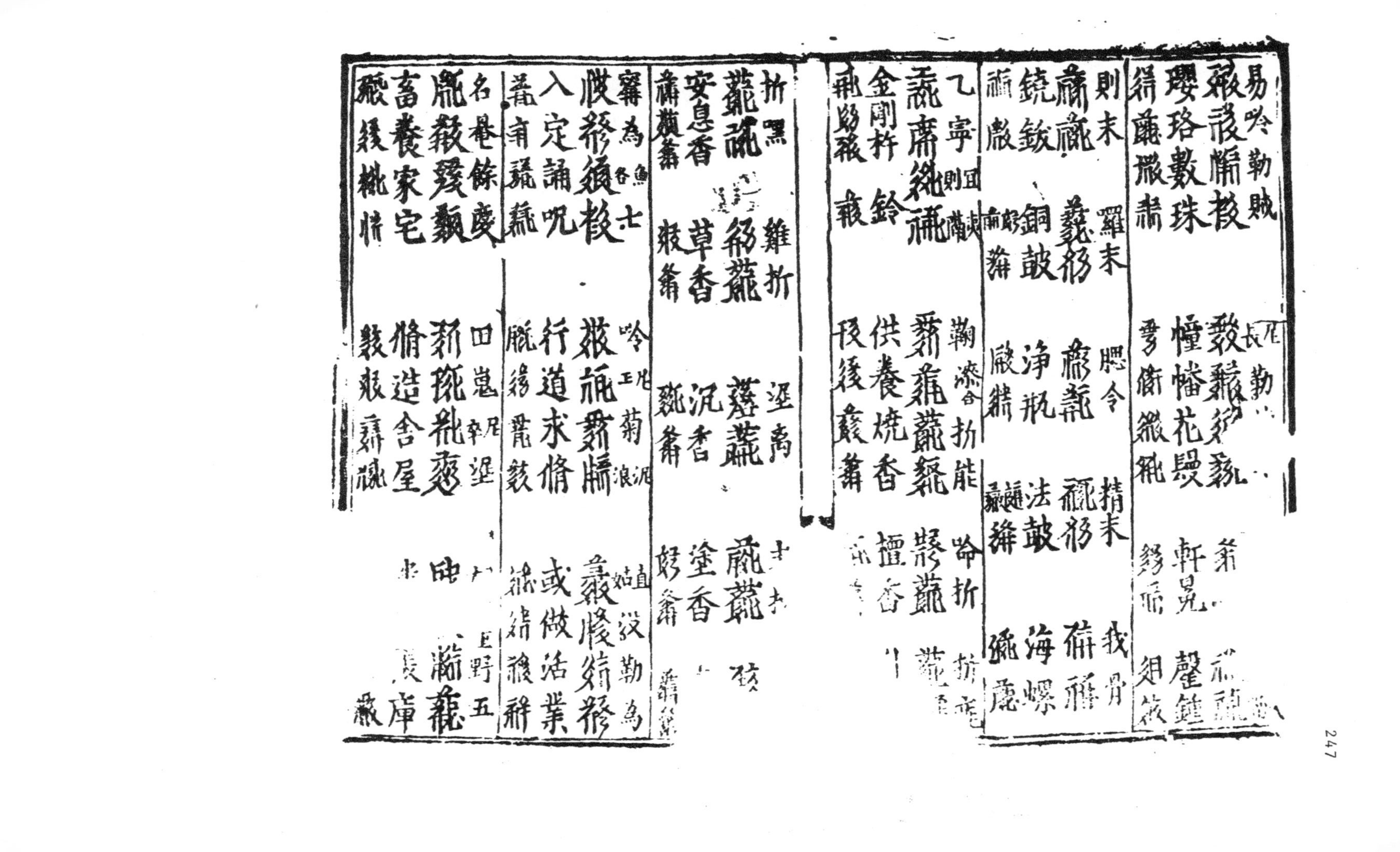

易吟 勒賊
瓔珞 數珠
長尼 勒
幢幡 花鬘
軒冕
磬鍾

則末 鐃鈸
羅末 銅鼓
腮令 淨瓶
精末 法鼓
我骨 海螺

乙寧 金剛杵
則囬 鈴
鞠 供養
折能 燒香
吟折 檀香

折黑 安息香
雜折 草香
涅离 沉香
塗香

寧為 入定
各魚 七 誦呪
吟尼 行道
菊浪 求脩
直姑 没 勒為 或做活業

名 畜養
餘慶 家宅
四崑 脩造
卒涅 舍屋
野五 庫

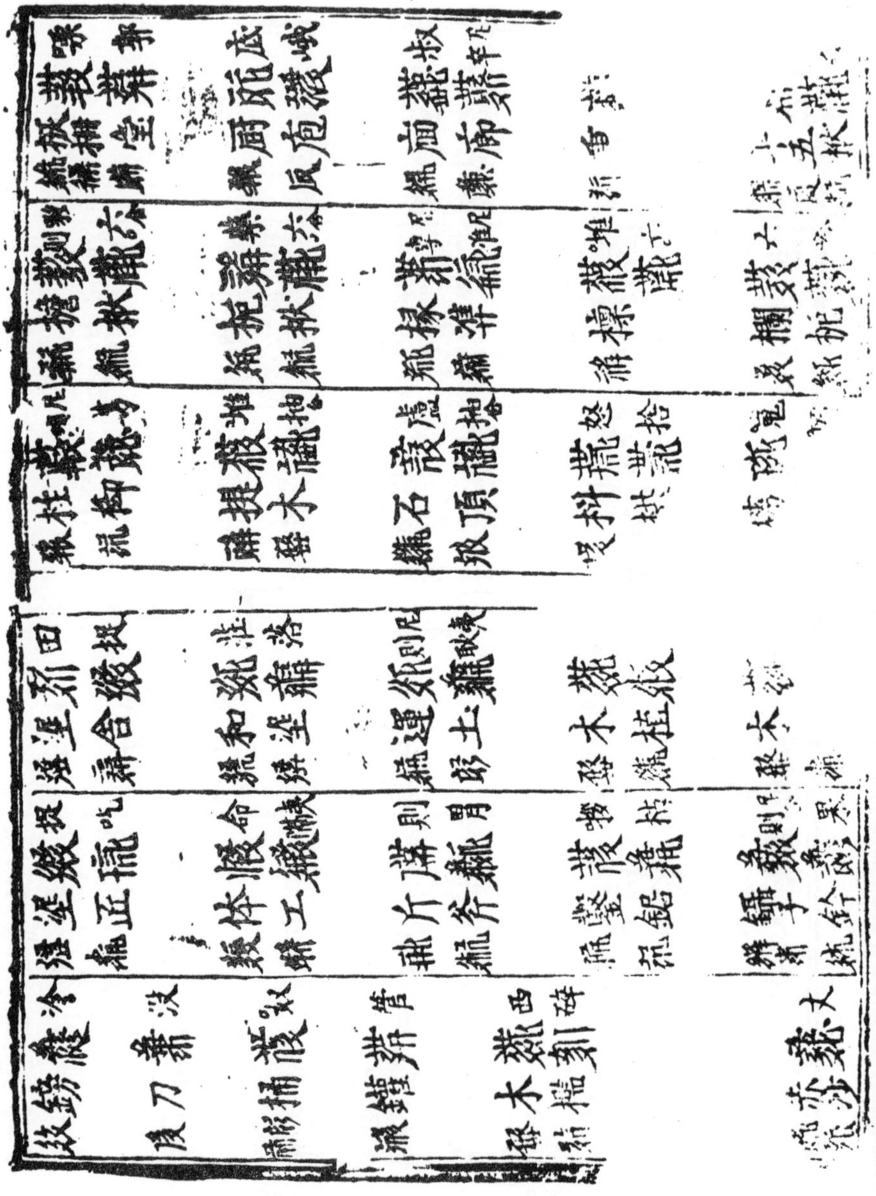

剌兎 [Tangut] 白土 [Tangut]
則 [Tangut] 作物 [Tangut]
為一 [Tangut] 做造 [Tangut]
[Tangut] 帳 [Tangut]
[illegible] [Tangut] 手冊 [Tangut]

野昝 [Tangut] 門簾 [Tangut]
野兎 [Tangut] 天窓 [Tangut]
客昧 [Tangut] 沙窓 [Tangut]
貢王 [Tangut] 器皿 [Tangut]
枯稅 [Tangut] 杭匙 [Tangut]

則 沉得合 [Tangut] 筋 [Tangut]
無郎 [Tangut] 杓笊籬 [Tangut]
能積 [Tangut] 藥子 [Tangut]
能積 [Tangut] 棟 [Tangut]
鎮 [Tangut]

吟 [Tangut] 鐺 [Tangut]
會 [Tangut] 鼎 [Tangut]
足合 聒 [Tangut] 急燧鋅 [Tangut]
絶 則宜 [Tangut] 火炉鐵 [Tangut]
[illegible] [Tangut] [illegible] [Tangut]
[Tangut] [Tangut]

普 [illegible]昝 [Tangut] 床 [Tangut]
羅昝 [Tangut] 紗草 [Tangut]
則 足 [Tangut] 茶銚 [Tangut]
井玉 [Tangut] 茶臼 [Tangut]
六 丁合 [Tangut] 瓶盞 [Tangut]

丁 普 [Tangut] 燈樹 [Tangut]
丁 丁合 [Tangut] 燈盞 [Tangut]
丁 浪 [Tangut] 燈毬 [Tangut]
[illegible] [Tangut] 燈 [Tangut]
沒 葉合 [Tangut] 火爐 [Tangut]

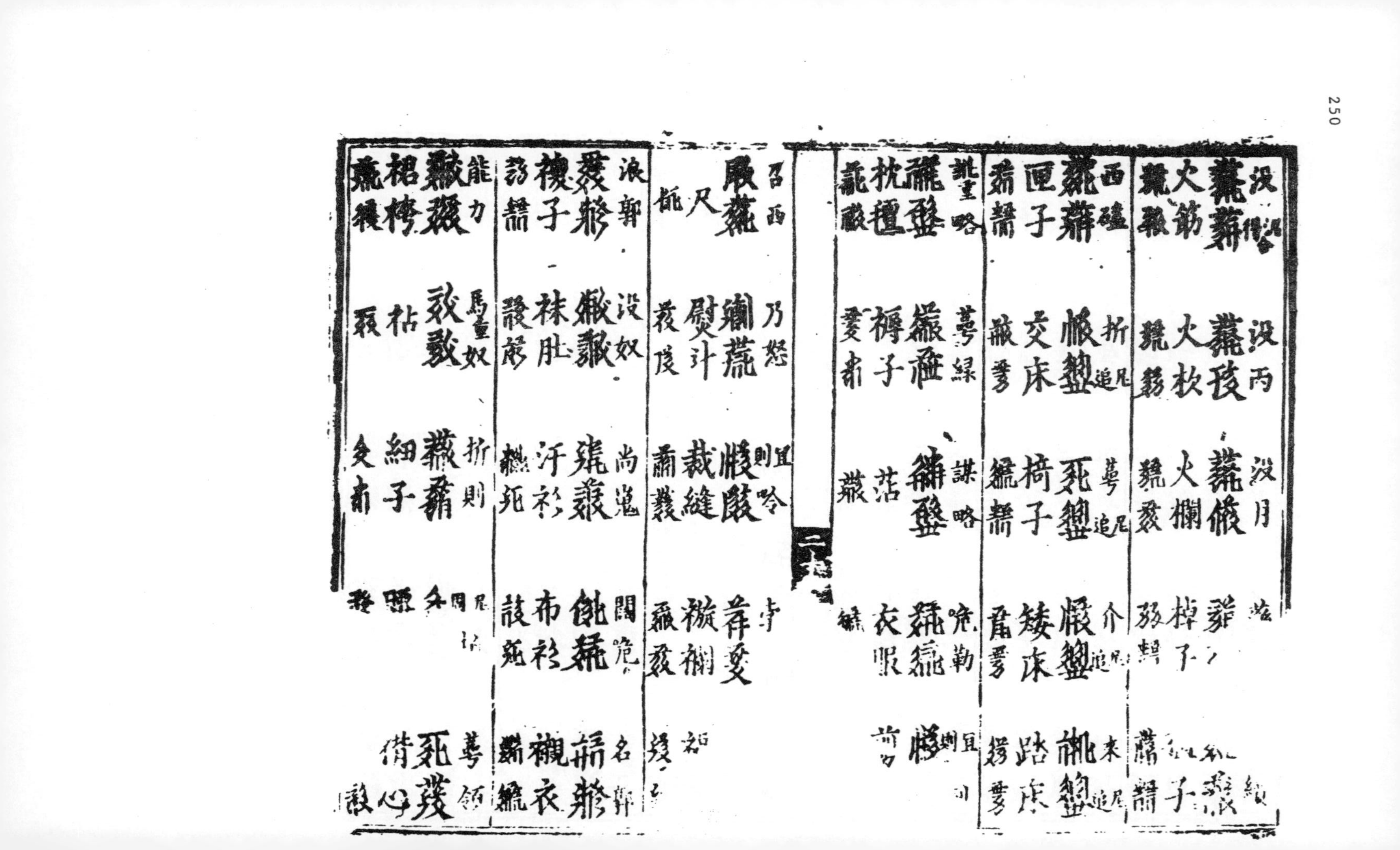

没僧合 火筋 | 没丙 火杴 | 没月 火欄 | 㳁 棹子 | 子

西碮 匣子 | 折追尼 交床 | 蕚追尼 椅子 | 介追尼 矮床 | 来追尼 路床

芈里略 枕氈 | 蕚緑 褥子 | 諜略 | 啰勒 衣服 | 则且 前

二

召西 尺 | 乃怒 熨斗 | 则且吟 裁縫 | 字 | 绍

浪郭 襖子 | 没奴 袜肚 | 尚嵬 汗衫 | 閭危 布衫 | 名鮮 襯衣

能力 裙袴 | 馬重奴 枯 | 折则 細子 | 尼 | 蕚領 借心

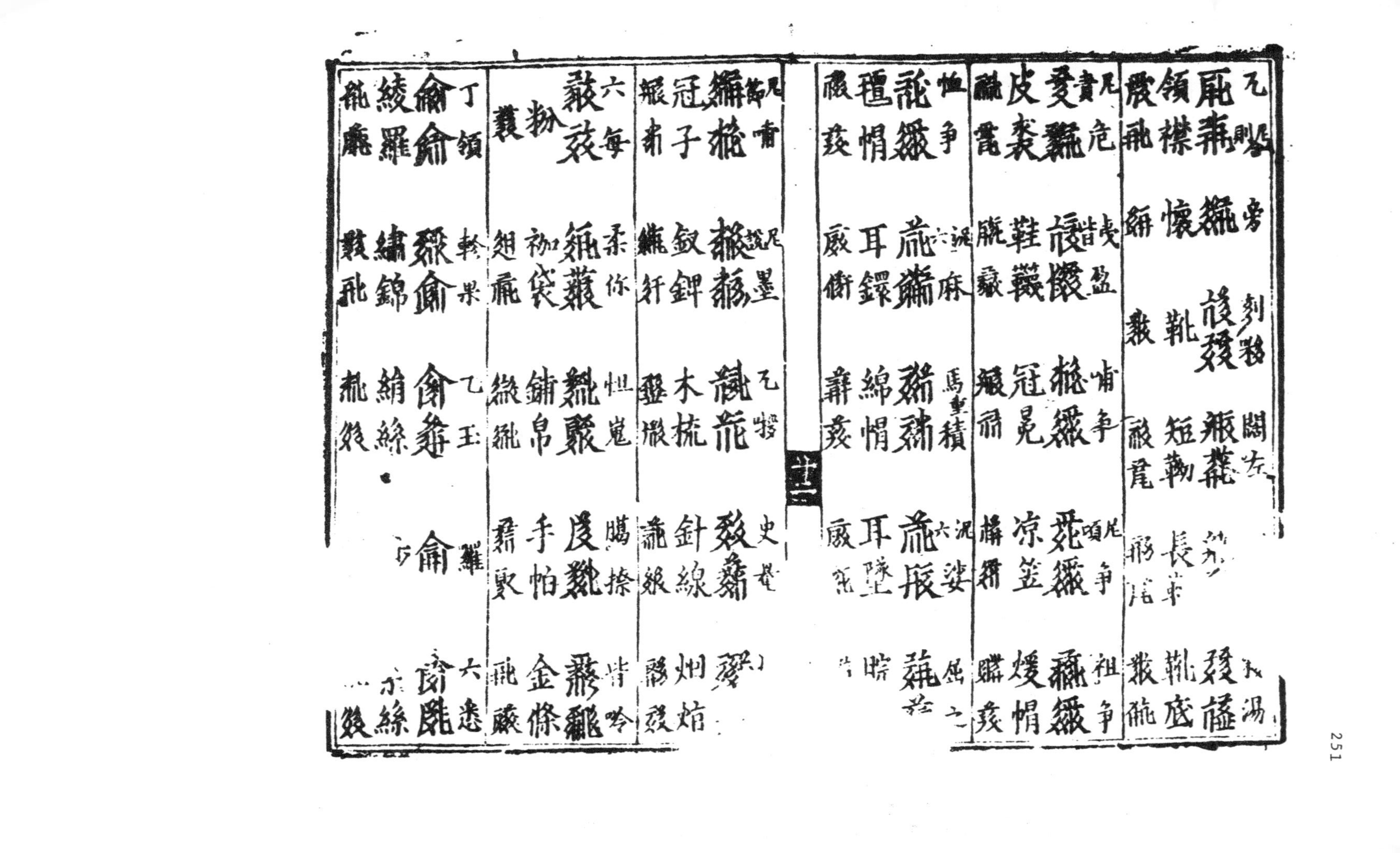

廿二

乙尼則 領襟

旁 懷

刻 靴

閼 短靿

[illegible] 長

湯 靴底

尼賁危 皮裘

皆盈 鞋襪

哺爭 冠冕

尼嗄爭 凉笠

祖爭 煖帽

恤爭 氈帽

泥六麻 耳鐶

馬重積 綿帽

泥六婆 耳墜

[illegible] [illegible]

尼節青 冠子

尼說墨 釵鉀

乙[illegible] 木梳

史[illegible] 針線

[illegible] 烟焰

六每 [illegible]粉

柔你 [illegible]袋

怛嵬 鋪帛

[illegible]搽 手帕

背吟 金條

丁領 綾羅

輪果 繡錦

乙玉 綃絲

羅

六[illegible] [illegible]絲

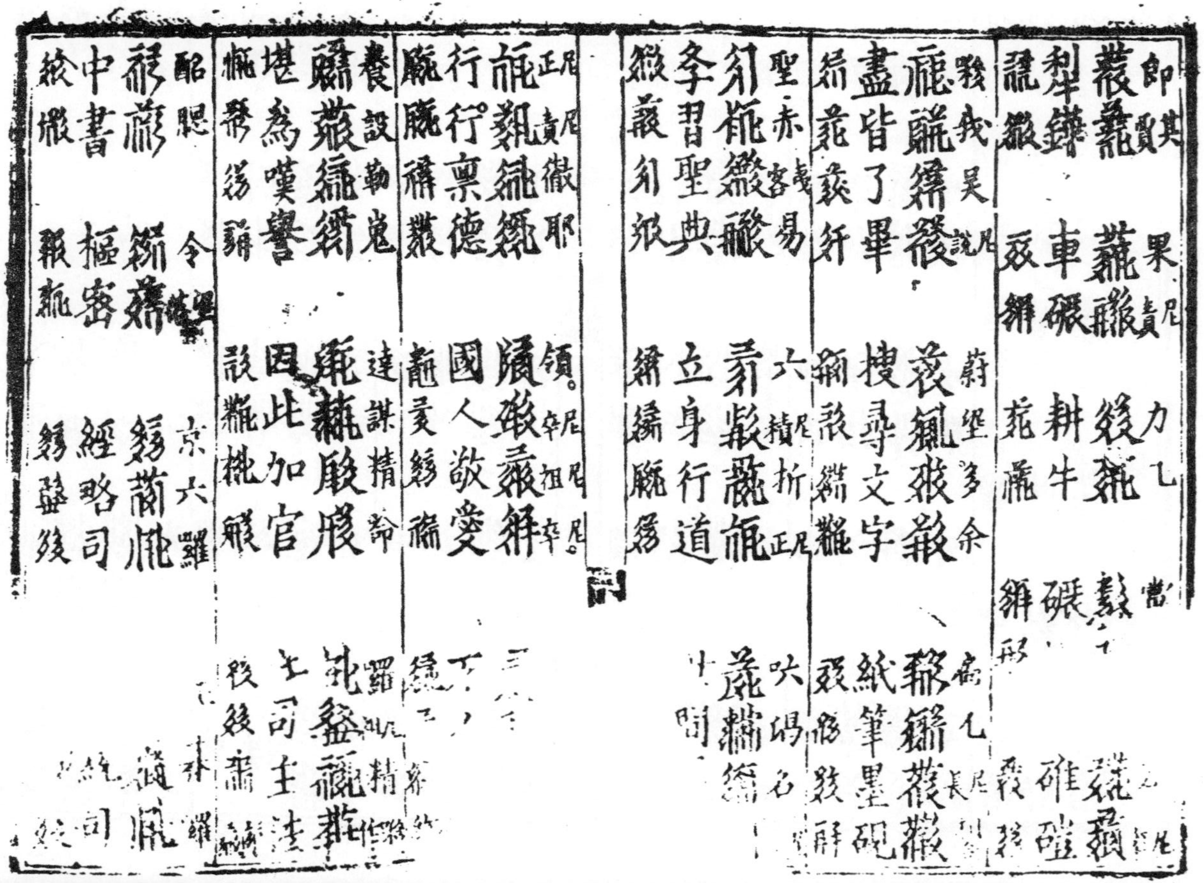

過暮羅 統軍司
北与羅 殿前司
辛尼訛 御史
皇
形訛 宣徽

則尼割 三司
姑要羅 內宿司
西正尼羅 巡撿司
吃訛 工院
力訛 馬院

能羅 陳告司
赤剋羅 磨堪司
与合力羅 審刑司
頂赤 大恒

羅 農田司
馨羅 群牧司
嚷張羅 受納司
頂 閤門司
監軍

嵬足尼 州主
托精尼 通判
正祖尼 正聽
足尼領 承旨
阿六由 都案
案頭

羅繾尼 司吏
倉尼哥 都監
竹領栽兕 為分大小
足尼迷 指揮

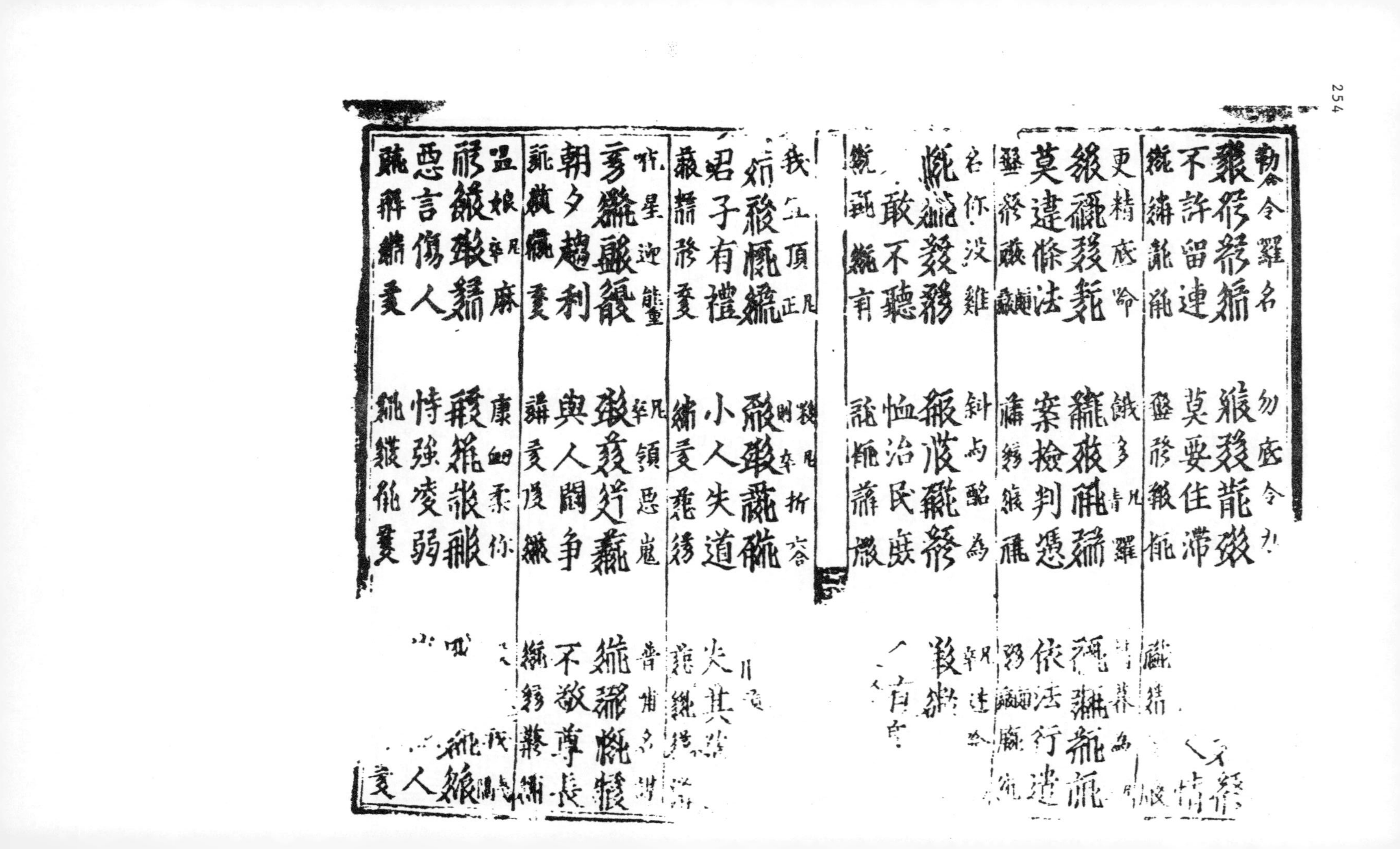

[Tangut]
勑令 令 羅 名
不許留連
[Tangut]
更 精 底 嶙
莫違條法
[Tangut]
名 你 没 雉
敢不聽
[Tangut]

我 丘 頂 正凡
君子有禮
[Tangut]
作 星 迎 鑒
朝夕趨利
[Tangut]
温 娘 卒凡 麻
惡言傷人
[Tangut]

勿 底 令 力
莫要住滯
[Tangut]
餓 多 青凡 羅
案檢判憑
[Tangut]
斜 勾 貂 為
恤治民庶
[Tangut]

我 卒凡 折 六合
小人失道
[Tangut]
卒凡 領 惡 嵬
與人鬭爭
[Tangut]
康 四 柔 你
恃強凌弱
[Tangut]

[Tangut]
依法行遣
[Tangut]
[illegible]

失其
[Tangut]
不敬尊長
[Tangut]
人
[illegible]

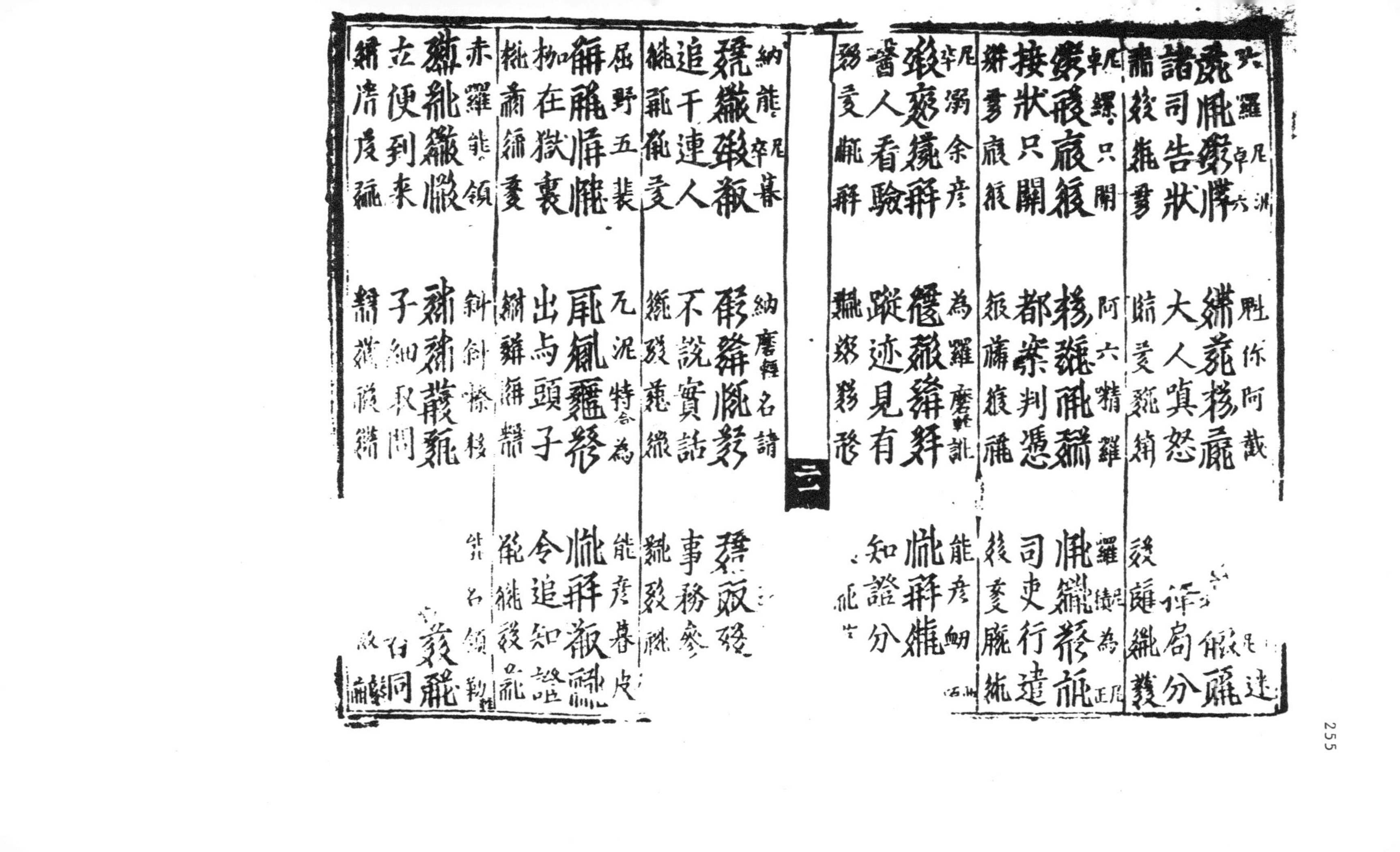

諸司告狀
接狀只關
醫人看驗

大人嗔怒
都案判憑
蹤迹見有

司吏行遣
知證分

二

追干連人
物在獄裏
立便到來

不說實話
出与頭子
子細取問

事務參
令追知證
同

不肯招承
愚蒙小人
父母髮身
你名星勒
心不思惟
我乃愚人
我聞此言

凌持打拷
聽我之言
不敢毀傷也
可謂孝乎
不曉世事
罪在我身

孝經中
你
心下思惟
彼人
[illegible]人

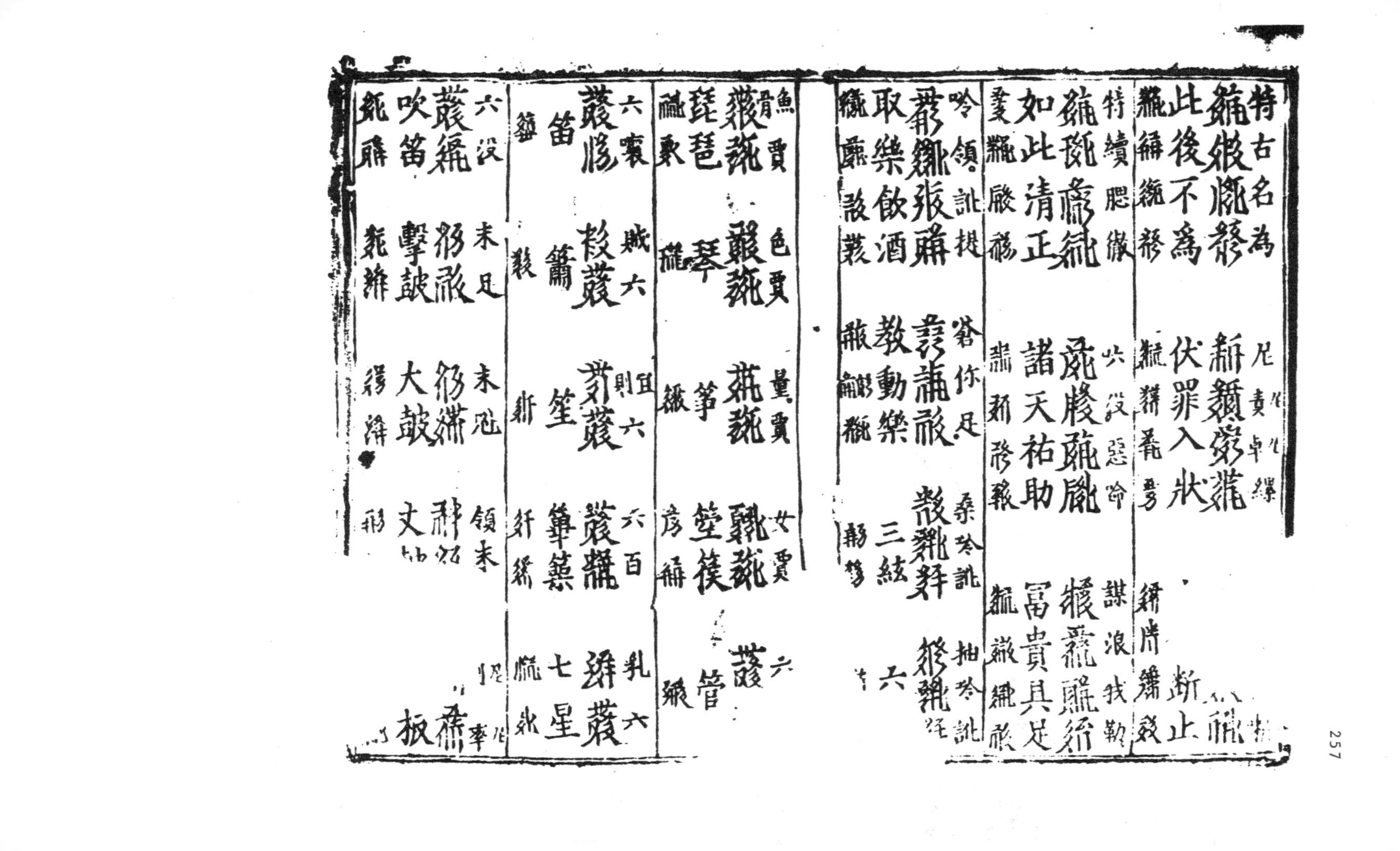

特古名為　尼責卓縲

[illegible]

比後不為　伏罪入狀

[illegible]

特續腮徽　吠沒惡吟　諜浪我勒

[illegible]

如此清正　諸天祐助　富貴具足

[illegible]

吟領訖提　咨你足　桑苓訖　抽苓訖

[illegible]

取樂飲酒　教動樂　三絃　六

[illegible]

魚骨貫　色貫　量貫　女貫　六

[illegible]

琵琶　琴　箏　箜篌　管

[illegible]

六囊　賊六　則六　六百　乳六

[illegible]

笛　簫　笙　篳篥　七星

[illegible]

六沒　末足　末泡　領末

[illegible]

吹笛　擊鼓　大鼓　丈　板

[illegible]

樂人打諢　折花　戴花

細麵　粥　乳頭　油餅　胡餅

蒸餅　乾餅　燒餅　花餅

饆饠　角子　饅頭　酸䤈

設筵已畢　教被　馬　馬鞍　馬韂

盡皆准備
奉送
本家

名番惡竹
勾管家計
名務啰唐
男女長大
夷使正為
遣將媒人

吠吠乙嚳
諸處為婚
逆聆成為
索與妻眷
野名

設盈識日為
嫁與他人
息路永為
送與沿房
親家翁

娘吠你羅
并諸親戚
務我令則尼
盡皆聚集
名務吾說凡
見女了畢

丈你乜叻
忙斜恤勢
乍六吡啰

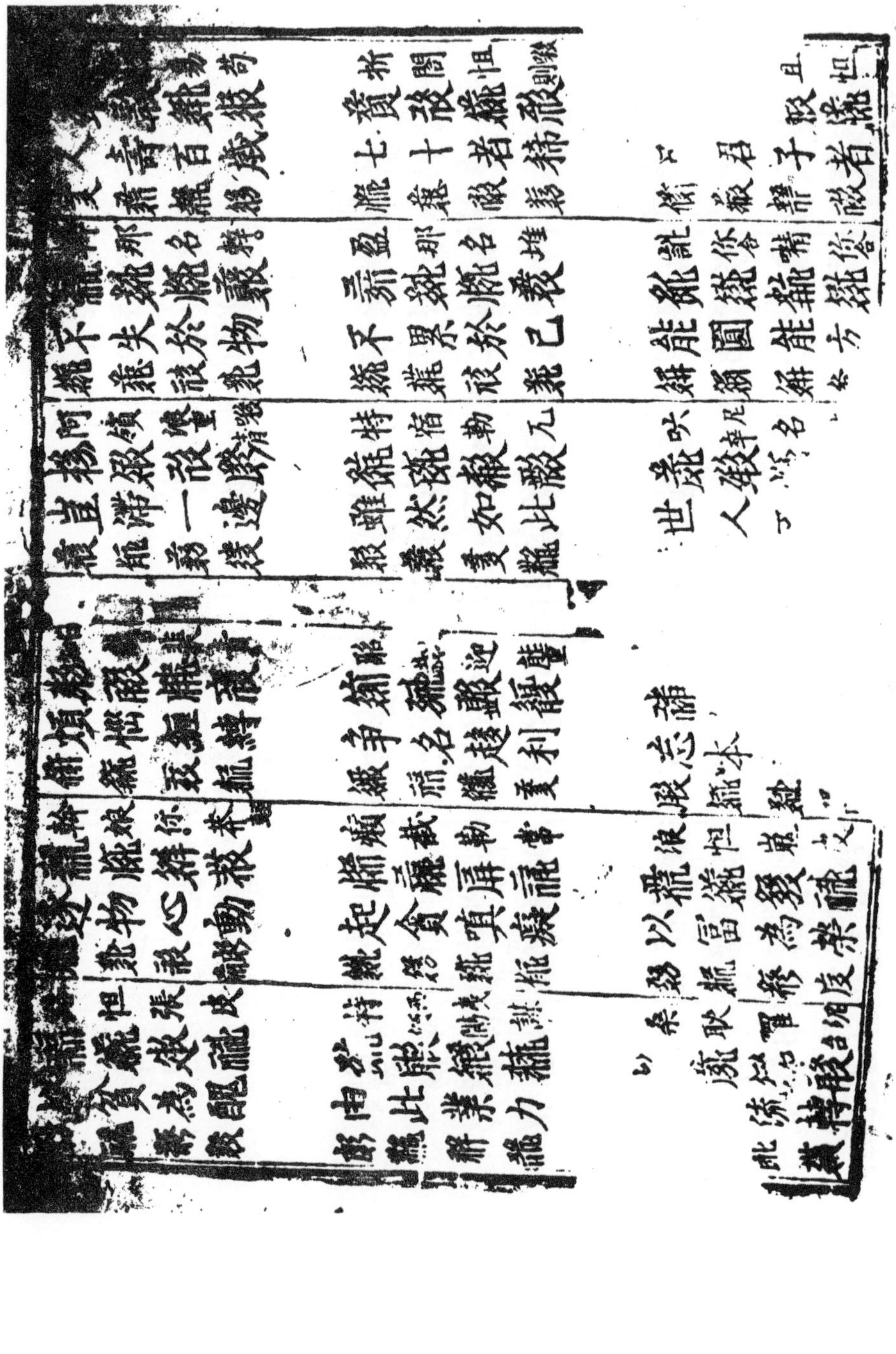

[illegible] 各 音
人 形 上

天 形

人 [illegible]

天 乾
皇 天
[illegible] 天

九 霄
一 清
虛 空

天 相 中

日 月
金 烏

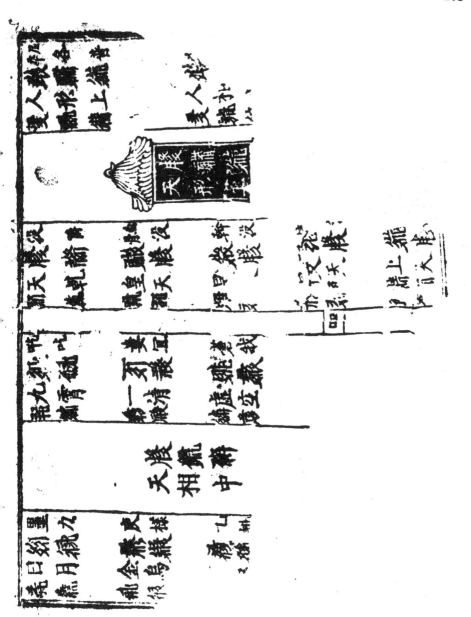

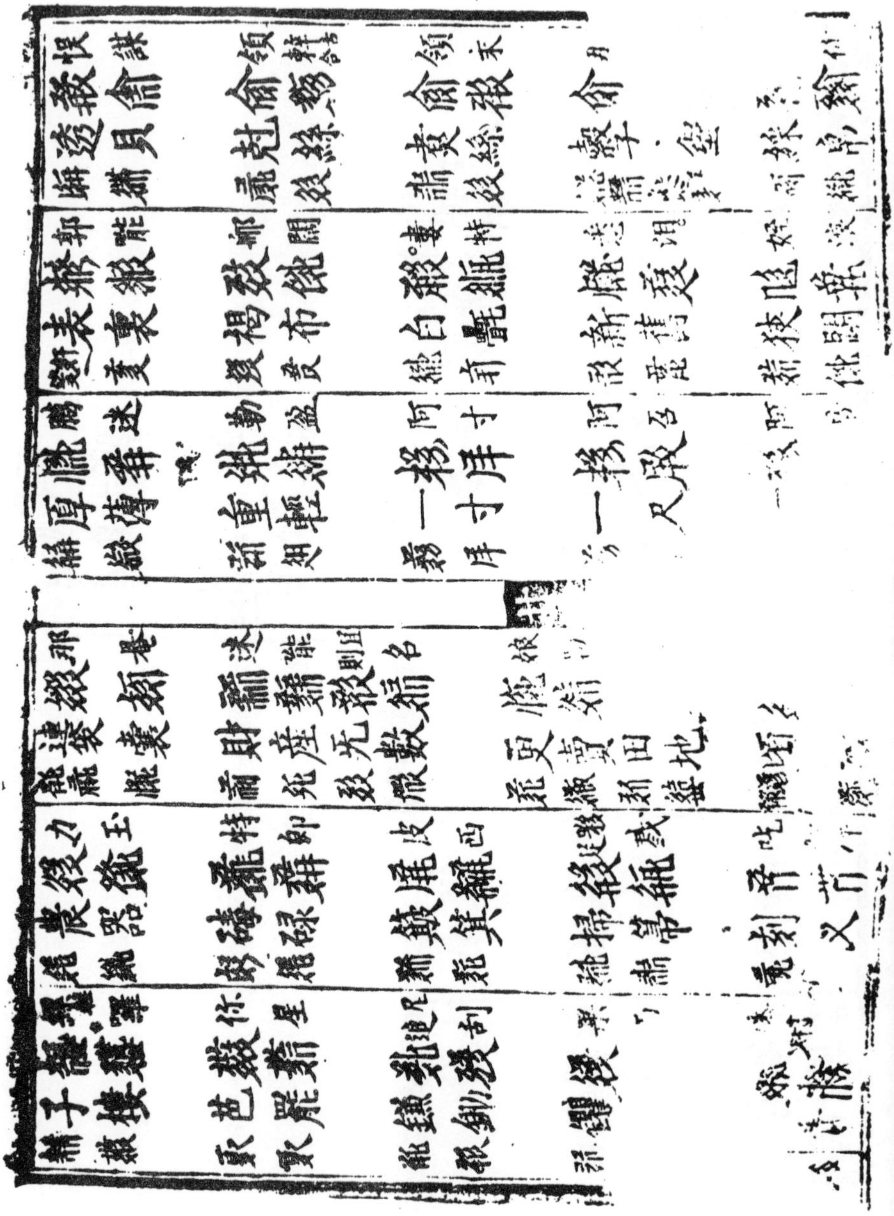

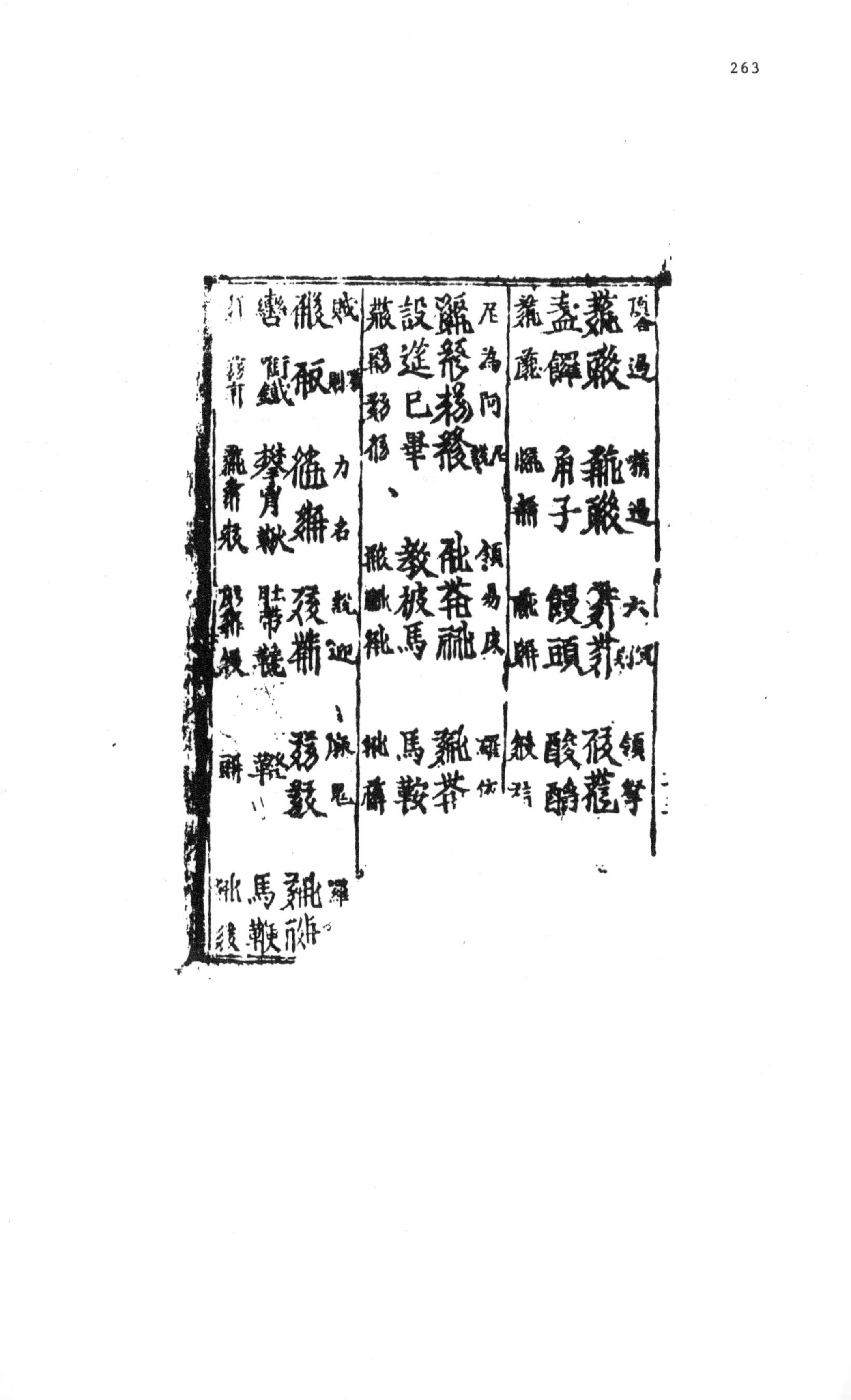

頂合過 [illegible] 盞解 [illegible]

精過 [illegible] 角子 [illegible]

六則 [illegible] 饅頭 [illegible]

領擘 [illegible] 酸餡 [illegible]

尼為問 [illegible] 設筵已畢、 [illegible]

領易皮 [illegible] 教被馬 [illegible]

羅依 [illegible] 馬鞍 [illegible]

賊則 [illegible] [illegible] [illegible]

力名 [illegible] [illegible] [illegible]

救迎 [illegible] 肚帶 [illegible]

脉尼 [illegible] [illegible] [illegible]

羅 [illegible] 馬韉 [illegible]

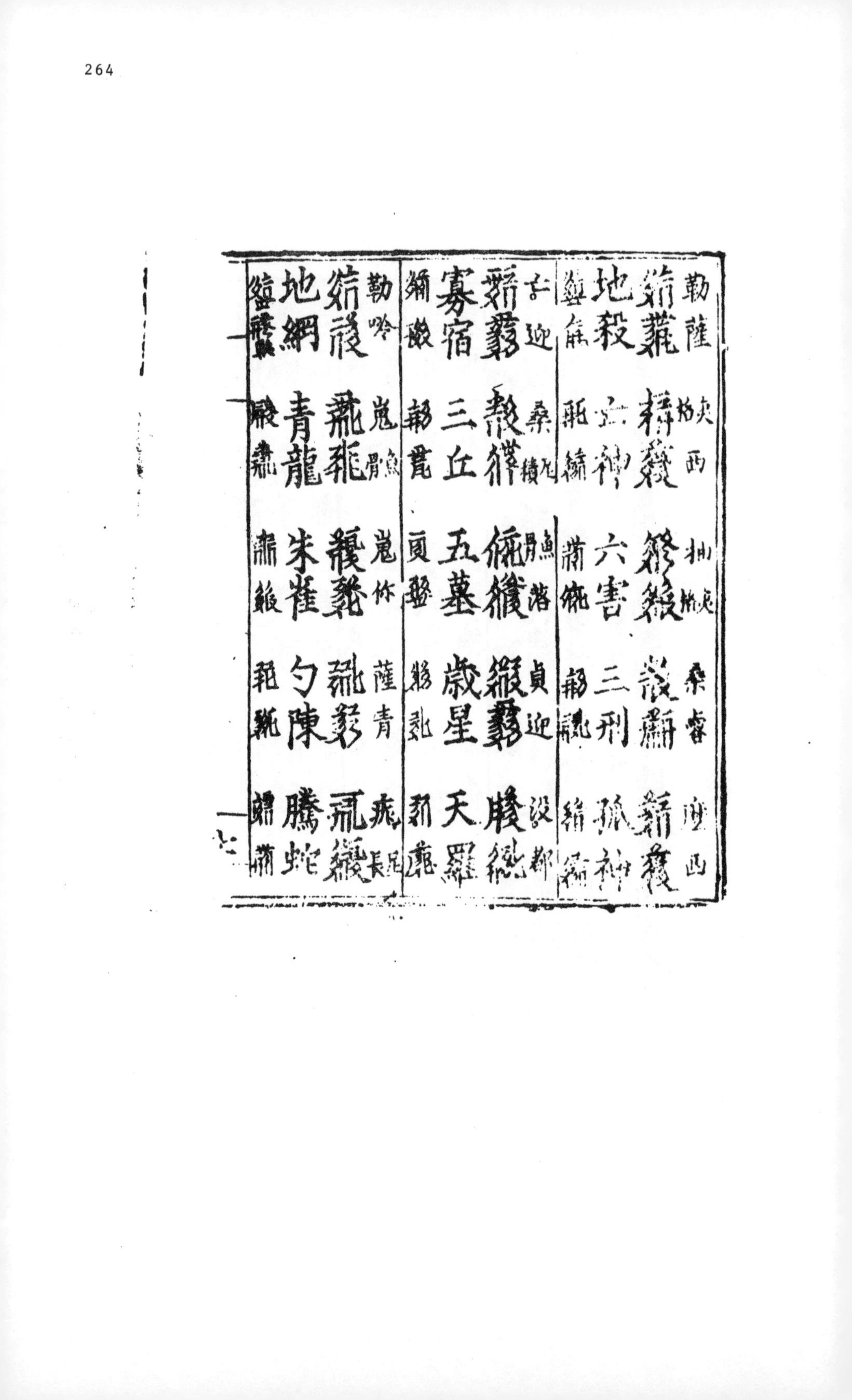

勒薩	地殺
夾西	亡神
枷尼	六害
桑睿	三刑
麼西	孤神
卞迎	寡宿
桑積尼	三丘
骨魚落	五墓
貞迎	歲星
没都	天羅
勒吟	地網
嵬骨魚	青龍
嵬你	朱雀
薩青	勾陳
疣長尼	騰蛇

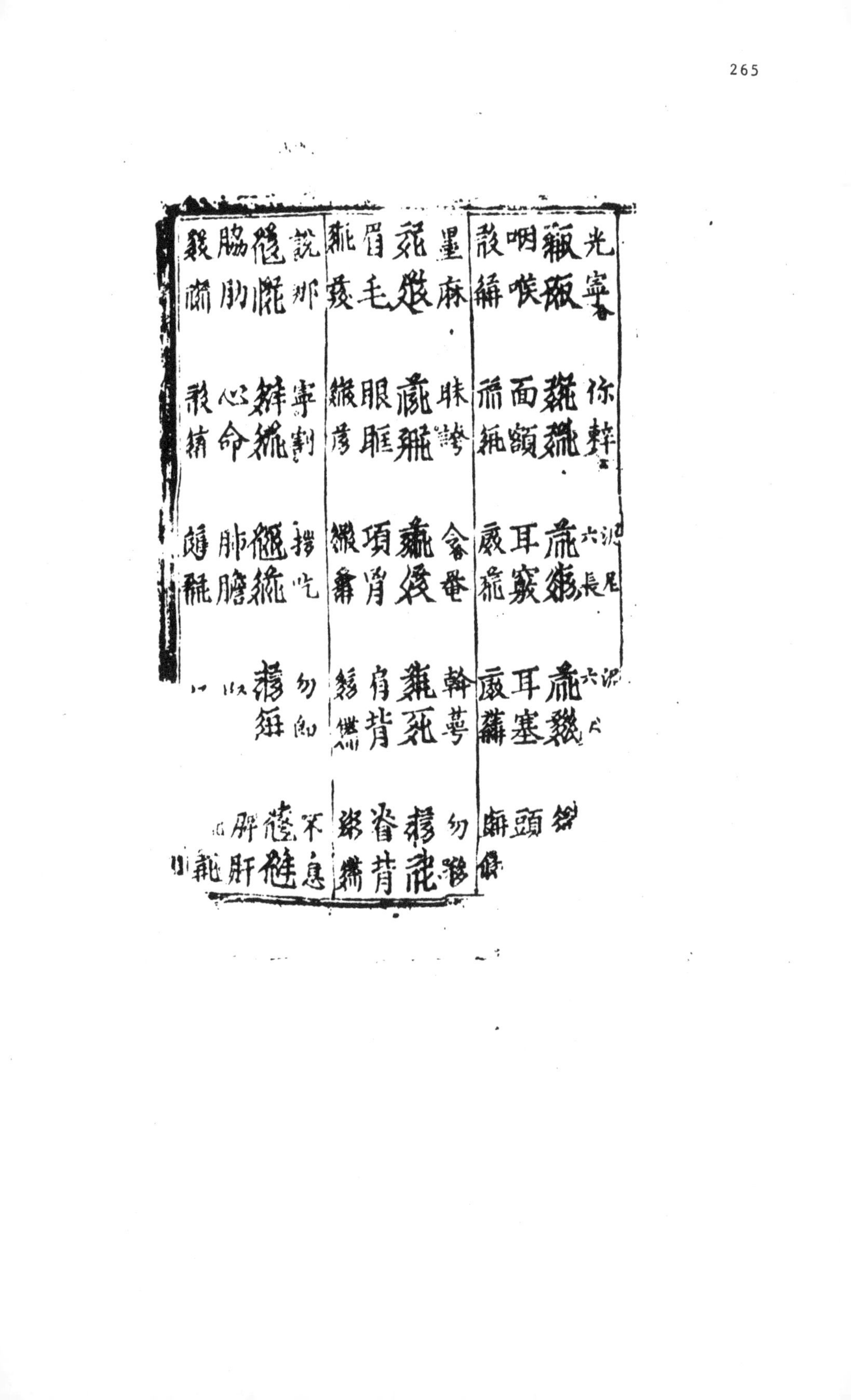

光寧 咽喉

你韓 面額

泥尼 六長 耳竅

泥 六尺 耳塞

頭

墨麻 眉毛

昧彎 眼眶

會罨 項背

翰萼 肩背

勿勝 脊背

訛那 脇肋

寧割 心命

捺吃 肺膽

勿囟 以

不息 肝肝

Milton Keynes UK
Ingram Content Group UK Ltd.
UKHW030916190924
448478UK00001B/29

9 780933 070103